Praise for *The Nake*

Non-fiction Book of the Month for the

'A hugely enjoyable anti-tour, and a wonderful eulogy to an implacable ocean' Joanna Kavenna, *Times Literary Supplement*

'A wonderfully bracing journey around the North Sea. His gaze misses nothing, and his robust prose glitters with story and lore and surprise' Philip Marsden

'Captivating … Rich, evocative prose' *Independent*

'A cold, muddy, delicate world of marginalia … Full of brilliant findings and unforgettable rediscoveries' Adam Nicolson

'Perfect escapism for those enduring long days on sun-baked Mediterranean beaches, this is a bracing journey around less-celebrated shores' *Financial Times*

'Rich, illuminating and enjoyable' *Observer*

'Who would have thought that a book about a treacherous expanse of freezing, grey-green water, feared by mariners through the centuries, could turn out to be such a delight?' *Daily Mail*

'Meanwhile, beneath the comparatively recent historical record, something dark, magnificent and primordial is patiently being assembled … This is a beautifully written book of travels. Trawling stories from around the coast, it transmutes the North Sea into something dark, heroic and fascinating' Barnaby Rogerson, *Country Life*

'Riveting. So extremely good … It will bring a warmth and richness to your early spring reading' *Guardian*

A Note on the Author

TOM BLASS studied anthropology, law and politics, and has earned his living as a journalist and editor specialising in issues relating to business, law, human rights and foreign policy. He lives with his family in Hastings.

THE NAKED SHORE

Of the North Sea

Tom Blass

BLOOMSBURY
LONDON · OXFORD · NEW YORK · NEW DELHI · SYDNEY

Bloomsbury Paperbacks
An imprint of Bloomsbury Publishing Plc

50 Bedford Square   1385 Broadway
London   New York
WC1B 3DP   NY 10018
UK   USA

www.bloomsbury.com

BLOOMSBURY and the Diana logo are trademarks of Bloomsbury Publishing Plc

First published in Great Britain 2016
This paperback edition first published in 2017

British Library Cataloguing-in-Publication Data
A catalogue record for this book is available from the British Library.

ISBN: HB: 978-1-4088-1549-6
PB: 978-1-4088-3403-9
ePub: 978-1-4088-3402-2

2 4 6 8 10 9 7 5 3 1

Typeset by Newgen Knowledge Works (P) Ltd., Chennai, India
Printed and bound in Great Britain by CPI Group (UK) Ltd, Croydon CR0 4YY

To find out more about our authors and books visit www.bloomsbury.com.
Here you will find extracts, author interviews, details of forthcoming events and the option to sign up for our newsletters.

For my parents

Contents

THE
NORTH
SEA

A North Sea Crossing

A grey green expanse of smudgy waters grinning angrily at one with white foam-ridges and over all a cheerless unglowing canopy, apparently made of wet blotting paper . . .

Joseph Conrad, *Mirror of the Sea*

Swaddled in jumpers, jackets and gloves I looked down from the deck of a freight ship upon a fairy-tale city of lights stretching along the south bank of the River Humber. The tide was still in flood, and the freighter, the MV *Longstone*, bound for the Swedish city of Gothenburg on the far side of the North Sea, had yet to slip its moorings. But it hummed and throbbed in anticipation of doing so. Dock-workers in bright boiler suits spread out along the dark quay, and even against the deep rumbling of the ship's engines snatches of their conversation rose up like handkerchiefs to where I tried to catch them, though they were easily lost in the autumn night breeze. In the warm-looking bridge, to whose occupants I had not yet dared to introduce myself, screens and instrument panels flickered and glowed.

I'd passed through a confusion of checkpoints and transit zones on the way to boarding the ship, donning hard hat and dayglo jerkin and signing a disclaimer to show I entered the dock at my own peril. More than half a dozen unchaperoned footsteps beyond its gates were *verboten* – and rightly so, given my own clumsiness and the profusion of strange vehicles threading their way between ever-changing canyon walls of shipping containers. (One, in particular I thought, a trunk-less towering pair of legs on wheels, its cabin some twenty feet above the ground, smacked both of Georges Braque and Hieronymus Bosch.) Far safer, I was told, to be passed along a chain of clipboard-toting men until safely delivered into the vessel's cavernous, echoing hull.

At mid-afternoon the colour-scape had been muted and utilitarian. But just before sunset the windscreens of a thousand factory-fresh estate cars glinted like the shields of warriors at some hot and distant battle between ancients. One hour after, with the sun banished to the west, a quite different luminescence, unearthly flashes of halide orange, magnesium white and peridot, cut through the gloom, silent and rhythm-less drumbeats beating off the night. Just before midnight, everything came together. The engines hummed deeper, and the *Longstone* tugged free of the quayside to canter out into the dark channel.

For a good hour the fantastical lights strung out to starboard remained etched bright in the darkness, while to port the river, widening to the sea, loomed, black, brooding and intransigent.

I slept in a spare but large and comfortable cabin on the other side of the corridor to the (steaming, odorous) galley. Scattered in the mess were relics of those who had travelled before me – well-thumbed back copies of *Truckstop* magazine and other reading matter. Patrick the first mate (in *loco parentis* for me but uncertain as to the reason for my presence) apologised for the lack of travelling companions. At weekends, he said, the ship was full to the gunwales with Irish truckers taking sides of beef to Sweden. I assured him that my own company would suffice.

In the morning I woke slowly, gazing through the porthole at a disc of grey before heading up to the bridge, where I cradled a coffee mug and watched the freighter's great hull beating down on spry but pliant waves.

The measures of progress are painfully infrequent at sea and the general train of events unfolds slowly. Only Patrick, the second mate Steve and I were on the bridge, watching the horizon and the dipping gulls. The captain was in his cabin, where he'd stay for most of the day. Patrick told me that this would be a good crossing. He had spent most of the last year on the Falklands run, three weeks each way, arriving in Port Stanley feeling numb and listless through over-consumption of DVDs and lack of conversational stimulus. This trip was like a bus journey, a mere four-day round trip from the river mouth to Gothenburg a thousand miles distant on the coast of the Skagerrak.

'Skayraak', it's pronounced, like the rasping of a crow.

In earlier centuries the ships on this route, so much smaller and more fragile, made the same journey laden with bolts of wool and bundles of petticoats, returning with warm pelts from the deep north, ancient amber and timber. We were taking car parts and cat food to Sweden, and the boat would return with Volvos and Christmas trees.

This had become the regular beat of the *Longstone*, which, named after the lighthouse, rekindled the memory of an expedition to the Farne Island of the same name, where beneath the gaze of the candy-striped column of Portland stone that had once been home to the lighthouse keeper's daughter, Grace Darling, my son had startled a seal cub, and the cub had startled him. Both retreated to watch each other, the one peeking out from behind me, the other seeking sanctuary in a rock pool, eyes and twitching whiskers just visible above the dark but limpid waters.

That was at the height of a glorious day when ancient rocks daubed with yolk-coloured lichen showed a kind of rough-textured mirror to the sun, and the surface of the sea was so unruffled as to seem dormant. Wearing T-shirts and sunglasses we had eaten ice creams and counted guillemots. By the autumn the Farnes would be murderously inhospitable. In early times even September's equinoctial gales drove ships into safe harbours, where they would remain until the spring. But there is no such let-up for a modern vessel like the *Longstone*, which treads and retreads the seaways in almost any weather, out of the Humber, steering south of the Dogger Bank as prudent skippers always have when there's a chance of a northerly wind.

In a day we would come close to the necklace of the Frisian Islands – Sylt (pronounced 'Zoolt'), Amrun, Terschelling, Schiermonnikoog – and head north towards Heligoland and the *Halligen* – half-islands – on the way passing a forest of oil rigs sucking up the slick pools of what once were ancient trees, the flared gas like distant match flames. Only a generation old, these are among the North Sea's newest accretions. But other features of the scar-impervious sea hold their course through all its moods – the grey-green smudginess Conrad described and the water's angry grin, the gloomy sky above. The Phoenicians and Romans, he pondered, 'had experienced days like this, so different in the wintry quality of the light from anything they had ever known in their native Mediterranean'.

Sea journeys are waymarked by mealtimes. At noon a call to the bridge scratched through an intercom from the galley. 'Tell the passenger his lunch is ready,' was the message from Lewis the Liverpudlian cook, grey-skinned with a scalp as smooth as an eel's, who on introduction had fixed me with a skew-eyed stare and asked, 'D'ye speak English?' Moved to muteness, I could only nod, thus failing to convince him.

At the galley door he handed me a glistening hubcap of an omelette and urged me in the direction of the lonely mess room, where I ate a morsel, bolting it down with a nugget from the letters page of the *Meat Trades Journal*.

As the *Longstone* lurched and yawed, I took pleasure in the few birds studding the maudlin expanse. Gulls were in abundance. Scarcer and more thrilling was the sight of an occasional kittiwake or swarm of tiny black petrels skirting the wave tops with giddying audacity. (On 17 September 1798, aboard a German-bound packet, Samuel Taylor Coleridge, leaving England for the first time, observed, 'A single solitary wild duck – You cannot conceive how interesting a thing it looked in that round objectless desert of waters.')

At sea every vessel within eyeshot becomes worthy of remark, as one might discuss the features of passing strangers on a lonely country walk. First, a handful of trawlers, then an improbably top-heavy container ship, and next another 'roll-on, roll-off' vessel or 'ro-ro', a direct competitor of ours, heading back from Gothenburg. Our mate knew its mate, and he regaled me with an impenetrable tale of commercial rivalries, undercutting shipping companies and not-to-be-trusted employment agencies, lest I should be duped into the misperception that the freight business was as simple as transferring goods from place to place. The ships recalibrated the horizon, lending scale to the near-eternity of interminable wave tops.

It was easy to be lulled into forgetting why I found myself aboard the *Longstone*, mesmerised by her slow roll, the passing of hours, the cups of tea. But the endless churning mass of water was the very reason. I had set out to write a book about this sea and its world, too often snubbed by writers, derided for its moody lugubriousness, its inclination towards inclemency, damp chilly sands and a decidedly utilitarian aspect when glanced at from a certain angle. But both the sea and the shores it beats upon possess their own allure. Just as the sparkle of the

Mediterranean out-twinkles a multitude of vices, do not the mists, miasmas and surliness of the North Sea cloak a multitude of gems?

True, the sea so deftly erases the clues to its own history. Already many of the coastal defences built during the last world war have crumbled into oblivion. Relics from previous centuries and millennia are more elusive still.

Early inhabitants of the North Sea basin, the Chauci and the Frisians, constructed *terpen* – earth mounds that rose above the floodplain upon which they built their homes, granaries, livestock stores and places for growing crops. Such structures yielded to the temper fits and ill-humoured sorties of the waves, which seldom left lasting damage. The move to build dykes – pushing back the chaos of the sea – coincided with the spread of Christianity. Surely, archaeologists have suggested, there is some parallel between the reclamation of the land and the saving of the pagan soul?

It took classical minds born of warmer waters to name the sea and its parts and preserve their observations for posterity. These early voyagers felt out of their depth in all sorts of ways. The tides were a perennial puzzle. In 325 BC a Greek, Pytheas of Marseille, described their rising and falling as 'the lungs of the sea' when he encountered them off the coast of the Netherlands. Pliny the Elder, on being told of the twice-daily transformation of the mudflats of the Frisian Islands, was uncertain as to whether they should be regarded as belonging to land or sea, challenging, as so often the North Sea continues to, the long-held axiom that the one is not the other. Pliny called the sea adjacent to Britain the Oceanus Britannicus, and that adjoining the German coast the Mare Germanicum.

Both were tricky places for the Romans. Partly on account of those treacherous tides, but also because they were not the masters of these waters. It was the Frisians and other tribes that possessed the upper hand, and the Pax Romana applied less readily out of reach of land. In AD 69 Roman vessels fought a pitched naval battle with a cohort of mutinous Germans who had had the audacity to steal twenty-four of Caesar's finest galleys. A century on and the Picts were the most assiduous of the piratical tribes. Later it was the Franks and the Saxons. The last straw was a maritime assault on Roman Britain and northern Gaul in AD 367. Described as a *barbarica conspiratio*, this was a hellish combination of Picts, Scots, Saxons, Franks and even the Attacotti, elusive British barbarians, possibly cannibals.

As Roman influence waned, so the North Sea frothed and swirled with new, turbulent movements. Picts swooped down the coast from Scotland, while Saxons flew fast and light across the Mare Germanicum, the vacuum left in the wake of the legions drawing traders and invaders (the distinction was blurred), their undoubtedly well-earned reputations for rapine and pillage, but also new words and phrases to contribute to the creation of England and the English.

In Whitby once, among the stones of the 'Dracula' abbey, I was struck by the starkness of the difference between the accents of a visiting family from Newcastle and that of the natives. Geordie's origins lies with the Teutonic Angles, hence 'gan' – as in 'gan doon toon', from the German *gehen* for 'go', while their Yorkshire hosts' linguistic ancestry lay further north (arse, bairn, dollop and flit all have Norse heritage). Some fifteen hundred years after their arrival, fifty miles of English coast still reflect ancient ethnic diferences, the origins of which lie on the far side of the North Sea.

History dwells on the sacking of monasteries and the clash between the one god and the many. But in that *aperçu* between empires the North Sea lands were alive with a prolixity of tongues and the deities they prayed to. Mediterranean invaders had brought wine, olive oil, marble and underfloor heating, shipping out skins, salt, gold and hunting dogs, but exotic tastes outlived them (and were never uniquely theirs).

Among the treasures unearthed from the seventh-century burial mound at Sutton Hoo were Merovingian coins, silver from Byzantium and amber from the Baltic. The peoples of the North Sea were spreading their wings and their sailcloth. Ships not only reached distant shores, but represented sacred spaces conjoining the realms of the living with eternity. Vikings, Saxons and other maritime people buried their queens, warriors and shamans in, beneath or above them, sacrificing entourages of handmaidens, concubines, horses and gaming sets to accompany the deceased on the great sea voyage to the land of the dead.

The Oseberg ship, discovered beneath an earthen mound in 1914, contained fifteen decapitated horses, a cart and a sleigh. Other sites have yielded chess sets, dog harnesses, swords and drinking vessels. No archaeologist has ever wholly penetrated the mind of a Saxon or Viking undertaker, and the symbolism of the boat is only hazily apprehended. An academic called Martin Carver has described the Sutton Hoo burial as a poem drawing 'on the time and space of the imagination, creating not a direct statement but a palimpsest of allusions', and in so doing outlined the parameters of our understanding of an event so dark, so bright and so distant. Another, Robert Van de Noort, argues that the souls possessed by the ships accompanied the deceased, but a ship burial might also have made another statement, affixing a community's sense of belonging to the sea.

Perhaps because the tonsured, peaceable monks ultimately found themselves both on the winning side of history and with a free hand to write it, their former tormentors have been sidelined within the European narrative, dismissed as part of its misspent youth. Proper, respectable, history begins with the payment of taxes and tithes and the consolidation of the power of the Church.

These changes transformed the North Sea as a political space, and the Scandinavian kings and warlords were pushed to the fringes of a Europe whose centre of gravity now lay further to the south. Trade flourished as burgeoning cities inland demanded more in the way of goods from overseas.

Naval architecture responded in kind. In middle age, the once sharp-prowed longboat, so well suited to slipping (viciously, inquisitively, lustfully) in and out of estuaries, lost its sleekness. The fat capacious *cog*, its successor, was sluggish and portly in contrast with the svelte beauty it replaced, but suited the purposes of a general trading ship, with sufficient bulk to carry cargoes of grain, timber, wool and leather. This too would become outmoded, supplanted by the smaller, faster but still beamy *fluyt* better serving the need of merchants of the times – for the reason that it was less of a catastrophe to lose a small boat than a large one. Boat design reflected the topography of the coast, the needs of trade and contemporary perils, whether tides, pirates or jealous rivals.

And over time, taller, straighter dykes and sea walls and ever more efficient means of bleeding the land of the polluting sea sapped away the ambiguity of the shoreline. The very identity of the sea altered. Once a proving ground for warriors, it acquired a new role as a hinterland, serving the interests of elites whose greater concern was the possession of estates and castles than mastery of the waves. Soon the sea would fall into the purview of scientists and navigators, their new mathematical arts enhancing and supplanting the ancient art of reckoning by 'cloud formations and the colour of the water, marine creatures and birds, iceblink, currents, driftwood and weed, the feel of a wind', as the writer David Hay put it. In the first century of the second millennium the chronicler Adam of Bremen coined the term *Nachtsprung*, 'to leap in the night', to describe the practice of steering a ship in such a way that the Pole Star remained visible above the same part of the masthead at all times when sailing on the same tack.

No less illuminating than the stars above were the mud and shingle below. Many sailors forsook the astrolabe and compass, which were fiddly, expensive and prone to error, but no ship would leave port without lead and line, a hollow lead bell filled with tallow at the end of a long rope. By lowering the bell to the bottom of the sea and retrieving it, a captain knew both the depth of the water beneath him and the constitution of the sea-bed. Given the ephemeral appearance of the surface, these gave a more reliable indication of location than any other available clues.

By the late seventeenth century, the navigator Captain John Hammond was able to give the 'Directions To Be Observed Going and Coming From Norway' in around a dozen sentences, half of one of which follows.

On ye North edge of Well Bank, if you have 28 fathoms of water, stony ground, without you be Easterly, the SW part ye same and 12 and 13 fathom, but on ye middle of this bank, 17 or 18 or more depth, sometimes fine sand and other times coarse and black specks, ye soundings on this Bank being Variable but Steering East you deepen your water and sometimes meet with coarse ground and 27 and 28 fathoms water and then less before you fall off your east side between the Well Bank and white water, where you'll find at 24 and 25 fathoms nothing on the lead . . .

If the bearings are approximate, the descriptions of the sea's bottom are almost tender in their precision. Of Swart Bank he notes, 'the middle . . . is like oatmeal'. Other features are to be identified by their 'fine yellowish coloured sand', 'fine light coloured sand', 'Muddy foundings', 'Darkish Rock' or 'Whitish sort of foundings mixed with yellow particles'.

By this time, the 1660s, almost every acre of the North Sea had been mapped and named, its secrets disinterred. Cats, colliers, pinks and every other kind of vessel traipsed between Newcastle and the Thames, to Kiel, Crail, Amsterdam, Bergen, Lerwick, Ipswich, Hamburg, Edinburgh and Esbjerg. The riches of northern Europe, its timbers, furs and cloths, lured in traders from the south who sailed up from Mediterranean and Barbary Coast ports in exotically lateened caravels. And pirates, hungry for human commodities sufficiently pale to fetch a high price in the kasbah or souk, were known to chance their arms in the cold dark waters of the North Sea.

Not that the sea was free of local dangers of such a kind. Throughout the mid-sixteenth century fishermen, trading ships and coastal villages trembled at the exploits of the sea beggars – *Watergeuzen* – Dutch adventurers like Wigbolt Ripperda, Baron Lumey and the Baron of Middelstum. These often aristocratic outlaws had been rallied by William of Orange to the cause of independence from the Habsburgs. In their zeal to free themselves from the Catholic yoke, they were rumoured to visit terrible things upon anyone they chanced upon possessing anything of value. And more localised opportunistic piracy remained endemic to much of the coast; sometimes fishermen preferred to steal a rival's catch than catch their own. Privateers, 'licensed pirates' to all extents and purposes, added to the muddle of the sea's moral compass.

The reign of the *Watergeuzen* came to an end as Habsburg tyranny gave way to the Dutch golden age, placing Amsterdam at the heart of north European culture, the pivot of trade between the North and Baltic Seas and more distant oceans. Bankrolling the gilded glory was a silvery but modestly sized fish – albeit found in shoals sometimes several miles in length. The Dutch mastered the catching and curing of the herring in a way that no other nation could match. That their descendants have perfected the art of eating a whole fish in a single gulp and still possess affection for the herring while the English can scarcely stomach them, is perhaps a legacy of that.

Herring meant money, and money meant power and the right to trade. At the end of the seventeenth century the Dutch and English embarked on half a century of maritime pugilism: the Anglo Dutch Wars, I–IV. Their skirmishes, such as the Battle of Kentish Knock, the Battle of Texel, the Battle of Lowestoft and the Medway Raid, were slow, loud and carefully choreographed – almost like courtly dances set to a pyrotechnic accompaniment, and as such not without entertainment value. Onlookers from the shore would be spellbound by the sight of upwards of sixty or eighty ships of war, entirely at the mercy of the vicissitudes of their own clumsiness and the shifty, changeable North Sea winds, enveloping themselves in great plumes of smoke, spewing round shot and musket balls, frequently to uncertain tactical effect.

Not all such encounters were inconclusive, neither were they mere theatre. From Dutch dykes, cliffs and beaches, relatives would watch for the return of the fleets, hope sometimes crumbling to despair as the smashed ships limped into harbour with their bloodied, blinded menfolk – or without them. Though sluggish and the trajectories of their primitive missiles were erratic, seventeenth-century warships could inflict damage reaching deep inland: the Battle of the Gabbard, fought off the coast of Suffolk, resulted in so comprehensive a victory for the English that they were able to impose a blockade on the Dutch, many of whom, reliant on imports of rye and wheat, were pushed beyond the edge of starvation. And yet, so necessary to each other's economic and cultural survival were the two nations that the packet service between Harwich and

Holland, a small fleet of single-masted, shallow-draughted galliots and hoys, traversed the North Sea unmolested even when Dutch and British relations were at their blackest.

For some years in Oslo a batch of correspondence passed between the Dutch, German and British embassies and the Norwegian government as a sort of parlour game. The letters had been written in the 1600s by the owner of a repair yard at a town called Gismeroya on the southern coast of Norway. None of the ambassadors could translate these letters in their entirety, but each could pick out individual words and phrases, for they were composed in a jumble of North Sea languages. Their author was native to no single country but a true denizen of the North Sea. (Earlier still, the Hanseatic League had operated through the medium of its own language comprised mostly of Middle Low German, embellished with a smattering of Dutch, Danish, Finnish and a touch of Slav.)

What these letters proved was that by the beginning of the eighteenth century the North Sea rim had almost become a world unto itself – not cut off from that beyond, because of course there had been trade links with Africa, the Baltic and the Mediterranean since well before recorded history. Nonetheless a communality of experience now bound together North Sea peoples almost regardless of nationality and sometimes with greater cohesion than that bonding coast dwellers to their inland compatriots. Small coastal towns, perhaps dependent on the export of a single product or handful of products or raw materials – coprolite, rye, coal, hemp, mutton or whisky – became cosmopolitan trading centres and their inhabitants accustomed to, even conversant with, languages that were not their own.

Such was the appetite of Amsterdam for imported labour that long after the golden age it drew thousands of domestic labourers, journeymen, shipwrights – a kind of New York of its day. (What is now New York is fittingly built on the bones of New Amsterdam.) Moreover, advances in navigational technology and even the contested sharing of the wealth of the sea created both a lingua franca of experience and opportunities for coastal dwellers to live well beyond the confines of their own parishes. Rates of literacy were significantly higher than they were inland, just as the incidence of witchcraft accusations was lower, coast dwellers being that much better acquainted with human variety and difference.

The waves sparkled brighter still beneath the enlightened gaze of the eighteenth century, the sea acquiring a new, more abstract identity and a role as a source of pleasure and health – in essence, more than a mere resource, a conduit for trade or theatre of war, rather as a *thing* in itself. Around the same time Europe was drawn to new markets and the promise of greater riches in the Indies, East and West, in North America and Sub-Saharan Africa. The North Sea remained at the hub, but of ever-spreading concentric circles of wealth, power and possibility. Now the use of larger ships with deeper draughts relegated coastal towns with shallow harbours and channels to second-class trading posts or made them entirely redundant. Meanwhile, improved roads and canal networks spread like a mesh of capillaries throughout Europe, undermining the importance of the old sea routes.

Communities that had relied on cultural and economic ties with their equivalents across the North Sea or along the coast began to look inland for markets. Smaller settlements dependent on trade or on artisanal fishing from open boats or nets worked from the shore could no longer compete with the bigger fishing towns with their large trawler basins and deep-water docks equipped for transporting by rail.

But the railway was coming, bringing a new breed of seasonal migrant, the tourists with their bathing machines, dance cards and donkey riding and the descendants of whom continue to return in droves each summer.

By the early nineteenth century the North Sea was very much safer than it had ever been. Piracy had been rooted out, the sea too well policed to permit its existence. Following the defeat of Napoleonic France, Europe was mostly at peace, and the glory days of smuggling, which had begun with wool and only later included the more glamorous contraband commodities of tea, brandy, wine and hollands (gin), were fading, although there must have been those who ached for its return.

Once it had been possible to lure, bribe or terrorise whole communities into complicity with the illicit trade, and fortunes could be made from outwitting the red-coated and ill-equipped customs authorities. Smuggling even expedited the evolution of the sailing boat. The invention of the cutter, a vessel with a fore-and-aft rig, faster before more points of wind than any predecessor, is attributed to what in effect amounted to an arms race between the smugglers and the revenue officers pursuing them.

Governments, especially in times of war, made strenuous if often futile efforts to prevent the loss of customs duties. A typical British ordinance was a 1779 act of Parliament that demanded that 'All Dealers in Tea, Coffee, Chocolate and Foreign Spirituous Liquors, who have not those Articles painted or written in large legible characters over their Outer Door, or some conspicuous Part of their Houses . . . forfeit two hundred pounds.' But officers of the law could be induced to turn a blind eye for very much less.

Smugglers and wreckers, prostitutes and dealers in duty-free chocolate, these were the dark side of the seaside. Then as now such pursuits coexisted with the effete cosmopolitanism of the surging tide of summer visitors, the latter smoothing away the sharper edges of the former, the former adding spice to the latter.

If the twentieth century saw North Sea waters placated by science, trade and other totems of nineteenth-century rationalism (tide tables, timetables and the hiss of steam), it still simmered with a tension that would boil over fourteen years after its start.

Strangely enough, on the day that the Archduke Franz Ferdinand was shot by his Serb assassin Gavrilo Princip in Sarajevo the top brass of the Royal Navy were in the Baltic town of Kiel with their German counterparts, celebrating with oompah bands and bumpers of champagne the expansion of its eponymous waterway, now sufficient to allow a dreadnought battleship to pass from the North to the Baltic Sea (and vice versa) without necessitating the trip around Denmark.

Maps from before 1914 describe the North Sea as the German Ocean, but ironically Germany's poor access to the North Sea and its lack of harbours suitable for berthing battleships fed the strident ascent of militarism and hence its march to war.

Within a few years of his country's creation in 1871, Admiral von Tirpitz of the German Imperial Navy had masterminded the doctrine of *Flottenpolitik*, which held that if it were to enjoy its 'rightful' share of colonial spoils and trade Germany would need to match its rivals in naval strength. The North Sea, seen through such a prism, was the anteroom to the world and all its riches.

The boat-loving Kaiser Wilhelm II became infatuated with the idea, and by the turn of the century, the arms race had started in earnest.

The British regarded Willy, grandson of Queen Victoria, as pompous, silly and erratic. Victoria herself was aghast on hearing in 1890 that her prime minister Lord Salisbury had agreed to sign over the British resort island of Heligoland to Germany in exchange for a free run in Zanzibar, and came close to exercising her royal prerogative to prevent it. Many Heligolanders, having experienced the 'despotism' Victoria despised in Wilhelm, came to wish she had.

In 1903 an upper-class government clerk, keen yachtsman and former soldier in the Boer War published a ripping yarn which saw its protagonist – strangely enough, an upper-class government clerk – uncovers a German plan to send an invasion force across the North Sea in a fleet of barges.

Erskine Childers's *The Riddle of the Sands*, perhaps the greatest North Sea novel written and still riveting despite its sometimes laboured prose, has not been out of print since. It had an incendiary effect on the British public, convincing it that the government was lackadaisical in its response to German shipbuilding and putting pressure on Lloyd George to step up production in the shipyards of the Clyde and Tyne.

Through both world wars the coasts of each side of the North Sea were tense with anticipation and barbed wire, and the sea itself hosted thunderous and terrible sea battles. Just as many of the shoot-outs between the fleets of the Anglo-Dutch wars concluded with exhausted and expensive stalemates, so First World War encounters were often of a similar kind – who or whether anyone won the Battle of Jutland remains a moot point; that nearly 10,000 men lost their lives is not. Thick with mines and shot with submarines, the abstract politics of the sea exploded into life, and death.

The North Sea was more subdued during the Second World War – heavily mined and criss-crossed by submarines. But with the Allied victory in Europe in 1945, it was if the North Sea littoral states collectively exhaled with relief. Peace allowed the return of trawlers to waters which, having been only lightly harvested for five years, were now burgeoning with fish, while business-hungry resorts lured pleasure-craving tourists from Whitby to Wilhelmshaven. The maritime centres of gravity of the new conflict between the communist bloc and the capitalist West lay far to the north, in the Atlantic Ocean and the Bering Sea, and fishing communities, at least those in the United Kingdom, found themselves hard hit not by the Cold War, but by the Cod Wars, a series of disputes over fishing rights with Iceland, upon whose fish stocks much of the British industry relied.

Britain played its hand badly and greedily, and the Icelanders, whom even the UK press invariably described as 'plucky', prevailed, raising their tiny sub-Arctic nation to new heights of prosperity while the social and economic structures of some British coastal towns began to come undone.

The discovery of oil didn't quite step into the breach left by the decommissioning of trawlers, but it did promise new opportunities.

Only two countries stood to benefit from the deposits of valuable goo deep beneath the seabed. Norway, a thrifty country with a small population to support, took prudent measures to ensure the windfall would benefit future generations. In Britain the prospect of oil money threatened to raise as many issues as it could ever solve. Most dangerously it threatened to reignite the fitfully dormant issue of Scottish independence. And it created new physical hazards on the seascape culminating in an explosion on the Piper Alpha production platform in which 167 oil workers burned, drowned or suffocated to death on 6 July 1988.

North Sea Sybils have long whispered that the reservoirs would run dry. That has yet to happen. The platforms have however permanently altered the architecture of the sea to an extent that no single other thing did before them, though now they have been joined by the giant turbines of the wind farms – Gunfleet Sands off the coast of Kent, Princess Amalia in Dutch waters, Horns Rev 2, Alpha Venus, Beatrice, Thornton Bank – the push for renewable energy adding a new layer to the process of place-naming the North Sea that began before it became a sea.

Oil and wind cast the North Sea in an industrial, functional light, but not everything changes. Even in the face of cheap flights to 'sunny Spain' and Phuket, we continue to chance a North Sea holiday. Freighters ply many of the same routes as the *fluyts* and *cogs* of centuries past. Fish, despite the gloomy auguries of scientists and conservationists, still spawn and shoal and are caught and grace our tables. But the North Sea is a so-so repository of its own physical memories, in places erasing its inheritance with the reckless speed of a spendthrift heir. And it can be a lonely place. Just as the Mediterranean is garrulous, busy and bright even where its shores are empty, its North Sea counterparts tend towards the sombre, the still and the stern, even where trampled by happy summer crowds.

For all that, I reasoned, in conceiving this book and these journeys, it scarcely deserves our indifference. Other seas may be more photogenic, more televisual, their ports and harbours exotic and sensual, but was it fair to permit the North Sea to become unfamiliar through being overfamiliar? What did I know previously of the courtship rituals of the island of Föhr, the tragedies inflicted upon Heligoland, the mysterious language of Norn, the genius of the Ostend painters, the trials and tribulations of the German *Warft* dwellers who each year confront the power of the *Sturmflut,* or even the boozy pleasures waiting behind the portals of the Nordern Lights Pub? Indeed, what had I experienced hitherto of the magic of a winter's evening in the marshes of the estuary of the Thames, from where I set out, by bus, boat, bicycle and train, to explore the sea that lay beyond?

In Defence of the Estuary

> Ours was the marsh country, down by the river, within, as
> the river wound, twenty miles of the sea . . . that this bleak
> place overgrown with nettles was the churchyard . . . and that
> the dark flat wilderness intersected with dykes and mounds
> and gates, with the scattered cattle feeding on it, was the
> marshes; and that the low leaden line beyond was the river;
> and that the distant savage lair from which the wind was
> rushing, was the sea.
>
> Charles Dickens, *Great Expectations*

Descend slippery steps from the embankment at Gabriel's Wharf
to poke along a furlong's length of foreshore and the tenor of the
Thames shifts abruptly. There is an odour, cool, dank and ancient,
pertaining to the very bedrock of London. Here among the
broken bricks and stones are the smashed atoms of the city, the
pipe stems, bones, bullets and crockery shards (willow-patterned,
heavy-glazed, IKEA), revealing a history in fragments, tantalisingly
and magnificently jumbled with no regard for hierarchy or
pomp.

The sanitised and trammelled Thames is only an echo of its
former self. Before embankment filtration its tendrils branched
everywhere, feeding and poisoning the city in almost equal
measure. Where river and man now stand aloof from each other,

they were once intimate. Wherries, lighters and barges clogged the banks and watermen jostled for fares. At the rat runs where the wharfmen unloaded – Kidney Stairs, Pelican Stairs, Pickled Herring Stairs, Mason's Stairs – vice, pleasure and business thrived and could scarcely be distinguished. Mudlarks, children caked in the river's grey ooze, inhabited its banks, scraping a half-life from the recovery of the accidentally lost (buttons, nails and pennies), the washed up in the tide, the long since forgotten.

It stank long before the coining of the term the Great Stink in 1858. Tobias Smollett had complained ninety years before of a river 'impregnated with all the filth of London . . . human excrement [being] the least offensive part of the concrete, which is composed of all the drugs, minerals and poisons used in mechanics and manufacture, enriched with the putrefying carcasses of beasts and men, and mixed with the scourings of all the wash-tubs, kennels, and common sewers within the bills of mortality'.

A myriad of quotidian and extraordinary tragedies contributed to the stench. There were those that could stun even the most hard-nosed of cities.

Early in my forays I chanced upon a plaque at the bankside at Woolwich which remembers (or reminds us) how on the warm and clement evening of 3 September 1878 a 220-foot steamboat called the *Princess Alice* was returning from the long-vanished Rosherville Pleasure Gardens at Gravesend, its 700 passengers, women, children and day trippers, in high, holiday spirits.

It moved me, this story – an abrupt beginning to my estuary adventures.

Alice was fast and narrow, built as a blockade runner for the Confederate army during the American Civil War and, such being the curious life of ships, recommissioned for pleasure on the Thames. At a notorious bend near Woolwich she was struck amidships by a Newcastle collier steaming out towards the North

Sea and her bows almost severed. *Alice* sank quickly, dragging her passengers into the flooding and opaque current.

A city no stranger to shocks, London was seized by a collective frenzy. At Woolwich a makeshift mortuary was soon choking with swollen bodies and grief. Scarcely mentioned by the press, which otherwise gorged on the *Princess Alice* story, was that the victims were covered in the raw filth released by Joseph Bazalgette's famous sewage works, which saved London from the excrement which had coursed through its streets but failed to treat it.

Londoners possess short-lived and selective memories. The sinking of the *Alice* is forgotten bar the plaque, but the horror of the accident resurfaced in 1989 when another pleasure boat, the *Marchioness*, sank following a collision, claiming 51 lives. Just as it had in 1878, the press laboured the youth, beauty and potential of the victims and the public clamoured for new measures and a safer river.

Ghosts dance with shades of glory on the waters of the London Thames. But what lay beyond the shimmering lights, the prettified river walks, the temples to Mammon? Indeed it was a pleasure boat trip (unhampered by disaster) that spurred me to explore the lower reaches of the Thames, which my naive and cosmopolitan mind's eye could only imagine as mute, disquieting and beyond the pale. Who were its inhabitants, flung by the city's centrifuge to its outer edges? Where does the river become the sea? And did the silvery notes that glanced, sometimes, from its otherwise stalwartly green waters, presage some deeper, more intriguing beauty beyond? Thus charged I ventured, if not without apprehension, east towards the long-eclipsed estuary.

At Tilbury the river pilot hands the baton to the sea pilot, who in his trim-as-a-captain's-cap launch guides the big ships into dock, where they unload cargoes of timber, toys and shiny cars, and fill up before heading out again, waterlines set by the balance-of-trade deficit. And from here the cruise ships dinner-dance to Nice, St Petersburg and Bergen. On sunny days I've seen couples sitting upon their fold-up chairs on the foreshore, beamingly content, watching these vessels which come and go like un-murmuring servants, bulk light on the water, disarmingly quick, ponderously silent. But back from the ordered riverbank the land gives way to a patchwork of unkempt pastures, where travellers graze ponies among the wreckage of burned-out cars, and where amid a haphazard smorgasbord of allotments, pylons and pockets of bucolic countryside I came across a city built on shoes.

The faded vision of Bataville at Tilbury has its twin in the Czech town of Zlin. Its founder Tomasz Bata said he was inspired by Henry Ford to create a metropolis devoted to the manufacture of footwear in which, in return for loyalty and labour, his workers would receive housing, training, childcare and something respectable to put upon their feet. Drawn by cheap land and labour, Bata replicated the entirety of Zlin's Corbusier-inspired work-life complex of factories and houses replete with school, cinema, hotel and ballroom in a patch of wasteland beyond Tilbury dock.

Life in East Tilbury, for five bizarre decades, was dominated by a micro-economy driven by the manufacture of heels, soles and uppers – which also added wholly new elements to the gene pool. The county district of Thurrock became almost a colony of Czechoslovakia, all the more so when the Soviets established their own foothold in Prague, nationalising the Zlin factory and putting greater pressure on Tilbury to make up the volumes if the shoe company was to maintain its profits. By the late 1980s Bata had succumbed to the charms of cheap Asian labour, and wound down its operations. The factories, once famed for their light and airy interiors, are now unlit and patrolled by men with dogs. Terraces of workers' cottagers born on a Bauhaus drawing board have turned native, acquiring a peculiarly English cast of dishevelled pokiness.

Above many flies the ubiquitous standard of the scowling and dispossessed, the George Cross.

For all that, the Czech connection has yet to wither. I met a man called Peter Cermak mowing grass outside a storage hut. Peter's parents arrived at Tilbury in the 1930s to train the locals in the Bata method of sole adhesion. War and the Iron Curtain interrupted their return, and he grew up in what he remembers as 'half idyll, half authoritarian state'. The dance hall, he said, was the best in Essex. But the bosses were heavy handed, demanding unquestioning loyalty and fiercely intolerant of dissent or unionism. Cermak, who also worked for Bata, spent some time abroad but returned. 'Here I am now, tending the lawn in the ruins of my childhood.'

He warned me that Bataville's inhabitants were not friendly. Old linkages had been broken, and unemployment was high. A scheme for massive redevelopment and thousands of new homes loomed over Thurrock like the shadow cast by some voracious raptor, hence the unequivocal demand to FUCK THE THAMES GATEWAY sprayed in several choice locations. I stole a surreptitious photograph of this, catching a fish and chip shop in the frame. The fryer turned in my direction and raised an angry finger.

Tomasz Bata's detractors accused him of espousing a philosophy with fascistic overtones. Ironically for a man who made his fortune by helping the masses keep their feet firmly on the ground, he died in an aeroplane crash in 1932. It was, said those who had known him, characteristic of Bata that he'd goaded his private pilot to fly to Switzerland in the face of an oncoming storm. Close to the long-abandoned reception building, in a privet-hedged garden on a fading patch of lawn littered with cigarette papers and beer bottles, stands his statue.

'Do you know,' said Cermak, 'that Henry Ford built a city in the Amazon called Fordlandia, which was overgrown by jungle within three decades of the first stone being laid? That's what comes of outsiders and their grand schemes.' And he turned away, drowning me out with the sound of his strimmer.

Beyond Tilbury lie the marshes: the Cooling Marshes, Whalebone Marshes, Cliffe Marshes, Fobbing Marshes, Allhallows Marshes, Lee Marshes . . . It is a landscape little changed since Pip's fictional and fateful encounter with his future benefactor Magwitch – who threatens to cut his throat, turns him upside down to empty his pockets and dislodges no more than a piece of bread – a tableau of tidal creeks and paths through smuggler-beloved water meadows, the domain of patrolling harriers and owls. Very low tides reveal the bones of the hulks, decrepit prison boats of the kind from which Magwitch escaped, protruding from the rank bed of the river and its offshoots.

It is the tide that takes, brings, hides and sculpts the estuary – and sometimes musters forces of extraordinary destructive power, rolling up the seas, flinging them at the shore. On the night of the Great Flood of 31 January 1953 a tidal surge swept across Canvey Island, drowning 53 people, many in their own beds. In Essex and Kent another 200 met the same end. And in the Netherlands, where the surge swept across low-lying polders, briefly reclaiming them for the sea, almost 2,000 people perished in what the Dutch call the *Watersnoodramp*, the most devastating natural disaster in post-war Europe. Most of those who died on Canvey were the inhabitants of jerry-built shacks, uncounted and unregistered, 'temporary accommodation' for victims of the Blitz that no one had seen fit to condemn.

There's an irony that Canvey and the Netherlands should have borne so much of the brunt of the Great Flood. Canvey would not have existed had it not been wrested out of the mud by the Dutch engineer Cornelius Vermuyden, who at the invitation of James I brought a boatload of dyke-building labourers from across the North Sea to drain the marshes. They settled, built octagonal cottages like fancy cakes utterly at odds with the vernacular clapboarded dwellings of Essex and set up their Dutch homes beneath the north bank of the Thames.

Then England fell out with Holland. In the first week of June 1667 the legendary Admiral Michiel de Ruyter drove his fleet into the maws of the Thames and the Medway and set about burning British ships and forts and throwing London into convulsions of panic. Samuel Pepys, on hearing that the underwater chain that protected the capital had been broken, confided to his diary, 'all our hearts do now ake . . . I do fear too much that the whole kingdom is undone.'

It was, in a sense, a false alarm. De Ruyter wasn't bent on invasion, only on punishing perfidious Albion for its duplicity – plotting with France against Holland while purporting to negotiate with Amsterdam in good faith. Duly humbled, Charles II signed a peace treaty with the triumphant Dutch, and their erstwhile tormentor rose so high in the estimation of the relieved British public that when De Ruyter was struck down by Spanish grapeshot in 1677 there was little celebration among his former foes. The relationship had been both intimate and intricate. De Ruyter's ships had been the scourge of the North Sea throughout the Anglo-Dutch Wars, but he was never vicious. Within weeks of his death a biography of De Ruyter became a Cheapside bestseller.

In life, wrote its author Robert L'Estrange, the man who had sacked the estuary was 'not fat, but fleshy, of a gracefull and majestic countenance, his aspect pleasant and chearfull, not terrible by too much fierceness, nor by too great mildeness un-awful; of a complexion sanguine, and a constitution temperate and healthfull; sober in his diet and moderate, though free in his words, neither sullen with rigid and morose reservedness . . .' (De Ruyter's nightshirt, a lasting testament to the 'fleshiness' L'Estrange describes, takes pride of place in the maritime museum in the

Dutch town of Vlissingen, which the English have long known as Flushing.)

In the sore weeks after De Ruyter's raid anti-Dutch feeling ran rampant. Vengeful mobs of Englishmen put the little cottages to the torch – punishment for their inhabitants' imagined crimes of sending signals to the enemy fleet and general treachery. Overnight Canvey lost the character it had assumed, bar its dykes, sea wall and two cottages – one of which now houses a collection of corn dollies. That the causeway connecting Canvey to the mainland is called the Avenue of Remembrance is a nod to the victims of the flood, not to the creators of the island, who were brutally dispossessed. Today Canvey sounds like a joke, a third-rate seaside resort for anyone lacking the money or imagination to travel further afield. It is almost wholly the product of post-war sprawl. But within the (unmistakably Dutch) high sea wall that encloses it there's a Netherlandish gentleness in its quiet, grid-like and idiosyncratic cul-de-sacs.

Occupying an acre or so of the island's northern shore is a ramshackle marina at the candidly named Small Gains Creek, a veritable dogs' home of yachts, smacks and working boats, many in an advanced state of decay, ribs jutting defiantly from mud-wedded keels. Many are houseboats, either by destiny or design, reachable by rickety plank walks suspended on stilts in approximations of garden paths. Few of these vessels will ever float again, but nor will anyone remove them, so they stay, disintegrating by degrees. But the mess and entropy of the marina provide an antidote to the civically sensible order imposed on Canvey by the planners of the early 1960s, with their boxy vision of spirit-sapping dullness. It helps Canvey resurrect (against a backdrop of tanning parlours, carports and takeaways) something of the flash of De Ruyter's cannon, of fireships and musket shots, all of which can be conjured by squinting into the old-gold river-sea.

Canvey, like Tilbury and towns across the river in Kent – Chatham, Rochester, Gravesend – is long steeled to the threat of invasion, whether by Dutch, French, Spanish or Germans (less so to 'foreign' fauna like the Asiatic clam and zebra mussel). In 1795 an ex-military man called George Hanger wrote to the Admiralty:

I have seriously reflected on my pillow on the danger the capital has been exposed to within these few months, since the French have been in possession of Holland, *the easterly winds prevailing, with dark and long nights*, and not a ship in the mouth of the Thames, or near it, or any defence whatever, that I know of, to protect the capital. I confess it is to my utter astonishment that they have not run a body of men over in the long nights from Holland into the Thames, for in seven hours after landing, they might have been in London *without opposition*; indeed, they have had their hands pretty full of business, which I believe is the only reason they did not, but this is no reason why we should think they *will not do it*.

The forts at Tilbury and Gravesend, which squat like crabs, almost invisible from the river, Martello towers like sandcastles and Maunsell Forts, are perhaps only the physical extrusions of a general sense of fear that has persisted over generations. In the First World War the Martellos, built to defend against French invasion more than a century previously, were reactivated – Tower C in Jaywick, for instance, became a picket post for the 8th Cyclist Battalion of the Essex Regiment – while the soft contours of England's hazy eastern flank were stiffened with pillboxes and rumour.

In November 1914 German warships fired a salvo of shells at Great Yarmouth in Norfolk. It landed ineffectually on the beach but still showed Britain's vulnerability to seaborne threats. In the same month the German spy Carl Lody was executed by firing squad at the Tower of London having been found guilty of, among other crimes, spying on the movements of the British fleet while masquerading as an artist. Soon afterwards the *New York Times* giddily ran an article suggesting that the raid had only been made possible by the existence of a German spy network working on the English coast. The Lody trial, it said, 'showed how easily information could be transmitted to Germany through Holland', explaining that flashlights and pigeons were the secret behind the 'spy peril', with agents on the British coast sending signals to boats flying neutral flags. These would steam close to the German shore and release message-carrying pigeons.

All this put pigeons in the firing line: 'The bird shot at Framlingham, a short way inland from the Suffolk coast, on Tuesday, has been identified definitely as a *foreign pigeon*, and the police are following up information which has come into their hands.' Further proof of a spy network was furnished by villagers in Norfolk and Suffolk who told of 'big cars rushing wildly through the night'. No doubt there were *some* spies and, archaic as they might seem now, pigeons, torches and big cars could be powerful tools for the agents of the Kaiser, especially in conjunction with a submarine and a handful of dreadnoughts. In a churchyard in Harwich there stands an empty German shell case turned collection box, which, says its plaque, is 'enduring testament to the perfidy of the invidious Hun'.

Less than a fortnight after that *New York Times* article was published, a fleet of German battlecruisers and destroyers shelled Hartlepool, Scarborough and Whitby, killing 137 people and wounding a further 600 before the vessels returned to their home ports almost unscathed by the British fleet. A US newspaper, the *Independent*, reported how, 'Sudden as a lightning flash in a lowering storm half a dozen cruisers of the Black Eagle shoot out of the mist that hovers over the North Sea and bombard the coast of the boasted invulnerable isle.'

Of all the estuary's sulkiest corners, Shoeburyness is among its most wary and impenetrable. Or so it seemed on a day of scattered showers punctured by interludes of intense, almost hallucinatory sunlight. The Ministry of Defence owns much of this shoreline, but at weekends it lowers its guard, and when I arrived with a photographer friend at an entrance – high mesh gates prettily garlanded with unfriendly-looking fencing – men in berets waved us through neither querying nor demurring. We drove slowly onto a dead-straight road, a steep ditch on either side, coming to an abrupt halt at the sea wall where it would have otherwise tumbled into the estuary.

The transition from civilian to military worlds is sudden, dark and exciting. Painted signs warn against picking up strange objects and the (strictly prohibited) taking of photographs. It is all somehow Wyndhamesque, old-fashioned but suffused with menacing potential. Or from another stance sublimely beautiful, looking out towards the estuary at a vision that Turner might have held in his mind's eye, of waves heavily tinted with silt marching in from the North Sea, uniformly khaki, no foam breaking and the sky above soot grey.

We watched as a flock of waders scattered itself across the gloom like cinders. The southern shore of the Thames was just visible in silhouette, and haphazard platoons of black geese unevenly dispersed across both the fluid elements. Out of the long cold grass a panting yellow Labrador brushed hot and wet past our legs holding in its mouth a limply quacking teal. In pursuit of the dog came a red-bearded man clad in a green hunting jacket, and our first thought was that, although we hadn't heard the shot, he had bagged the duck. He scowled after the dog, but she was far off down the path with her prize.

The skeins of geese continued gathering in the sky as if conjured from the clouds – they had beaten down the spine of the North Sea from their nesting grounds in Siberia to shelter in the relative clemency of the estuary. 'Oh no!' The red-haired man had stopped by us to apologise for the savagery of his Labrador. 'It's instinct, I guess,' he said, and we agreed and fell into step and conversation.

I don't know who we'd expected to meet on the walk, if anyone at all, but I don't think it was Chris, a north London Jewish history teacher working with young offenders who had moved to the nearby village of Great Wakering to be closer to his wife's parents, who, he said, were part of the well-established Jewish community around Southend. Jews, he said, had moved out of the East End like so many others. 'There's more space here. It's closer to the sea,' he said, 'like Miami.' And he gave a shrill chuckle. Nothing ever stayed the same. Until recently Southend had possessed two proper Jewish delicatessens, as good as those in Golders Green, but a kosher food section in Sainsbury's had killed them off. At least there were still two synagogues. I asked to which he belonged. 'Definitely the Reform.'

Around his neck Chris wore an improbably large pair of binoculars built for star-gazing. And he discharged excited puffs of knowledge about the coast and the birds he'd seen. As he did so his elbows sat close to his body while his forearms and hands opened and closed with a kind of rabbinical rhythm like the wings of a mechanical bird, his fingertips briefly interleaving. The gradual dispersal of the local Jewish community was not, he said, a cause of any great sorrow. Now there were thriving Polish and Nigerian communities and new foods and delicatessens. And he loved his new proximity to the wild, strange, quasi-military coast and its curious connections with history. He, the grandson of Jewish refugees, had made friends with men who had fought with the *Wehrmacht* and, having been confined in POW camps, had chosen to settle close to the North Sea for the rest of their lives.

Chris's path veered left inland; ours went right. The mysterious architecture of war was everywhere: half hidden among the flats and marshes was a necropolis of crumbling bunkers, discarded machinery and windowless structures, the purpose of which was neither clear nor, I guessed, remembered. And at ebb tide the sea pulled back to reveal a shore-scape of rusting sheets of iron, shell holes blasted through the middle, jagged and mangled at the edges. It's a lethal beach, the kind to which a child would be compulsively drawn. Indeed, my friend Alex tripped on a slab of slippery concrete and smacked his head on a rock, narrowly avoiding losing an eye on a vicious and random spike. Shoeburyness has yet to be made safe.

Still more dangerous, just across a tiny creek lies the island of Foulness. Once an atomic weapons research establishment, access to strangers is utterly forbidden, but peering from a hummock we could just make out the shapes of improbably leaning towers, unorthodox derricks, structures poised at preposterous angles. I had heard that the beef reared among this junkyard of Cold War detritus, grazing on thrift, aster, milkwort and other exotic seagrasses, is piquant, tender and well-seasoned, almost as true a taste of the estuary as that denizen of its ooze, the cockle.

The drum-shaped ruin of Hadleigh Castle – decrepit as painted by John Constable, more so now – is deliciously reminiscent of a sandcastle that has withstood the lapping of a first wave but will topple at the second. Baron Hubert de Burgh had it built some time in the early 1200s; a century later Edward III improved Hadleigh, and from the windows of its long-vanished solarium gazed out beyond the marshes towards the sea from which a French invasion might have come but never did.

The turn-off from the A12 (follow the sign to Essex World of Beds) is unpromising, but one majestic, sweeping view from the castle redeems the visit, taking in the glistening spike of Canary Wharf and on the Kent side of the Thames the Isle of Grain refinery spewing too-white smoke and other fumes. Falling away from the castle itself, a soft wooded escarpment rolls down to the marshes and to Two Tree Island, which is neither as bare as it sounds nor in any obvious way an island, but a place where stalks of shoulder-high fennel flourish and infuse the air with the fragrance of aniseed and liquorice. Signs – yet more signs – caution that nesting avocets are not to be disturbed, but fail to dampen the petrol whine of the radio-controlled aeroplanes climbing and tumbling above the island's scrubby heath.

A mile's walk east along the estuary, and the path stops at Leigh (-on-Sea, lest anyone be in doubt as to the status of the river), where I supped with royalty.

Michael Bates is the second-generation Prince of Sealand, a former World War II gun platform built seven sea miles out from the Suffolk coast as a defence against the Luftwaffe. His father Roy was a natural adventurer who fought demob boredom through a series of erratic business ventures and an attempt, culminating in his prosecution, to start a pirate radio station somewhere in the English Channel. On 2 September 1967, driven both by revenge and by entrepreneurialism, Bates Senior sailed out to one of the many fortress islands built around the British coast during the war to defend against invasion and declared himself its monarch.

What was Roughs Tower he renamed Sealand, arguing that as it lay beyond the recently redrawn UK territorial limit and had been abandoned by the War Office in the 1950s, the platform was *terra nullius* with little or no legal impediment existing to prevent the appointment of himself and his wife, Princess Joan, as its heads of state. The incensed government set about the destruction of other forts so as to prevent imitators or even any aspiration Bates might possess to establish an archipelago nation, but even now the sovereignty and very existence of Sealand is a question about which Foreign Office lawyers feel decidedly queasy.

Sealand has accrued a near-mythical status among aficionados of quirkiness, something the Bates family has worked hard to achieve, playing on its patchwork heritage of stories, such as the attempted 'theft' of the platform in 1973 by a consortium of Dutch businessmen which resulted in a helicopter shoot-out, fisticuffs and the Bates family taking hostages. Apropos of God-knows-what, a Sealand passport was rumoured to have been found at the scene of Gianni Versace's murder.

I wanted to visit the platform. Michael Bates suggested we meet to discuss things over a pint of cockles.

Bates as good as grew up on Sealand, an isolated steel and concrete pile of nothing, and by his account his adolescence was terrifying at times, with him often being left alone to watch against chancers and the Royal Navy, with no one for company but imaginary voices carried in the battering seas and winds.

In the manuscript of the autobiography that he showed me he boasted of having done bad things – not least during the hostage/ helicopter episode. After meeting me off the train at Leigh station he whisked me away in his silver Range Rover. There were reasons of state behind our destination – it was all, he said, 'a bit political'.

Deteriorating relations between Michael and his girlfriend meant he was back at his ex-wife's semi-detached house in Westcliff. She made tea, and we sat in a tidy but not regal kitchen as toy dogs and fancy cats skirled around our ankles and the prince regaled me with tales of plots and coups and dirty tricks. He was already in discussions with Hollywood about the biopic, he said, and had a strong vision of how the movie should be. Had I ever seen a film called *Lethal Weapon*? But I sensed that Michael was himself beginning to tire of Sealand. I'd seen him on a Canadian chat show telling the world that he was looking to sell it for something in the region of £75 million.

Not a lot, he pointed out, for an independent state that generated decent revenue. It was 'no secret', he told me, that

Sealand made money through the sale of peerages – a knighthood can be purchased for ninety-nine pounds. 'How much do you make?' I asked. 'A *lot*.' When we'd finished our tea and looked through the family albums (his daughter had been a local beauty queen and took up many of its pages), we drove down to the quayside to take a peek at his other line of business.

Leigh-on-Sea is a glorious surprise of pubs, whelk and winkle stalls, ice creams, coffee shops and even a strip of sand, which for want of any other purpose serves fairly successfully as a beach. The train to Fenchurch Street takes only an hour. It is the perfect Dickensian day out, neither la-di-da nor 'ow's your father but friendly, well mannered and non-judgemental. Ancient black-tarred cockle sheds exude steam and pleasant fish smells, while behind them on the quay sit a jaunty little fleet of boats and a tangle of gear.

Until the early 1970s cockling was a dangerous, body-wrecking pursuit. The small boats would sail out to the cockle beds, and as the tide ebbed men would wade to the exposed sands and rake up the molluscs into large hand-held scoops. The whole job is undertaken now with vacuums, which suck up cockle colonies in one slurp. Michael owns two boats, and we watched as one drew alongside the quay, a lorry came to meet it, and cockles were hauled up in one-tonne sacks to be driven away. The cockles, said Michael, would be in Spain by the end of the next day. They couldn't get enough of them there, where they were known as *almejas* – so much more appetising than 'cockles' with its connotations of poor-man's food.

'We don't appreciate them like the Spanish – they pay fortunes for good cockles,' he said.

'How much will one of those big sacks make?' I asked.

'A *lot*.'

Later, a well-informed source suggested that each cockle boat could make up to a million pounds in a summer's work, and if the Spanish recession had dented that figure, it hadn't been by much.

Michael never delivered on the half-promise to take me out to Sealand. My interest seemed to have been eclipsed by that of a celebrity journalist with whom he was in yet more talks about a possible visit. But in most respects I'd gleaned what I wanted to know over tea. There was less to Sealand than met the eye. And Prince Michael, perhaps like Emperor Hirohito or Lady Jane Grey, had reluctantly accepted the burden of monarchy which his line had imposed.

Some fifty miles north-east of Leigh sprawls the Suffolk settlement of Shingle Street, a long, hard and lonely stretch of mist-muffled East Anglia between the estuaries of the Rivers Orwell and Deben. This part of the coast is a quiet mecca for sailors who enjoy poking and nuzzling at its estuaries, the Stour, the Twizzle, the Deben and the Ore, where sometimes the tawny-coloured, loose-footed sails of Thames barges can still be seen breaking the monotony of the flat marshland.

This is challenging sailing. Shoals and tides rip and ripple through the seabed like spitting snakes, and as breakers leap from the water full of threat it's hard not to imagine them as slathering dogs on the cusp of snapping their chains. Like an anvil for the breaking of boats, here the shingle steps down into the North Sea and piles into banks that break the surface like the backs of whales. But there's a magic in listening to the thump and clap of the waves and their sizzle as they draw back like an archer's arm.

The name Shingle Street is self-explanatory. Three miles long or so, it is armadillo-like and serpentine, its curves unyielding, not easily conquered. The Street now comprises a defiant armada of coastguard cottages and other little houses, weatherboarded and brick, valiantly facing off against the sea, and a curious cluster of Martello towers, so many that you'd think whoever planned them found they had a surplus at Shingle Street and dispensed with them all at once. One is now a holiday let. Another has fallen to the temptation of becoming a 'luxury home', albeit without windows. Above all this snaps and shakes a Union Jack, jeered and goaded by the hard wind glancing off the stones.

What has sometimes been said in the saloon bars of local pubs is that, some time in August 1940, a flotilla of ships set out from the ports of Germany and Belgium in a manner not dissimilar to that concocted by Erskine Childers a generation before. Even before it appeared on the horizon the British military's new-fangled radar detected its presence, the army set the sea alight with an impenetrable barrage of flame, and the would-be invaders, stealthily crawling towards the English shore, were devoured in swathes of burning petrol. For weeks after, those who tell the tale say, the North Sea spat charred bodies onto the late-summer beaches, where they lay, quite defeated, pending their silent removal by 'the authorities'.

The strange thing about Shingle Street is that even now this may-have-been episode wobbles like a mirage. Believers argue that the Shingle Street Incident was covered up by the government to protect the morale of a public that would have lost heart to know it had come *this close* to invasion. But then there are the others who insist that the Shingle Street story was invented by a government anxious to spread the rumour that perhaps as many as 50,000 German soldiers burned to death on a single night and that a similarly dreadful demise would be visited upon other unwelcome strangers. And indeed, no clues can be found in the trembling tendrils of sea beet, the sea-clanked stones, the sea-borne miscellany of rubbish and weeds, or the hiss of the sea itself to suggest anything other than that the near-invasion of England by way of Shingle Street was a masterful exercise in black ops.

On the Dengie peninsula, squeezed between the Rivers Blackwater and Crouch like a fist, a different war story has taken root. Defoe warned of the high probability of catching the 'Ague' (malaria) on Dengie, where he said he had met a man who had married twelve women, all of whom had died of it, rife as it was in the undrained meadows and semi-swamp. More recent fears of illness stem from Bradwell nuclear power station, around which rumours of increased incidents of cancer and leukaemia have been reported, discounted and resuscitated. It was recently decommissioned, but its bulk still manages to unsettle the quiet of the fields, sharpens the cawing of rooks and lends to the rustle of the hedgerows just the slightest hint of something untoward. And more signs (KEEP OUT! THIS IS THE PROPERTY OF THE NUCLEAR DECOMMISSIONING AGENCY) imbue otherwise placid pastures with an aftertaste of something apocalyptic.

Dengie demands some kind of pilgrimage nonetheless for it is lilting and beguiling, in summer expansive and generous, its sands hot and uncontrived. Even in winter, when the tide draws great breaths and hurls the waves back upon the marsh, it is savage but not unkind. There is always, on account of its emptiness and the sense of being far from anywhere (the great metropolis of Bradwell boasts under 900 souls), an undertone of sombre quietness and the oxymoronic sensation that the absence of conspicuous glories creates its own presence.

At the north-east corner of Dengie, two miles' hard, noisy walk on shingle and broken shell from the power station, is a building some fifteen hundred years old that constitutes an architectural statement so elemental as to exercise a kind of unshakeable authority over the surrounding fields, sea and marsh. There was a Roman fort here, housing a garrison charged with keeping watch for the pirates who periodically poked up the Blackwater and upset the Pax Romana. In its current incarnation it is a church, the Chapel of St-Peter-on-the-

Wall, founded by Cedd (brother of Chad, Cynibil and Caelin), one of a brood of saints that poured out of the Northumbrian monasteries in the wake of their sacking by the terrible Vikings.

It has also at various junctures served as a hayloft, and is now tended by a religious group called the Othona Community, established by a former RAF chaplain in 1946 as an attempt to foster reconciliation and draw together people of different faiths and which, as befits the generosity of its guiding principles, is open to anyone caring to stroll through its compound of timber-framed dormitories, kitchens and allotments scattered among hedges and trees. When I visited I found the complex pervaded by the kind of institutional smells (yesterday's spaghetti Bolognese, tumble dryers, Vim) that comfort the noses of some but get up those of others. I had called in advance so as not to take the Othonas by surprise with a quiver of intrusive questions, and found that my name had been written on a whiteboard, below that of a Pastor Rupert and above a washing-up rota.

In my own mind I had attempted to draw a link or comparison between the presence of the power station and the Othona Community. Nuclear power stations are built at places like Bradwell (or Sizewell, a little further north) because they need to be both close to the sea, from which they draw their cooling water, and also far away from any large settlement, which might be affected in the event of the reactor melting down. Communities like Othona gravitate towards the periphery for other reasons. Remoteness allows them to create their own sense of singularity unchafed by the scorn, curiosity and abrasion of the rest of society. Does the sea also play a role as a kind of meditational tool, a simile for the ever-changing but eternal truths underpinning the human condition?

The young pony-tailed deputy warden who kindly volunteered to have coffee with me wasn't about to indulge my hypothesis. It was true, he said, that the sea could be calming if he was feeling wound up. Sometimes he took himself on long walks and returned relaxed, but at other times he found the waves too repetitive and wanted to be as far away from them as possible. I didn't press him on the point. He had some photograph albums for me to look at, charting the community's early black-and-white days in Nissen shelters and army tents, and then a sudden leap into colour and checked shirts around 1963. It could have been any kind of grass-roots slightly radical movement of the kind of which sing-songs, loosely organised group activities and table tennis are common denominators. But, said Mike, there wasn't a good relationship with the Bradwell villagers, who were suspicious of the Othonas and their constant stream of visitors from outside Dengie, though the community had done everything, he said, to share what they had with the locals.

Generously, Mike suggested that I stay for a meal. I could see that he was trying to impress upon me the community's lack of dogma and that the chapel, with its simple, unfussy lines and interior untrammelled by ornateness or imagery, was a space in which anyone might find their own god. Uncharitably perhaps, I found it claustrophobic. Raring to commune with my own deity of the sea, I escaped out to where the fields and hedges came to an end and the Cockle Spit began. Beyond was a dark expanse of salt marshes – saltings – and then banks of shells where the tide rolls dead cockles into huge crunchy drifts.

Feigning in the twilight to have missed another finger-wagging sign (DO NOT WALK BEYOND THIS POINT), I walked out ginger-toed to the very edge of this strip of land, borrowed from the sea. In the shingle's dips and hollows grew fat and juicy clumps of scarlet-hued glasswort, or 'chicken legs', and other curious botanical inhabitants of the intertidal netherworld. Towards dusk groups of birds staked their claims to parcels of beach. A flock of golden plover moved in from the sea, flying low with the sound of rustling skirts. Ivory-white egrets colonised the sluices; a hysterical crescendo of oystercatchers startled the low horizon. And most spectacular – the sky was by now violet and the shadow of St Peter's dark and austere – a hare cantering heavily across the salt marsh, with each turn kicking up cockle shells or a brackish puddle, attempting to elude whatever it imagined pursued it.

Soon the tide would turn and re-embrace the land with its frothy caress, bidding and beckoning it to return to the sea.

The Question of the Scheldt

Through the flats that bound the North Sea and shelve into it imperceptibly, merging at last with the shallow flood, and re-emerging in distant sandbanks and less conspicuous shoals, run facing each other two waterways far inland, which are funnels and entries, as it were, scoured by the tide. Each has at the end of the tideway a narrow, placid, inland stream, from whence the broader, noisier sea part also takes its name. Each has been and will always be famous in the arms and commerce of Europe. Each forms a sort of long street of ships crowded in a traffic to and fro. For each has its great port.

Hilaire Belloc, *The River of London*

Belloc saw the Scheldt as the Thames's twin. They do possess similarities, and their mouths are roughly latitudinous. But the Thames is old, and the sinuous, serpentine Scheldt a mere upstart by comparison. Only a thousand years ago it was one of a litter of many nascent waterways wriggling like kittens in a maelstrom of riverine change. Now it rolls into the basin of the North Sea with youth-belying stately grace.

Its apparent peacefulness is also a lie. The history of the Scheldt is one of squabbling and blood, smashed timbers, flooded dykes, blasted spars and lingering deaths from aguey vapours. It is true that one brief skirmish – fought in 1781 between the Holy Roman

Emperor Joseph II and the Dutch state – resulted only in the denting of a kettle hit by the ricochet of a musket ball. Few of the others were so Gilbert and Sullivan-esque. However – and it must be the sea air – the scars have healed well. Things change quickly on the Scheldt. The stretch of coast from north of Bruges to the Hook of Holland is as geologically mercurial as any around the North Sea. The very name of Zeeland (Sealand), the province that lies to the north of the Scheldt, boldly and breezily grasps the dualism of this land and seascape: a hodgepodge of islands, a concertinaed archipelago in a near-constant state of bunching and unbunching.

What floods take away with one hand, silt gives with the other. The quiet fields are always only a broken dyke away from a disaster which in time will heal. Two millennia ago a great flood submerged the entire coast of the southern North Sea. The local warrior-hunter Frisii were accustomed to occasional inundations of their low-lying reed-bedded landscape (rich in eels, carp and fowl), and in times of flood would retreat to their *terpen*, settlements built upon mounds protruding above even the highest flood waters. A landscape of plains became a mosaic of islands like a patchwork quilt come unstitched.

Over the following centuries the early Netherlanders began to claw land back beyond the limits of their *terpen*, building successive dykes in expanding rings first to defend against the sea, and then to push it further and further outward, the dykes becoming longer and straighter, the *terpen* broadening into polders – larger areas of reclaimed pasturage and meadows. And they learned to shore up the banks of the rivers to counter their erratic seasonal variations. The tides too pitched into this permanent revolution. The unsteady ensemble of all these forces resulted, by the thirteenth century, in the Scheldt emerging as a navigable river worth the price of a good fight.

The chance arrival of a spice-laden caravel from the Indies was all it took to transform the Scheldt-side city of Antwerp. Though she was by no means unaccustomed to wealth, a ship's hold groaning with pepper, cinnamon and cloves enthused and infused her with a new lust for sensual, distinctly foreign delights. Baggage trains arrived from Trieste, Genoa and Zaragoza. New connections with Lisbon and Cadiz brought the Americas within reach of the Flemish. Spanish silver mined in Mexico and Argentina stoked an appetite for speculation, conspicuous consumption and architectural testaments to the accumulation of wealth.

I had my first eyeful of the Scheldt from this city. A broad steel-blue ribbon mirrored the evening sky, the horizon pockmarked by a low constellation of lights and the gas-flaring chimneys of the chemical works on the other side of the river. I was promenading on a raised walkway built at the height of Belgium's imperial ambitions as a platform from which young men waved goodbye to home before heading off to brutalise the Congo.

The esplanade was empty aside from its ghosts, a squabbling couple and a lonesome girl. The 'long street' Belloc described was almost devoid of ships. But a solitary barge made its way seaward, hugging the slack channel close to the shore. Through binoculars I could see the bargee sitting louchely at the wheel, his wife (I supposed) making coffee on a gimballed stove as their long bluff-bowed hull ploughed through the flood tide. They may have come through the filigree mesh of waterways that stretches deeply east, linking the North Sea with the heart of Europe. According to a river pilot I met in Vlissingen the bargees not only refuse the services of pilots, but take dangerous short cuts, playing fast and loose with the tides and banks, or at least as fast and loose as a barge is able to play. But in that protracted moment, between the barge chugging into and out of view, riding those slow strong currents seemed a noble calling.

By morning the river, dubiously lit by an overcast sky, appeared to have shrunk and lost some of its sheen. Still it was fine-flowing and broad, and Antwerp's winding old streets and hobbled houses and chiming bell tower were scarcely less charming – so much more so than the diamond quarter, not glittering and exclusive but careworn and low rent, though Hassidim hurrying by on their bicycles lent a carat of Levantine charm, and the red-light district appeared not to burn too bright.

It is Antwerp's docks, though, not diamonds and doxies, that have been the *casus belli* of most if not all of the Scheldt's woes.

However easily it may flow, a river shared by nations invariably gives rise to friction. The Scheldt has the mixed fortune to be embanked by three countries. Rising near Aisne in France, it broadens considerably in Belgium and debouches into the North Sea in what is now the Netherlands. From at least the fourteenth century almost until today a muddle of dynasties, dictators and powers (the Habsburgs, Napoleon, Dutch stadtholders, dukes of Orange, duchesses of Parma) have squeezed, blocked or haggled over the river to maximise their own or restrict others' access to North Sea trade. The Scheldt question was once a staple of billiard-room debate in diplomatic circles. It may conceivably rear its head again. An academic called S. T. Bindoff, writing as recently as 1945, confessed to having misgivings about 'raking over the embers of the past' by researching the Scheldt. And, he said, he had been warned by a Belgian archivist that 'as many scholars had been drowned in the Scheldt – figuratively speaking – as sailors'.

In the late sixteenth century the Dutch led by William the Silent had sloughed off the yoke of Spanish rule, seizing towns and forts on both sides of the Scheldt including Antwerp. William's nemesis, the haughty Duke of Parma, responded with Castilian vigour, retaking Antwerp but leaving the territory further down the Scheldt in rebel hands. To consolidate his gains he built a bridge of ships across the river to prevent waterborne traffic from reaching the North Sea. The Dutch responded with their own blockade, starving Antwerp of the oxygen of trade.

The more Antwerp wilted, the more glorious grew Amsterdam. Merchants, artists and intellectuals moved north, and Antwerp quite literally became a backwater. North Sea traders also suffered, denied access to lucrative upriver markets. Whether the Dutch were in breach of international law – such as it was – was a difficult question to answer. The river, after all, flowed through their country. Did other riparian states possess an inalienable right to access the sea? Napoleon 'solved' the question by taking possession of both countries, although as continental Europe was now under blockade by Britain, it was something of an anticlimactic gesture.

France's ambitions for Antwerp were less about the restoration of her former glories than about transforming the city into 'a pistol loaded, cocked, and pointing straight at the heart of England', by which Napoleon meant that it would be his launch pad for the conquest of his perfidious enemy across the North Sea. It was an aspiration that would have terrible consequences for those who dwelt on the banks of the Scheldt, particularly the inhabitants of pretty, steep-pitched copper-orange-roofed Vlissingen downriver from Antwerp and across the Dutch border. Sitting on the southern tip of the island of Walcheren where the river meets the sea, this diminutive sometime fortress town and sometime fishing port has for centuries found itself an unwilling watchman at the mouth of the Scheldt.

Wilbert Weber, the curator of the town museum, had warned that the train journey between the two towns was time-consuming, considering that they are so close: 'You are still crossing a frontier remember. These things take time.' And it was true. It seemed that, because the line marking the Dutch and Belgian border had so frequently shifted, the driver lavished ceremonial lack of celerity upon his engine's progress.

Little evidence of this Byzantine political geography was visible from the window of the train as it stopped and started on its way through Zeeland and across the island of Walcheren, a latticework of parallel lines and right angles, the land protected from the sea by the clever construction of drainage channels and dykes, with small copses of beech and poplar at their interstices.

Here, geometry cleaves sea from land. I remember walking the top of a dyke listening with one ear to the gentle cymballing of waves, and the other to a choir of songbirds. In the fields hares lay out in the sun's last gold, worn out with their antics and nearly invisible in furrows of chocolate-rich soil. As if fanning the remaining warmth of the dying day, a crane flapped slowly by with melancholic reptilian grace.

Functional as they are, there's poetry in the polders. Those closest to the sea and possessing the greatest responsibility are called *wakende* dykes – waking dykes. The next are sleeping (*slapende*) dykes, and in the event that these both fail only a *dromende* (dreaming) dyke stands between the sea and oblivion. The Dutch response to the North Sea is one of guile and negotiation, proportionate response in place of counter-attack. But it can fail, and when a tidal surge breaches the dykes only the elevated roads and the roofs of buildings sit clear of the brine.

The British have had a long-standing relationship with Vlissingen – which they call Flushing. During the interminable war between the Dutch rebels and the Spanish Habsburgs the rebels offered Elizabeth I sovereignty over the United Provinces in return for her guardianship. Elizabeth baulked at the responsibility – and at the danger of goading Spain – but eventually the Earl of Leicester was sent to Flushing in the capacity of governor. Then England had Walcheren thrust upon it. But in 1809 the British would hurl themselves upon its shores in a surge of anti-Bonapartist passion, retreating as a ragtag army haunted by failure and sickness.

When the Dutch decided to throw in their lot with Napoleon, England determined that the 'pistol' must be made safe, its armaments and shipyards destroyed and the Scheldt rendered unnavigable to North Sea traffic. The mission would also assist beleaguered Austria by diverting French forces from the campaigns in the east. The first stop would be Walcheren.

It was, in the beginning, a bold affair that began in July with the mustering of some thirty ships of the line, forty frigates and transport ships for 40,000 men – the largest British expeditionary force that had ever been assembled. Command was given to the Earl of Chatham, the elder brother of Prime Minister William Pitt and a man known for the pains he took to ensure the comfort and welfare of the collection of tortoises that he liked to fondle in stressful situations. Then and ever since his appointment has been regarded as inexplicable, settling 'a pall of sloth' over the expedition, according to the naval historian N. A. M. Rodger. Indeed his choice of animal friend seems also to have had an overt influence on his punctuality (his nickname was the 'late Earl' for his inability to get out of bed), a fault which would be compounded in months to come as critics rounded on the planners of the campaign as 'imbecilic and accident prone'.

Though handicapped by their leader, the British had to their advantage the fact that Napoleon was convinced that Walcheren, and Flushing in particular, were almost impregnable. 'Write and tell everyone,' Napoleon told his brother Lucien, 'that Flushing cannot be taken, unless by the cowardice of the commandants . . . and that the English will go off without having it. The bombs are nothing – absolutely nothing; they will destroy a few houses, but that has no effect upon the surrender of a place.'

In response to the British threat, Napoleon's commanders opened the dykes, but the island refused to flood. On 2 August 1809 Chatham wrote breathily that despite a westerly gale forcing a 'huge swell upon the sands' at their intended landing spot at West Kapelle, they had succeeded in landing further south, bagging some early triumphs. The island's capital of Middelburg shuddered beneath British rockets that looked like bonfire-night fireworks, but were larger, steel-barrelled and packed with explosives. Its citizens, wholly unused to modern warfare and agnostic as to the relative merits of British or Bonapartist justice, sent a deputation to secure terms, among them that 'security is to be granted to every person . . . whatever their political opinions may be or now are'.

Next the British captured a fort, taking 516 prisoners, including ten drummers, three pipers, four farriers, one boy and five 'artificers', all of whom, Chatham congratulated himself, were permitted to keep their knapsacks. Flushing held out longer, but the British were prepared to burn it down in pursuit of its liberation and thus succeeded in killing over 2,000 people, the good citizens of a place which merely had the bad fortune to be en route to Antwerp. Amid this carnage a William Keep of the 77th Regiment wrote that he and his comrades in arms were able 'to spread our tables under the shade of luxuriant fruit trees and enjoy all the pleasures of rustic life'. It was looking like a good campaign. Antwerp was sure to fall next.

It was in August that the expedition took a sickly turn, when (according to the letters home of a hospital inspector) the beds of the drainage canals became

> thickly covered with an ooze which, when the tide is out, emits a most offensive effluvia. Each ditch is filled with water which is loaded with animal and vegetable substances in a state of putrefaction, and the whole island is so flat and near the sea that [it is] little better

than a swamp, and there is scarcely a place where good quality water can be procured. The effect of all these causes of diseases is strongly marked in the inhabitants, the greater part of whom are pale and listless.

Worse, Napoleon's troops were gathering their strength, and by early September the capture of Antwerp looked impossible, not least because 7,000 British troops were either dead or laid low by a mysterious illness which a doctor described as coming on 'with a shivering, so great that the patient feels no benefit from the clothes piled upon him in bed, but continues to shiver, as if enclosed in ice, the teeth chattering and the skin blanched . . . It subsides, and then is succeeded by another paroxysm, and so on until the patient's strength is quite reduced, and he is received into the arms of death.'

Which is more or less what would happen to Chatham's reputation. In late August the late Earl, so full of brio only weeks before, wrote,

However mortifying to me to see the progress halted of an army from whose good conduct and valour I had everything to hope . . . my duty left me no other course than to close my operations here, and it will always be a consolation to me to think that I have not been induced lightly to commit the safety of the army confided to me, or the reputation of his majesty's arms . . . I [shall] hold [troops] in readiness to await his majesty's command which I shall most anxiously await.

By December the entire force had returned to Britain with none of its objectives accomplished, and parliamentarians rounded upon the conduct of the campaign. To rousing cries of 'Hear, hear' Mr Windham Quin told the House that the adventure was 'remarkable only for ignorance, imbecility and mismanagement' and the litany of 'egregious blunders' accompanying its every step. Calls for a full inquiry failed, but the public believed with Quin that

> In the military annals of Great Britain . . . there was no precedent of such extensive, complete, and unqualified failure . . . here was an Expedition terminating in great disgrace and unparalleled disaster, and with numerous presumptions of misconduct. It was not that the Expedition failed, but that it could not succeed . . . It was generated in calamity, and your troops were marched from their own shore to destruction. [Ministers] should have been aware of the nature of the climate, of the poisonous air of Walcheren. But the event proved that they either did not know of them, or knowing that, they disregarded them. They marched the British army to its grave, to be extinguished amidst the pestilential air of Walcheren, to go out like a candle in a vault.

Walcheren Sickness, or Flushing Fever, has baffled medical historians ever since. It exhibited some of the symptoms of malaria, but also typhus and cholera, so it seems this was not a single disease but a portfolio of ailments for which there was neither prevention nor cure. Many returning soldiers continued to suffer for several years, with the result that survivors of the Walcheren campaign were seldom taken back into the army again.

There are places, and Walcheren must be one such, that invite the repetition of history. In the Second World War a British force would again attempt to oust a despot from the island, though whether its commanders had an eye on the failure of its predecessor is unrecorded. Bulky and beautiful ships of the line had long passed into obsolescence; this time small groups of men would attack from small, fast rocket-launching ships and assault craft.

After the D-Day landings the Allies began probing weak spots in the German defences on the North Sea coast. The Netherlands was keenly defended, but just as Napoleon had regarded Antwerp as critical to his designs on Britain, so the British knew it was crucial to the retaking of Europe. Once they had secured the Scheldt, Antwerp would be a hub for unloading the supplies and materiel necessary for the big push to Berlin. But a division of German troops would need to be neutralised if Antwerp were to be taken.

The joint British and Canadian plan was to assault Walcheren by concentric assaults from the east, south and west, involving the crossing of the estuary, mounting a seaborne assault from the Channel and neutralising the defences of Walcheren by bombing the sea dykes and flooding the island – this last, the very tactic Napoleon had planned to defend Walcheren, the Allied generals sought to use as a means of attack.

Unlike the 1809 campaign, things started badly. Early assault craft were fired upon by their own side, and the attempt on the eastern side of the island turned into a bloodbath on the causeway linking it to the adjacent island of Beveland. One officer recalled 'a long line of weary, muddy infantrymen which plodded back down the road which would take them [to safety]. The men were indescribably dirty. They were bearded, cold as it is only possible to be cold in Holland in November, and wet from having lived in water-filled holes in the ground for 24 hours a day.' Failing to take the causeway, the Allies made an attempt to cross the adjacent Slooe Channel, 'just such a muddy and ambiguous creek as you will find among the Essex Marshes', flanked on each side by grey and glutinous mud and once crossed giving way to muddy creeks 'just wide and deep enough to stop an armed man from either wading or swimming across and also quite impassable by armour'.

The messages back to London are remarkable for their similarity to those sent by Chatham and his colleagues 135 years before: long rostas of casualties, snatched jerky narratives to convey triumphs, mishaps and minor victories, petty recriminations, requests for ammunition, water and instructions. But this time the operation on Flushing was more successful, and a dawn crossing of the Scheldt succeeded despite dismal rain. Soon the river was lit by countless muzzle flashes and fires that cast an eerie, sickly glow and revealed in silhouette, an officer recalled, 'the unmistakable outline of the Oranje Mill'.

I allowed myself an excellent coffee at the café which the Oranje Mill has become. Out in the estuary, just as in its twin the Thames, ships crawling in from the North Sea disembark their sea pilots and wait for river pilots to guide them into the Scheldt. The sleek profile of a US warship steamed past Flushing, heading, I was later told, towards the south Mediterranean, where combat missions had just begun against Libya. The weather was indulgently fine, and on the beach below a sort of *passeggiata* unfolded of figures in apparent Brownian motion wheeling pushchairs, eating ice creams, dawdling, tugging upon and tugged by happy spaniels and frisky poodles. This is where the landing craft had beached amid a rain of artillery fire.

Vlissingen was warming up for the summer invasion. The Iguana Mini-Zoo on Bellamy Square boasted a freshly painted sign, and early tourists ambled in the pretty backstreets. Although not all the shops had opened for the season, fragrant herbal smells wafted from the guitar repair clinic on the main drag behind the harbour, and Mr Van Houff at the bicycle hire shop by the station was whistling in anticipation of heavy demand for his heavy-framed back-pedal-brake machines.

There are newer apartment blocks around the edges of town, but the buildings in the centre, which the British attacked with rockets in 1809, remain at the core of the town and its identity.

Some were already war-seasoned in the sixteenth century when the Duke of Parma fought William the Silent. In 1944 German snipers shot from their open windows, from derricks and pillboxes and bombarded their attackers with mortars.

The decision to bomb the sea wall was made with the reluctant consent of the Dutch government-in-exile. Grainy, flickering propaganda films show smiling women in traditional bonnets and shawls lifted from their flooded homes into evacuation craft by soldier gallants and removed to makeshift shelters. There was just time to move some livestock to the few remaining pockets of higher ground, much of which was mined, with the curious consequence that while the Walcheren islanders would lack almost every other comfort, their meat ration ballooned to five times that of their compatriots further north. The Germans, sodden and defeated, eventually withdrew.

It was not long afterwards that the villagers began to drift back to their blighted homes, to lead lives not unlike those of their *terpen*-dwelling ancestors a millennium and more ago. The fields remained semi-flooded, and the pastures, trees and shrubs had been poisoned by the saltwater. Against the backdrop of the European war's thunderous closing stages, the islanders now battled hunger, exposure and the threat of disease, surviving on air-dropped provisions and what they could scavenge.

On 3 November 1947 British Prime Minister Clement Attlee and his wife Violet travelled to Walcheren for a ceremony marking the replanting of the island's trees, arriving with Dutch dignitaries at Flushing station to a solemn reception. The party, said a correspondent from *The Times*, headed towards the town's main church, Jacobskerk, 'through streets densely packed with intent but undemonstrative crowds . . . scarred by war and hardened with toil. The flaunting jubilation of the first day of liberation was absent; it did not need the evidence of recently drained polders and patched up houses to show that this was a people that had had a hard field to harrow.' First, hymns and Dutch folk songs were sung, and then, assisted by 'a little girl with two pigtails done in orange ribbon and three small boys in outsize plus-fours', the Princess Regent of the Netherlands planted the first of the 1,500,000 trees paid for by subscription, and the Dutch prime minister 'made an address of welcome in which he emphasised the stoical understanding displayed by the inhabitants in never for one moment blaming the British for the terrible hardships inflicted in the course of attaining ultimate victory'.

I had an unexpected glimpse of how a war-torn village on the banks of the Scheldt might look, having been given a tip by a woman working for the Antwerp Port Authority, who had described to me the 'desolate wasteland' her employer had created in its project to accommodate the very longest and deepest super-freighters. She and I were standing on a giant computer-generated projection of the entire region – the centrepiece of an exhibition in a marquee on the Antwerp waterfront – an attempt by the port authority to engage with the local population. In the course of an afternoon I appeared to be its only visitor, and the woman, who wore the company's logo and slogan on her sweatshirt, pointed with her toe to a small village on the left bank of the Scheldt. 'Here,' she said. 'This is where you should go. To the village of Doel.'

I had already heard about the inexorable spread of the docks from Mrs Peremans, the proprietor of the guest house in which I stayed for the duration of my time in Antwerp. She lived alone with her cats among bookcases groaning with religious tracts in a large and gloomy nineteenth-century terraced house close to the resplendently majestic station in a neighbourhood which had once been genteel but has gone to seed – at least in the eyes of those who regard Belgium's acceptance of immigrants as a 'problem' and take exception to an urban landscape where shops offering cheap phonecalls to exotic places and internet access have usurped traditional cafés and grocers, and where heavily accented Congolese French and Farsi have displaced French and Flemish as the dominant tongues.

Mrs Peremans said that she was trying to sell her house, but who wanted even such a magnificent dwelling when the area had the reputation it now did? She felt sorry, she said, for the rootlessness of the asylum seekers from Iran, Equatorial Guinea and the DRC, who lead 'sad, intransigent lives' before being made to return home.

'Why do they come to Antwerp?' I asked.

'Perhaps because of the docks. Because there is always hope in docks of some kind of work or a passage to somewhere else. But Antwerp's aren't those kinds of docks,' she said. Antwerp's dock workers are highly skilled and extensively vetted. They live tidy lives in grid-like suburbs. These are not the happenstance quaysides of yore.

Mrs Peremans was desperate to sell her house not because she had problems with her neighbours, but because she wanted to return to the countryside of her childhood. Notwithstanding, however, that it no longer exists. 'Now everything is docks. Docks docks docks. The fields are all devoured − eaten up!' she said over breakfast and asked why I hadn't finished my scarcely boiled egg.

What the Belgians have done to develop their side of the Scheldt is like an inversion of the polder building of the Dutch. Whereas the Netherlands has made land out of sea, Belgium has made sea out of land. Hidden behind security fences and earthworks, the presence of the docks is only betrayed by an unearthly almost supra-human topography. The funnels and bridge houses of ships loom above an elevated horizon created by the sea wall. Through a haphazard cubist fantasy mountainscape of shipping containers snake roads along which articulated vehicles pass with pulse-like monotony. But nothing, not even Mrs Peremans's soft-boiled egg, could quite prepare me for Doel.

Eight hundred years ago the luckless village was no more than an island surrounded by the river and a hinterland of permanent flood water. And for hundreds of years during the interminable wrangling between the independent and Spanish-ruled Netherlands its sovereignty was either unknown, in dispute or bartered between the two. At the middle of the twentieth century Doel remained a small town, its inhabitants mostly farmers before they took to seeking employment in the docks and refineries and chemical works that flourished after the Second World War. But in 2001 they were given notice that Doel had been earmarked for dock development. Given the choice of selling up on good terms or hanging on, risking everything as the value of their properties slid inexorably into the Scheldt, the great majority of its residents chose the safer path and moved to nice new houses nearby.

For the moment the bulldozers only cruise past Doel like small-town toughs putting on the frighteners. Pending resolution of a number of legal challenges, the developers have yet to move in, tempting some of its erstwhile inhabitants to question whether they made the right decision to leave. But with every passing year, their otherwise perfectly good houses sink into greater decrepitude. Windows creak listlessly on their hinges; gardens are overgrown, and every other square yard of wall has fallen prey to 'street artists', who like crazed cosmeticians in a firm of surreal undertakers have prepared the village for interment.

This is highbrow graffiti, macabre and darkly funny: the Olympic rings on the side of a house, DOEL 2018 beneath; Doel represented as various dead or dying animals – a buffalo, a festering rat, a jackdaw. In the churchyard the bell tower seems to have become a stranger in its own parish. There are indeed a handful of people for whom the automated tolling of the bells still transports them to the time when it was, they maintain, one of the most special places in

Belgium. The remaining inhabitants are either older people who have hung on in the hope that the descent into madness will be reversed or younger squatters, who see in Doel a free place to live where the writ of the law does not apply. It is a place which is both thrilling and threatening, the kind of vacuum which dangerous elements might and might not abhor.

Compounding the insanity is the pub at the crossroads that marks the centre of the town. At lunchtime and in the evenings it is rammed from the bar to the dingiest corner seat with happy people and beer-furred smoky voices – a babble at the heart of an empty bedlam. They are for the most part workers at the local nuclear power station, the great silent chimney of which towers over Doel.

At the suggestion of the (hurried, harried) barmaid, I knocked on the door of a house on the fringes of the village, by the windmill. The woman who lived there, Cécile, might possibly be interested in talking to me as a representative of the older generation that had hung on. Her house, with a pair of wellingtons on the porch and a car in something approaching running order in the drive, looked to be one of the few in a state worthy of respectable habitation.

My knock was met with a querulous barking. Through a frosted-glass window I could see a basset hound running up and down the stairs, sprung into disorder by my arrival. Cécile opened the door a fraction to reveal wide and apprehensive eyes. In such a blighted, lonely village, anyone would be wary of a stranger. But she invited me into her cosy, cluttered home, with its cookery books, oil paintings and old photographs, an enormous fern taking up half her sitting room, a brooding sense of loss occupying the other.

She was, she said, one of the original inhabitants of Doel. As a child in the 1960s she had swum in the Scheldt with her friends and spent carefree summers in the woods and fields. Even when the nuclear power plant was built on its doorstep, the sense of community – and apartness from anywhere else – remained gloriously intact. In fact, the power station had provided jobs and contracts for local businesses. 'It is true that some people got very rich, and some people didn't, so there were resentments. There was some crossness. But we were still a village all together,' she said.

Cécile said she had felt unable to leave. She had no wish to be bought out of her childhood and home, and besides she could think of nowhere else in the world that she wished to live. It was sometimes a little scary at night but for the most part beautiful and quiet. Her great regret, she said, was that she was no longer on cordial terms with her neighbour Marina, who lived a few doors along, barricaded behind placards that promised hellfire and doom for the scheming businessmen and politicians who were determined to destroy their *doorp*.

They fell out, said Cécile, because whereas she had been born in Doel, Marina had only moved here to work on the power station twenty years ago. 'But still she has all this activism and so forth, even though she is not *really* from Doel. . .'

I trotted along to Marina's house to hear her side of the story and found her tale sadder still. As Cécile had said, the house was surrounded by placards. One (translated from Flemish) read, ARROGANT POLITICIANS ARE BAD FOR THE ECONOMY, and another, GOD WILL PUNISH THE MURDERERS OF OUR VILLAGE. Marina, an attractive blonde woman in her forties, told me that the village in which she had grown up a few kilometres east was just as beautiful as Doel had been, just as peaceful, and just as strong in community spirit, but it had already been destroyed. Where once had been her home was now an expanse of water and concrete.

'And do you know what?' She pinned me down with bitter blue eyes. 'The ships do not even use it. They have massive overcapacity. They build and build far more than they can even use.' So even if she was not born in Doel, she was still anxious to save it from the oblivion her own town had suffered. For her part, Marina pointed out that Cécile had sold her house, taken the money and was now renting cheap (from the same company that wanted to oust her), so wanted 'the best of both worlds'.

And thus the two women continue their baleful mini-war within a war, both doing battle in their own way with forces that heavily outnumber them, and each failing, like others before them, to heed the warning of a nineteenth-century Belgian officers' manual that 'the polder country is generally unsuitable for military operations of any kind'.

With Ensor and Octopussies in Ostend

Ostend is my orphanage – there are probably places I'd rather
be but I think that right now I need to be here.

Marvin Gaye, 1981

A cynic might describe the shortness of Belgium's coastline as its
greatest quality. Either way, its entirety can be travelled in comfort
and relative speed by taking the Kusttram – Coast Tram – which
whistles its way between Knokke, a hop away from the Netherlands,
and De Panne, close to the French border, in less than two hours,
and all for the price of five euros.

Viewed from the deck of the ferry from Ramsgate, Ostend greets
its guests as a stiff rictus of concrete. Fixed and a little forced. First it
is only discernible as a bank of low dove-grey cloud, curiously clean
cut, and then, almost only at the very last moment, does the city
reveal its identity as a wall of apartment blocks looking belligerently
out at the waves. During the Eighty Years' War of the 1600s it had a
terribly bloody time under siege or assault by the Spanish and took
another knocking a century later during the War of the Spanish
Succession. But in 1784 an English entrepreneur called William
Herket transformed Ostend's fortunes for ever by obtaining
authorisation for the building of a lemonade hut. Herket had a
captive constant base such was the frequency of shipwrecks at Ostend
that watching vessels smash themselves to pieces on the shallow

shoals around the entrance to the harbour had become a popular local entertainment.

The patronage of Leopold, first king of the Belgians, assured Ostend's emergence as the resort it is now slowly unbecoming. Leopold was planted on the throne of the brand-new nation by the great powers in 1831. The grand design was that Belgium would act as a check against future French expansionism, which seems ironic given what would later happen. But the new monarch had the good humour to believe that he was a real king, deserving of a seaside playground. A hippodrome, spa and esplanade soon sprang from the dunes. With the passage both of time and the royal title to the second Leopold, the classical gave way to the belle époque, and long before the First World War arrived to knock on Belgium's door Ostend really was a handsome place. In the right light on the right day and in the right mood she can still make that claim. But she does so despite herself – in splintered chinks between the grandiose and dreary.

I paid my first visit in late November. It was a half-accidental detour from Brussels, a city to which Ostend possesses a sort of umbilical link by dint both of the Leopold connection and the railway. As the train thumped out of that great compote of Eurocrats and grime, I had a sense of the thinning of things (flatter fields, fewer people in the carriage, more Flemishness, the public address system giving up on earlier bilingual efforts). By the time we reached Ostend my fellow passengers looked bored and despondent, and convinced by their demeanour that whatever I would encounter would do me some disservice, I tumbled with some reluctance from the warm train carriage into a city of chilly boulevards, frozen footsteps and the occasional whisperings of a tram.

I'd booked a bed and breakfast on Eduard de Kuyperstrasse, well off the main drag – past the hippodrome with its statue of a cantering horse, along the colonnade of the Thermopylae Hotel.

I arrived at the door of an immaculately restored *circa* 1875 house a hundred yards from the scowling sea, ill-lit by orange halide beyond the esplanade, or *doigt*. It was a boutique B & B, and a stuffed herring gull was suspended artistically above my bed. That evening I ate supper – fish baked in butter and cream – alone in a nearby pub. (Calorific and satisfying but not exciting. I thought of something I'd heard, of how a sixteenth century Spanish ambassador to Flanders described his posting as 'a land where there grows neither thyme, nor lavender, figs, olives, melons, or almonds, where parsley, onions, and lettuce have neither juice nor taste; where dishes are prepared, strange to relate, with butter from cows instead of oil'.)

In the morning my host Annemarie gave me bread, jam, healthy cereals and camomile tea. She told me that she intensely disliked Ostend, even – especially – in the summer when her takings are sky high and thousands of Belgians come to frolic on the beach. 'They eat their mussels and frites and *pardy*,' she said with disgust. 'Personally . . . my husband and I want to move to Berlin. There's a *big* arts scene there. There's nothing here in Ostend. Nothing but unemployment and old people.' But Ostend is more than a seaside resort that has seen better days. Despite effusions of *haut bourgeois* conservatism, the city inspired an artistic movement as anarchic as it was subtle, and deeply wedded to the sea.

The bronze equestrian statue of Leopold I stands umpteen hands high above the beach huts and the Ostend sands, famous in the nineteenth century for nude female bathers and highly edible rabbits. The small bust of James Ensor by contrast is half hidden in a small park named after the king tucked a quarter of a mile behind the esplanade, overlooking a flower clock. Ensor died in 1949 only a few hundred yards away from where he was born eighty-nine years earlier, having created an *oeuvre* of paintings, prints, sculptures and musical compositions that defined genres and defied them, veering, or rather hopping, between deft naturalism and the gaudily grotesque via caricature, cartoons and the sublime.

Ensor's father was an upper-class Englishman who spent a lifetime consummately failing in a number of professions. His mother was one generation away from the Flemish peasantry. Her sister, Ensor's Aunt Mimi, ran a souvenir shop of a kind that can still be found in Ostend (there is a good one in the smaller of the market squares), and the class conflict within his family life seemed to manifest itself in Ensor in a number of ways. He battled with the art establishment, which was afraid of him, and yet became paterfamilias to a host of artists – Leon Spilliaert, Constant Permeke, Willy Finch, Théo Van Rysselberghe – who collectively came to embody the Ostend avant-garde, creating a prism through which the city and indeed the whole Belgian coast can be redeemed.

That first trip saw me hounded out by grim cold. Ostend's inhabitants had fled, either indoors or abroad. Cafés and museums were closed, bar a handful. In my journal I wrote,

> The yawning golden sands, that each summer stiffen beneath the feet of a hundred thousand Belgians, lie taut, silver and shivering. Silhouetted figures appear and disappear into the mist, in pairs or groups or tantalisingly alone, taking advantage of the chance to have the expanse almost all to themselves. But for these whirls and eddies of life and the warm glow of one or other of the few cafes to brave the off-season, the city, for the most part sleeps, its inhabitants elsewhere in body or mind.

The next autumn I returned, booking into a hotel remarkable for the hugeness of the proprietor's walrus moustache and a dark warren of sour-smelling, curled and long-unfitted carpets lurking beyond the reception desk.

If the Hotel Theresen was neglected to the point of the grotesque, the Ensor House museum – the house where Ensor spent much of his life – is macabre by design. It also is a terraced house though smaller than the Theresen (and opposite a branch of Subway, an international fast-food chain). Inside it is almost as though Ensor had just left for a stroll along the esplanade, and though imperfectly preserved gives the sense of the man. Grinning masks, oriental objects and joyously and deliberately flawed works of taxidermy are arranged among the pot plants, harmonium and trinkets in an assemblage of Edwardiana manqué almost horrible but also almost beautiful. Ensor's paintings – unaffordable for the museum – are absent.

James Ensor gave himself the nickname '*hareng saur*', or 'kippered herring', because it almost sounds like 'arts Ensor'. His work, he declared, was 'beyond classification', and the implicit challenge has yet to be refuted. But he also believed he knew the origins of his unique style, attributing it to nursery years spent in Aunt Mimi's trinket shop, 'in the midst,' he wrote in his *Écrits*, 'of gleaming, mother of pearl coloured shells with dancing, shimmering reflections and the bizarre skeletons of sea monsters and plants. This marvellous world full of colours, this superabundance of reflections and refractions made me into a painter who is in love with colour and is delighted by the blinding glow of light.' Mimi would dress James and her pet Capuchin monkey in identical sailors' costumes for the amusement of her customers. An early childhood memory was the sight of the monkey straddling a giant stuffed fish, their shadow cast on the shop wall by a flickering gas lamp.

Of all his inspirations, the sea was the most potent. He wrote about it often – how he was 'guided by a secret instinct, a feeling for the atmosphere of the seacoast, which [he] had imbibed with the breeze, inhaled with the pearly mists, soaked up in the waves, heard in the wind', and more playfully or mock-ironically, 'Beneficent sea, revered mother, I offer humble praise with a fresh bouquet to your hundred faces, your gleaming skin, your dimples, your rosy lingerie, your diamond crown, your sapphire coverlet, your blessings, your blisses, your unfathomable charms.'

Between them, Ensor and his entourage represented not only the Belgian coast but also its denizens in all their permutations, lifting the lid on life beneath crinoline and starched shirt front and undermining the official narrative of respectability. An early guide to Ostend reads, 'Probably no other seaside resort in Europe can present such animated scenes of pulsating life and vivid colourings . . . The sands literally "teem" with the rising generation, cosmopolitan in their sports as are the cafes across the way cosmopolitan in their provision for hungry, not to say thirsty, visitors . . . nowhere else is bathing indulged in with such joyous zest.' An Ensor etching of 1890, *The Baths of Ostend*, puts flesh and all its temptations on those wholesome bones. Beneath a smiling sun (the spirit of Ensor?) the 'teeming' bathers flirt imprudently in the waves. A small dog mounts a young woman who does little to protest. A couple vigorously snogs in bathing hut number 69 while voyeurs endowed with telescopes straddle its pitched roof.

Away from the crowds Ensor found a tauter beauty in the sea. A neat, immaculately simple oil painting completed when Ensor was only sixteen years old depicts another bathing hut, a white shed on carriage wheels on a golden beach against a background of blue sea and dove-grey sky with promising hints of lapis. In a letter to a friend he muses on the delights that might attend living 'in a big bathing hut whose interior is clad in mother of pearl shells, and to sleep there, cradled by the sound of the sea and an indolent blonde beautiful girl with salty flesh'.

Elsewhere, Ensor nodded to Turner with sunsets thickly daubed in rich colours and struck brutally realist chords by depicting rough-featured Ostend alcoholics, fishermen and sailors. He painted and drew his own portrait (a leonine large-featured face, both proud and self-doubting, whiskered and bearded but not disguised) obsessively and in a number of moods (self-mocking, self-quizzical), most famously wearing a woman's feathered hat, the effect more theatrical than suggestive of transvestism, or of layers of skin peeling away to reveal a skull which remains undeniably his own. In one painting his own head is served, *pace* John the Baptist, by waiters upon a silver platter. And in a series of staged tussles photographed on Ostend beach Ensor, wearing smock and sou'wester, and his friend Ernest Rousseau Junior (in tartan coat and fez) brandish herrings (held between the constituent parts of a dismembered skeleton) at each other in faux menace.

Ensor had co-conspirators in his mischief. Leon Spilliaert, whose high-contrast self-portraits show him as lean-faced, hollow-cheeked and wild-eyed, was a sometime acolyte, also producing a body of satirical etchings. But his paintings and pastels have an elegance and spareness all their own – low-key evocative quests for the elusive architecture of the waves. Felicien Rops, who also produced exquisite pornography, captures Ostend characters: in one, two men squabble over the telescope that's instrumental to their voyeurism; and in another, a pencil drawing simply titled *God*, a middle-aged man in a wide-brimmed hat stares out at the placid sea. Jan Toorop, another of the Ensor 'set', employs a kind of pointillism to portray his subjects, such as that of a figure dredging for scallops on the beach below a pink-imbued turquoise sky.

Ensor sat out both world wars and died five years after the end of the second having been made a baron by the very authorities he had often mocked and derided.

In dismal mood one might surmise that with him the city lost its wit and fizz, but the longer I've spent in Ostend, the greater the number of moments that shimmer (to use an Ensor word) like mischievous curios, dark and sparkling, that I've come to chance upon. Riding the coast tram in November – it was already cold and I was returning from a failed attempt to walk from the last town in Belgium to the first in France – I caught a glimpse of a girl who, beguilingly, fetchingly and improbably had strode into the North Sea until it caressed the tops of her knees. Entirely alone on the beach, wearing, as far as I can tell, a long charcoal-black dress, she could, should even, have been a fiction. But, hurtling past far too quickly, I watched her scoop up handfuls of foaming sea with which to splash herself, the dress's hem floating around her in the surf like a dark petal. The tram rounded a bend, severing the sight but not the sense of intrigue.

Taking tea in a park, I watched a man wipe the rectum of his toy schnauzer with a distressing degree of assiduity before flicking the tissue into the depths of a herbaceous border. Later, killing time in the Café du Parc, itself an Ensorian anachronism, perhaps the most perfectly preserved café in the art nouveau style in Europe, I gazed out at a courting couple. She was evidently of African descent, tall, ramrod erect, blessed with the most perfectly straight nose and utterly graceful and forbidding features. Her cropped hair was dyed crimson, and she wore a coat of dark maroon. She was perhaps in her early forties. Her lover, a septuagenarian in a camel-hair coat, swung an umbrella as if it were a swordstick, sported a trilby hat, a military bearing and a black patch over one eye.

It was war and its aftermath that degraded Leopold's Ostend. In the 1914–18 conflict the town of Nieuwpoort, half an hour's tram ride along the coast from Ostend, marked the beginning of a line of trenches running from the North Sea coast to Switzerland. The

Germans had hoped for total victory over the Belgians in order to push into France from the north. They were almost successful. But the Belgians prevented them from getting beyond the Yser Canal by opening the sluice gates and turning fields into impenetrable marsh, a centuries-old military trick in the Low Countries.

An aerial photograph of Nieuwpoort taken in 1917 shows its esplanade like the smashed jaw of a gargantnam, unfortunate beast. A single building protrudes from the rubble, with a handwritten note identifying it as the Grand Hotel which still exists, the one attractive structure facing the sea, now kept dubious company by the ubiquitous apartment blocks. Today Nieuwpoort is an almost excruciatingly dull suburb, its greatest attraction the canal that leads mournfully out to sea. It doesn't go out of its way to exploit its gorily fascinating history, which is ironic given that only months after the armistice, British tourists were heading to Belgium to enjoy the spectacle of its ruin. There's a sense in which the war has been buried with deliberate absence of pomp, as one might inter a roguish relative one would prefer not to have ever mentioned. You could find yourself looking all afternoon for traces of war before giving up and settling for *moules frites* in a local bar. But it is always somewhere.

Convinced that Ostend and Zeebrugge were being used by the German navy as submarine bases, the British launched a desperate assault on both ports on 23 April 1918. At Zeebrugge three obsolete concrete-filled cruisers, *Intrepid*, *Iphigenia* and *Thetis*, were to be towed to the harbour mouth, run aground and blown up to block the entrance. By the evening of the 24th an official narrative of what happened had been released:

Those who recall High Wood upon the Somme as it was after the battles of 1916 . . . may easily figure to themselves the decks of

HMS *Vindictive* [another Royal Navy cruiser, badly damaged in the raid] as she lies today, a stark black profile against the haze of the harbour amid the stripped trim shapes of the fighting ships which throng these waters . . . the broken tools of war, that lavish ruin and that prodigal evidence of death and battle, are as obvious and plentiful here as there . . .

The navy thought it had the best possible conditions for the raid – there would be no moon, and the tide was favourable for an easy withdrawal. But by the time its ships arrived the Germans had got wind of them, and the sky was 'illuminated by strings of luminous green beads shot aloft, the darkness of the night . . . supplanted by the nightmare daylight of battle fires. Guns and machine guns along the mole and batteries ashore woke to life.'

An agitated sea made coming alongside difficult, and when the gangways were lowered they scraped and rebounded from the high parapet of the mole as the *Vindictive* ground and bounced against it. The two officers leading the attack were killed even before the whistle was blown, Colonel Elliot by a shell and Captain Halahan by machine-gun fire sweeping across the decks. Even the attempt to get onto the mole must have felt desperately suicidal. 'A passage across the crashing splintering gangways, a drop over the parapet into the field of fire of the German machine guns which swept its length and a further drop of some sixteen feet to the surface of the mole itself. Many were killed and more were wounded as they crowded up to the gangways; but nothing hindered the orderly and speedy landing by every gangway.'

On another of the assault vessels – a former Mersey ferry called *Iris* – a 'single big shell plunged through the upper deck and burst below at a point where fifty-six marines were waiting the order to go to the gangways. Forty-nine were killed and the remaining seven wounded . . .' The cowardly Hun offered 'no resistance . . . other than intense and unremitting fire', which could apparently be heard in Dover. Such was the insanity that one naval officer was attacked by a member of his own crew 'with a hammer'; another man hit the water in a lifebuoy, igniting a calcium flare, and found himself 'adrift in the uncanny illumination with a German machine gun giving him its undivided attention'.

Inevitable telegrams duly followed.

> *Sir . . . It is my painful duty to inform you that telegraphic information has reached this Department that Charles Pool, Acting Air Mexchanic [sic] 1st Grade, Official number F. 12787, was killed in action on the 23rd instant during operations off the Belgian Coast. I have to request that you will be good enough to telegraph to the Commodore whether you wish your Son's body, if recovered, to be sent home for burial or whether you would prefer to attend the funeral at Dover.*

The Zeebrugge raid was played up as a great victory. The officer responsible, Admiral Keyes, was congratulated by King George, the prime minister and General Douglas Haig. Whether it achieved anything of military value is dubious at best. The block ships were not sunk at the correct location, and submarines left Zeebrugge on the next high tide.

More recently the apparently blighted Zeebrugge became a household name on account of the capsizing on 6 March 1987 of the ferry *Herald of Free Enterprise*. I was sixteen, staunchly convinced that Margaret Thatcher (along with the other culprits to whom adolescents tend to attribute blame – school, and parents) was responsible for most of the things that had gone wrong in my life or the world at large.

The official inquiry into the *Herald*'s sinking described what happened pithily.

Approximately 459 passengers had embarked for the voyage to Dover, which they expected to be completed without incident in the prevailing good weather. There was a light easterly breeze and very little sea or swell. The HERALD passed the outer mole at 18.24. She capsized about four minutes later. During the final moments the HERALD turned rapidly to starboard and was prevented from sinking totally by reason only that her port side took the ground in shallow water. Water rapidly filled the ship below the surface level with the result that not less than 150 passengers and 38 members of the crew lost their lives. Many others were injured.

A number of individuals took the rap for what happened. The easiest to blame was a crew member, Mark Stanley, who should have closed the bow doors. After opening them on the boat's arrival from Dover he returned to his cabin for a snooze and remained 'asleep in his bunk until thrown out of it when the *Herald* began to capsize'. The inquiry criticised Stanley but added that it was 'right to record that after the *Herald* capsized he found his way out of the ship on to her hull where he set about rescuing passengers trapped inside. He broke a window for access and . . . his forearm was deeply cut. Nevertheless, he re-entered the hull and went into the water to assist passengers. He continued until he was overcome by cold and bleeding.' The ship's bosun Terry Ayling was also in the firing line. He too could have closed the doors, but, he told the inquiry, 'it had never been part of his duties'. Also like Stanley, he behaved 'heroically' after the accident occurred, organising rescue efforts in the absence of a senior officer.

In this instance at least my teen instinct towards anti-establishmentarianism was perhaps not too wide of the mark. In retrospect the incident represented much of the spirit of the age of Thatcherism, with all its attendant social and ideological divisions. 'Free enterprise' was a flagship slogan for economic libertarianism. Critics of the government saw the ferry disaster as indicative of a greater evil than the shoddiness of one or a handful of crewmen. And when a minister of the day announced that the operator P&O would not face criminal charges, one parliamentarian described the *Herald* as 'a latterday *Titanic*, wrecked on an iceberg of Department of Transport indifference, managerial incompetence and working methods that were apparently designed only to shorten turn-around times, regardless of risks to passengers and crew'.

Had Ensor been alive, he would almost certainly have made something of it. The *hareng saur* was by no means so distracted by the fancies of his own imagination as to shirk his obligation to social commentary. In 1890 Ensor produced a series of paintings inspired by a demonstration by Ostend fishermen on the Visserkai. They were protesting against preferential treatment given to English trawlers landing their catch. Within eyeshot of Ostend's promenading swells and dandies the gendarmes came out in force to quell what was quite a minor uprising. Several fishermen were shot, enraging Ensor and no doubt Spilliaert, whose atelier directly overlooked the quay.

Ostend does little to give its artists their due. The Ensor House is halfway there but moulders for lack of funds. The MuZee, a repurposed 1950s department store in a backstreet beyond the Leopold Park, has a standing collection of works by the Ostend Set, but it is less than it could be. All the best paintings are somewhere across the North Sea and beyond. Every so often a major retrospective is held in New York or Paris, and the art world remembers that Ensor and friends were 'major' and 'important' painters, but then the dust settles, and they sink back into the shadows of the Belgian dunes.

Major and important, but not household names like Cézanne or Gauguin, or bequeathing gardens full of lilies. Were they to be, the rule would be broken by which nobody can recall the names of above half a dozen famous Belgians.

One wonders, indeed, whether Ostend underwent some collective trauma after the Second World War which severed its links with the past. On the front only two or three belle époque buildings remain. Nonsensically, they were vacant when I visited, their soft, elegant, sexy curlicues having lost the power to entrance. In their place are unremitting blocks, which, up close and singly, just escape being monstrous. But in sum they resemble a mile-long Stalinist vision of collectivist seaside fun.

I had assumed that the Germans (easy to blame in Belgium) were responsible one way or other – perhaps for blowing the original buildings to smithereens. In fact much of old Ostend survived after 1945 only to be broken on the anvil of Belgium's strange politics. Typically the buildings had been owned by rich merchant families, and a succession of leftist governments colluding with the spirit of populist capitalism implemented a policy of tearing down these totems of privilege, replacing them with apartments which are hideous but afford very many more people their proprietorial right to a view of the North Sea.

Many Belgians feel sad about the national loss, though still in the summer they descend upon the coast in French- and Flemish-speaking droves, kicking up and tickling the beaches until the very sands groan beneath the thudding of their feet. And the Ensor collection is far too elitist an attraction to inflame the breast of Ostend's city planners and tourist board. He is, as might be said, a 'speciality attraction' with limited pulling power.

Not like Marvin Gaye.

Gaye spent a year in Ostend at the invitation of the record producer and city native Freddy Clousaert, who offered him respite from the curse of drugs, women and unpaid taxes. For a brief, charmed spell, the soul music legend found sanctuary in this out-of-the-way seaside resort. He recorded his masterpiece 'Sexual Healing' in a studio not far from Waterloo and found a modicum of sanity away from the temptations of big-city life.

A film by the director Richard Olivier documents Gaye running barefoot across the dunes and playing darts with Flemish fishermen, one of whom asks whether he is from Paraguay, and though never having heard of Marvin Gaye is impressed that he is playing a gig at the Kursaal, Ostend's big casino-cum-conference venue. Gaye comes across as a man of extraordinary intelligence. Eloquent, modest, endowed with great powers of reflection. Ostend, Gaye declares, is 'a beat back in tempo from London or Paris – or perhaps two beats back', but he adds, 'It's where I need to be right now.' Two years later he headed back to the US to face his demons, one of whom, his father, would fatally shoot him.

In early spring Ostend plays up its Gaye connections. Tribute bands appear at the Kursaal, and the Marvin Gaye walking tour sells out each time, in contrast to the derisory sales for Ensor's. I like Gaye, but it struck me that Ostend has over-associated itself with him, given the accidental, cursory nature of their coincidence.

In the last days of my final visit I felt tender towards Ostend, strolling through the enormous market, where the city, sometimes so stifled and grey, now came to life in an ebullience of pâtés, sausages, cold meats, fruit, flowers, cheeses and scratchy-looking brassieres. The gruff market vendors' shouts and haggling made good earlier city silences, and the water, studded with stars of light, belied the North Sea's animus. Ostend isn't beautiful, but on that long esplanade I realised the pleasures of a place where appearances, both the keeping up of them and the letting them slip, are everything.

Just off the esplanade on Vlaanderenstraat I discovered the Galerie du Rat Mort – named after an annual dance started by Ensor and some friends and inspired by a debauched trip to the cabarets of Paris. Ensor conceived it as a kind of off-beam *bal* for the city's radicals, eccentrics, poets and artists – a counterweight to its starchy bourgeois façade.

At first sight, the proprietor of the gallery was a large sheepdog with a wary glance and a well-chewed novelty chicken. But fervent doorbell-pushing drew out Madame Devolder, elegantly coiffed and excellently dressed. For the greater part the works on show were sculptures and paintings dominated by a singular theme: men and fish, sometimes men-fish, sometimes fish-men. Men carried large fish, not as fishermen do, but with paternal *tendresse*, as one might a sleeping child. Or men ran races with fish. I found they touched an instant chord, as if in painting and sculpting these images their creator had delved deep into my own unconscious.

'These are the works of Roland, my husband,' said Madame. And soon he appeared beside her. Hair, beard and gypsum-white smile, short and spry, Roland was immediately likeable.

'What is it with fish?' I asked.

He shrugged as if to indicate that surely that was obvious. 'I am a fish. My spirit is a fish. When I was a child I would go to the fishermen's quay and see that the fish were so big –' he stretched out his arms '– and now they are so big.' He shrank the space between them. 'Maybe I'm trying to compensate!'

The three of us talked about Ensor and the *bal*. Ostend had lost its magic, said Roland. Now the tourist board was trying to sell it as a kind of quirky kitsch city-break destination 'for Philistines'. It was bringing in artists, but it was all so crass, brightly coloured and sensationalist. The current favourite, a landmark on the esplanade, an installation of four fluorescent red objects in the shape of crushed cans, each six metres tall, was a case in point. 'It's . . . it's . . . it's . . .' said Roland.

Madame interjected to point out that even when one of her husband's own paintings had been offered to the MuZee gratis, by a philanthropist, it had refused it on the grounds that it was 'too classical'.

'And this claims to be the city of Ensor!' said Roland.

I saw his point, though I'd entertained a fondness, as meaningless as its object, for the crushed cans.

I had my train to catch and wanted to visit the aquarium, with which, it being open all year round, I was acquainted from the very first of my Ostend sorties, and where, behind a turnstile in a dozen or so tanks with their grey and blue painted backdrops and patina of algae swam the inmates – a lobster, half a dozen brill, an elderly haddock, a turbot resigned to never gracing a dinner table and an assortment of blennies, weaver fish and bass. It sits a glance away from the small fish market, a squat oblong of concrete in which half a dozen stalls sell lobster, brill, haddock and turbot.

Dirk, manning the booth, took my two euros. I asked him where the fish came from. 'From the sea of course, eh!' he said. 'De fishermen brings 'em.'

'So these are the lucky fish? The unlucky ones end up over there?' I said, nodding towards the market.

'No! The lucky ones are still in de sea, eh?'

Dirk, a shortish man with a mild squint behind his steel-framed glasses, had that thick Ostend accent that sounds brusque and rough (but pleasantly so) and rounds off each sentence with a semi-affirmative and rhetorical 'eh?' It is the cherry on the icing of a dialect so its own that other Flemish speakers find it almost incomprehensible.

Dirk said he didn't work at the aquarium by choice but that the council had made him take the job. If he didn't, he would no longer be eligible for his pension. He liked the fish all right – in fact, he loved nature – but he didn't like to see them in a tank, and he didn't like the lack of respect his colleagues, in particular his boss, showed the animals.

Up until a few months ago, they'd had 'an octopussy – the fishermen bring it. Ja! And you know, de octopussy, it become really friendly wid me. I tell it, like, "Come here!" or, "Go like making a circle," eh? And the octopussy, he do it.'

'You spoke to the . . . the . . . octopussy?'

'No, but like, wid my hand, eh? But then something happened.'

Dirk came out from behind the booth and took me to a tank in which a bloated lumpfish blinked and pouted.

'Diss is where de octopussy lived. You see dese stones, eh? First, my boss, my boss who didn't know anything about de octopussy, what he like and everything, he moved the stones. You see dese stones?'

'Yes.'

'And I knew de octopussy had everything just right before, you know, comfortable. Dis arm here, and dat arm dere and hiding like dis, eh?' Dirk demonstrated to the extent that was possible.

'So de octopussy, you know, he wasn't happy about dis, and he couldn't get right. You know, he try to sit, here, and dere, but it wasn't de same and den . . .'

Assuming the denouement could only end in the cephalopod's death I wasn't sure I could bear to hear more.

'And den my colleagues – fuckin' stoopid! – my colleagues dey started to, you know, poke de octopussy – see if dey can make it do tricks like me – but it gets angry. And squirts its ink. And you know what happens if it squirts its ink tree times, eh?'

'Did it . . .?'

'Died. De octopussy died.'

Dirk had, it seemed, a personal relationship with almost all of the fish, at least those that had been there for a while. In one tank a dozen flatfish lay heaped on top of each other, a little too hugger-mugger, I thought, but he said that if he got rid of any, 'De fishermen, they come and check to see if we're looking after the fish dey bring, and if dey don't see them, dey don't bring no more, eh?'

That the trawler men of Ostend, to whom fish represent an economic resource, might actually feel sentimental about the individual specimens they deposited with Dirk was a revelation to me. But it seemed to be the case.

Dirk showed me his favourite since the death of the octopus – a butterfish. 'You see it eh? Just little. Behind de rock. Dese days dey never get so big any more. Not since the wind turbines . . .' Almost as close to his heart was a little snub-nosed seahorse. He had, he said, tried to get it to grow, even sending off for a special kind of live food that could only be purchased from Salt Lake City, but, Dirk having successfully managed to hatch the eggs, his boss had thrown away the whole bucket.

I didn't like the sound of this guy who treated Ostend City Aquarium with such callous disregard. Clearly there was no love lost between him and Dirk. 'I only stroke de little sharks when de boss is gone, eh? After what happened wid de octopus.' Dirk lived by himself, though with some fish of his own. He was looking forward to giving up the job.

I didn't say that my Ostend days were over. 'Maybe you'll have a new octopus when I return.'

'Maybe, eh?'

Dirk and I shook hands. I liked him and his affinity with the fish, as I had liked Roland's.

Then I passed through the turnstile, and turned in the direction of Leopold's station with a sea breeze and, I flattered myself, an approving Ensorial smile upon my back.

Shapes and Shingle on the Naked Shore

. . . Here leaves unnoticed thicken,
Hidden weeds flower, neglected waters quicken,
Luminously-peopled air ascends;
And past the poppies bluish neutral distance
Ends the land suddenly beyond a beach
Of shapes and shingle.

Philip Larkin, 'Here'

Spurn Point is a just-so four-mile-long bony peninsula which dangles from the upper lip of the Humber into the river's mouth. Mostly and loosely composed of dunes, it unfolds to a bunker-cankered bulbous expanse. On its beaches golden-horned poppies burst from the sands and yolk-berried sea-buckthorn flourishes in the thickets. It is a place where whales come to die and birds find succour from the North Sea. Poets, saints and hermits gravitate towards what Shakespeare called its 'naked shore'.

It feels like the end of England, but it has pedigree. Edward IV landed upon Spurn by ship, dishevelled and 'sore weather beaten' (Shakespeare again), and found lodgings at a 'poor village' two miles further up the coast. Five hundred years previously, the hermit Wilgils (sometimes Wilislig) made his soft sandal-prints in the sands and settled in for a long and lonely stay. Wilgils, out of the same mould as Cedd, was also in a state of recovery, seeking refuge from the Vikings' sacking of Lindisfarne 200 miles north.

And Philip Larkin no doubt was also fatigued when he arrived here on his bicycle 'past the poppies blueish neutral distance' to where 'ends the land suddenly beyond a beach of shapes and shingle'.

I arrived, with my teenage daughter in tow, having driven beyond Hull's outer circle of retail parks and refineries to the flat levels of Holderness, curiously reminiscent of Friesland, some 200 miles across the North Sea.

The geology of these fields is as fresh as rain, no older than the last ice age. And yet bones and boats are fetched up from the dark soil which dates from the time when men fought bears. Beneath the right sky – say at dusk in winter when amethyst, amber and violet shades cast the waves in tints of slippery bronze – the gaze of old gods can still be felt. So it was when my daughter and I arrived and stood full square to the affections of a puppyish half-gale on a low cliff abutting the threshold of the Sandy Beaches Caravan Park, the southernmost boundary of which marks the beginning of the peninsula, and whose inhabitants are no less appreciative of Spurn than the other pilgrims, aesthetes, ascetics and writers to have washed up here.

We wandered among Sandy Beaches as if through a ghost town, and came upon a spectral figure, more mackintosh than man, emerging from his rickety caravan (a glimpse of a flickering screen and steam from a stovetop kettle before the vision snapped shut). The man in the mackintosh joined us. He had, he said, decided not to return yet to his winter roost far from the sea. This was the season for long walks and contemplation, just 'thinking about things quietly'. He was forced to raise his voice above the wind, adding with no apparent regret that his wife had returned to Corby in September.

A loner but not a misanthrope, he was happy to point out landmarks, decipher distant lights, excited by the transience of the fast-eroding coast. 'One day soon . . .' he said, his arm making a slow and grave sweep towards the caravans and a scattering of abandoned white goods, 'this will be gone.' None of those things looked incapable of obsolescence. Just beyond the shoreline two great discs of concrete, each perhaps eighteen feet across, jutted from the oozing wet sand. They had been gun platforms, once standing guard against German bombers and now resembling the scattered pieces of an abandoned game.

Eight years after the end of the First World War the composer Ralph Vaughan Williams subtitled one of his English Folk Songs 'Spurn Point'. He had the melody from a former sailor called Leatherday whom he'd met at a Norfolk workhouse, but the piece was also inspired by the wreck of a ship called the *Industry*, stranded off Spurn in the winter of 1868, its captain refusing out of pride the assistance of a lifeboat, thus consigning himself and his crew to a cold and miserable death on the shoals.

The music is as svelte as the source of its inspiration – and politely melancholic. But it fails to capture Spurn's quirkiness, the shingle-scouring easterlies, opaline sunsets or its proclivity for oddity, indeed any of the qualities I like to imagine appealed to Wilgils, who found his sanctuary here and about whom little is known other than that, despite his hermitic condition, he fathered St Wilibrod, converter of the Dutch pagans.

I would have known little about Wilibrod – a footnote in the hagiography of the North Sea – were it not for the small library of books and pamphlets pertaining to Spurn's lifeboat service, gravel dredging and cobble gathering, lighthouses, butterflies, birds and moths that lined the shelves of a dresser in the breakfast room at West Farm B & B. The most compelling of these volumes was a log kept by the teachers who had taught between the late 1880s and the end of the First World War at a one-room school for the children of pilots, lighthouse keepers and lifeboat men, and of which stood in what is now the car park by the quayside. In terse prose this diary – its authors neutered by namelessness – etched the harshness of life on a wind-beholden near-island: a litany of measles, louse infections and vain attempts to inculcate the twelve-times table alongside the values of a waning empire.

And yet there are flashes of radiance in these accounts. One diarist recorded taking a class to picnic among the dunes, where they ran races, counted the nests of sandwich terns and collected shells and tide-stranded fish. Another entry recounted how, the morning after a shipwreck, the school closed in acknowledgement of its students' right to gather the spoils thrust upon the beach – a valuable supplement to meagre family incomes.

In the summer the children sold trinkets to the tourists who disembarked each weekend from the Cleethorpes steamer to play on the sands and ride upon the sail-powered 'bogey', a trolley on rails that hurtled from the very base of Spurn to its tip, commandeered for games when not in the service of the military camp maintained to protect the Humber from invasion. The tiny train was rendered useless decades ago by Spurn's refusal to adhere to the course of its rails. Now, where the old track is not overgrown or covered by dunes (sleepers dozing beneath a blanket of sand) it meanders hopelessly out to sea. For Spurn is perpetually on the cusp of change, lengthening and shortening and narrowing and broadening. At high tide it is less than a dozen yards wide. Walking the path that runs along its spine is like a giddying sortie across a tightrope or being caught between the jaws of a great beast almost safe in the knowledge that they will never quite meet. Sometimes when the tide is abnormally high and the wind blows hard from the east, the waves cut across the narrows and the jaws clamp shut.

We had a near miss, driving south from Sandy Beaches in fading light with the waves on the Humber side of Spurn lapping hard at the edge of the road. Where the road stops we encountered a car-load of sea pilots about to take the night shift in their control tower at the mouth of the river: 'Turn back!' they shouted over the wind. 'There might be a breach.' And turn back we did, holing up at the Crown & Anchor, a pub which must count among the most exposed in Britain, where the music was too loud, but where Larkin, on his long cycling trips from Hull, almost certainly once rested sore feet.

In the pub we ate battered cod and browsed back copies of the *Yorkshireman*. Only yards away the Humber carried on bullying at the shore. The wind had picked up, and the trees began to scream, and I felt for but almost envied our friend from Corby in his caravan. Rocked as he must have been by a storm that had hurled down the Humber from the west and was predicted to make landfall in the Netherlands by noon the next day.

When the wind blows from the north sweeping in from the North Atlantic, the sea rasps away at the coast like a great tongue. In 1843 the parishioners of a church at Kilnsea – a village as close to Spurn as it has ever been advisable to erect anything of substance – woke to find their cemetery ripped apart by such a storm, its dead tossed onto the beach and into the sea. Within days they had packed the retrievable remains into carts and headed five miles inland, reinterring the bodies and rebuilding the village. Erosion has brought Kilnsea back to the coast once more.

Holderness, the steep isosceles from which Spurn protrudes at the south-east corner, is soft, upstart land. A mere two million years ago this was a shallow bay in a warm sea. Then it froze, locking out life for a millennium before the ice retreated, depositing in its place the existing sediment of boulder clay, gravel and fossils. When the Romans invaded, the shoreline lay some three miles closer to the Continent than it does now, but by the time the

Domesday Book had been completed it had already lost a third of that breadth. Each year the land retreats another ten feet. It is the fastest-disappearing coastline in the world. With every passing month, the clay cliffs slump upon the beach in slices and dissolve. Most geological changes occur over the course of tens or hundreds of millions of years. On Holderness whole cycles are squeezed into human lifetimes.

Sometimes the owners of properties on the cliffs put them on the market despite or because of the fact that they are only a garden shed away from oblivion. Occasionally they find buyers, such being the quixotically entrancing hold of imminent doom, but ultimately Holderness has no hope other than to follow in the wake of a catalogue of towns – Tharlsthorp, Frismersk, East Somert, Penisthorp, Orwithfleet, Sunthorp, Ravenser and Ravenser Odd – each of which now lies beneath the waves. A locally produced guide to the lost villages of Holderness invites its readers to stand at Spurn Point, gaze out to sea and into the mouth of the Humber, and invest in the churning waters sufficient imaginative powers to resurrect those once-thriving communities.

Ravenser – Hrafn's Eyr, or Hrafn's Sandbank – was always a nowheresville, even at the end of the first millennium, but it warranted a mention in the Icelandic sagas as the place from which the Norse army of Harald Hardrada embarked on its voyage home following its defeat by Harold Godwinson at Stamford Bridge. Its near-namesake and neighbour Ravenser Odd grew up much more quickly, first as a place where fishermen could dry out their nets, and in quick succession were built a busy harbour, customs house, windmills, prison and churches. It boasted a royal charter, levied dues on ships and sent men to fight wars against the Scots, but against the ever-scouring sea all was hubris, all in vain. Within a few decades of its charter, Ravenser

Odd was taken back by the sea. The inhabitants had only themselves to blame.

> The town . . . lay open to devastation from floods and inundations of the sea which surrounded it from every side like a wall, thus threatening its imminent annihilation. And so with the terrible vision of waters seen on every side, the besieged persons . . . preserved themselves at that time from destruction, flocked together and tearfully implored grace . . . by all its wicked deeds, and especially wrong-doing on the sea, and by its evil actions and predations, it provoked the vengeance of God upon itself beyond measure.

Thus at least was the explanation provided by monks of a nearby abbey.

It was fanciful but pleasurable to imagine, as we lay beneath electric blankets at West Farm B & B with a wolf of a gale hammering at the windows and the trees, that timelessly entwined in the moaning and carrying-on were the howls of the penitents who may or may not be forgiven but are as good as forgotten. Ask any local where they believe Ravenser Odd to have been located and they'll point variously to any sandbank. 'We think it was possibly there – or there.'

Anticipating their descendants at Kilnsea, the surviving inhabitants of Ravenser Odd gathered up their dead and moved them for reburial to drier land, while at around the same time the town of Dunwich in Suffolk was suffering the same indignities, which the poet A. G. Swinburne captured hundreds of years later in his infectiously arhythmic (and excruciatingly long) poem 'By the North Sea'.

> Tombs, with bare white piteous bones protruded,
> Shroudless, down the loose collapsing banks,

> Crumble, from their constant place detruded,
> That the sea devours and gives not thanks.

He may also have had Ravenser Odd in mind.

By morning the wind that until dawn had been shaking the windowpanes had lost its thump, and we walked the four sandy miles to the point almost unmolested other than by a squall that blew out like an ambitious but abandoned fancy. Spurn had not been breached. The tide had ebbed, and where the water had come up to the road the day before, the foreshore shone like silver beneath bright sun. Almost as if in atonement for its earlier frolics, the sea had thrown any number of treasures onto the sands: lobster legs, whelk sacs, mermaids' purses, starfish and, most pleasing of all, sea urchin shells in every size but identically proportioned, like Russian matroyshka dolls. And though every discovery, whether moss agate, a sea-changed bottle or tree stump, constituted occasion for delightful meditation on how small things succumb to the forces of time, we succeeded in arriving at the little settlement of buildings that comprises the sum of human habitation on the point.

Before setting out for Spurn I had contacted the local wildlife warden, a man called Andy Gibson, who now waited for us by the pilot boats' quay. A big, ruddy, soft man in the Yorkshire mould, he made an ideal custodian for Spurn, a plain-speaking scholar, spending his working hours scratching the sky with his binoculars, tending, supervising and thinking – mostly about Spurn and about the birds that he delicately untangles (hot beating hearts, easily snapped legs and wings) with his large hands from the mist nets he sets to monitor seasonal migration.

Man, he said, had played push-me pull-you with the point for too long. Gravelling and cobble extraction, mostly for the paving of London mews, had weakened Spurn while the sea defences had prevented it from following its own course. What would happen if it was just left? It was a contentious issue. As a realist, he knew that the mouth of the Humber would silt and the channels quickly become unnavigable. Ships would founder and the ports of Immingham and Hull would lose trade. All of which he understood. But from one stance, even as a thought experiment, it would be intriguing to turn Spurn back to nature.

Not that it seemed to have been overly tamed. The human presence on Spurn is so obviously temporary, consisting of a pilots' tower rising from the dunes like a periscope, a scattering of ancient weatherboarded huts used as sheds, a jetty for the lifeboat and the pilots' boat, and the lifeboatmen's buildings – a cluster of modern(ish) but not unpleasant two-storey cottages. Simple and suburban as they are, the buildings represent the culmination of two centuries of remarkable history. For while the Spurn community has also included at various points pilots, naturalists, soldiers and hermits, the lifeboatmen are at the nub of it. Without them, Spurn would revert to the remote, unsocialised appendage of land jutting into the North Sea that it is always about to become.

Spurn had been hungry for a lifeboat for years before it finally arrived. In most coastal settlements the task of saving lives at sea was undertaken by local fishermen. On Spurn there existed no permanent community with the boat or other requisite wherewithal to step into the breach. Local newspapers had been petitioning for the establishment of a lighthouse station since before 1800. It was essential because, as one concerned local wrote to Trinity House around 1805,

When a ship takes the ground upon the Shoals called the Stoney Beach, as frequently occurs, the tide gradually leaves her in apparent safety and the crews, if strangers, imagine that on the return of the tide the ship will ride off without further damage or danger. The people on shore, from constant experience, know that on the return of the tide the conflict between it and the current of the Humber occasions such a surf that the ship will inevitably beat to pieces and the crew perish. Yet the people on shore have not means of affording help to the mariners or even of communicating to them, though within a comparatively short distance, the peril of their situation, so that the mariners might in many cases, find safety in their own boats.

Thus, he said, 'the mariners wait with patient confidence and the people on shore with the most distressing anxiety, till the awful period arrives – when the ship is lost and the people perish'.

In the early 1800s the Lord of the Manor of Spurn, Burton Constable, decided that the responsibility for establishing a lifeboat rested in his hands. The idea was that while the lighthouse commissioners of Trinity House would be responsible for the governance of the lifeboat, Constable would provide the land and commit money. He thus funded a lifeboat built to the latest design and a carriage by which it might be conveyed to the sea. Constable also (in his beneficence) provided the lifeboatmen with rights over his land, reserving for himself and his family the privilege of collecting fossils and such Royal Fish (whales, dolphins and sturgeon) as might become stranded. His motives were driven 'solely by motives of humanity', his agent told Trinity House, he himself having no financial interest in the shipping trade.

The much-anticipated vessel arrived in Spurn in the autumn of 1810 from the respected boatyard of Henry Greathead of South Shields. It was ten feet at the beam, three times as long, and shipped ten oars, moving with equal ease in either direction so as to obviate the need for turning. It was, Greathead acknowledged, not a boat easily managed by novices, and he advised that the crew should begin practising with their new boat as soon as its varnish had dried. The words SPURN LIFEBOAT were carefully painted in bold black letters across the shiny white gunwales.

On 4 November 1810 the boat successfully hauled a vessel called the *John and Charlotte* from the sand upon which she had run aground, and everyone involved with the rescue hailed Spurn's new enhancement as a great success – briefly.

Constable's plan envisioned sufficient funds (three shillings and sixpence daily) to pay the crew to train on a regular basis, building stamina, pride and morale, but for the most part the scheme was designed to be self-financing. A disused barracks building would be converted into a pub which the lifeboat master would run to generate income, selling beer and stores to the crews of passing vessels – but also to his own lifeboat crew, a perquisite they heavily resented. It was little inducement for the lifeboatmen to stay in their posts. They received only a breadline stipend, supplemented with the 'opportunity' to load gravel and cobbles onto passing ships. But locals ('Countrymen') came to the point and took the work from them, sometimes waving pistols. Being so far away from any justice of the peace or court, a brutish 'law of the dunes' applied on Spurn in which any semblance of order stood as close to being breached as the point itself. Thus the role of lifeboat master required mustering a semi-starving near-mutinous crew into something akin to a purposeful body of men while also defending their rights against resentful local interests.

The first master fled within a month. The second, Robert Richardson, was made of grittier stuff, committing himself to serving out a term of thirty-one years and a month. But the North Sea wind seldom brought him anything good. On 27 December 1811 he wrote to the Brethren at Trinity House: 'There is three

Countrymen that always brings guns with them to Spurn, which is William Wilson, Robert Bird, Thomas Bird, which if they are suffered to do I am confident my Life will fall a sacrifice the first opportunity.' Relations between crew and master were also strained, small grievances flourishing like weeds. Richardson complained that the men were often drunk and frequently challenged him to fights. On the occasion of one 1811 rescue he was obliged to take the lifeboat out alone – either for the reason that the crew were off the point at the time and couldn't be summoned, or simply because they refused to show up.

Intransigence and insubordination were not solely characteristic of Richardson's watch. One June day in 1858 a successor, William Willis, was having his three o'clock supper when a crewman he had dismissed, 'a blackguard by the name of Bell', arrived at his house accompanied by three cudgel-bearing companions and their wives, who collectively 'abused him most shamefully' to the point that he 'risked being maimed'. The wives, 'three viragoes of the first class, a disgrace to their sex', were, he said, most ferocious in their 'urging on' of Bell. Of Bell himself, whose language was so crude that it was unfit to be heard by 'anyone with a spark of decency', he had earlier written that he could find 'no better specimen of a bad man'.

Debt, poverty and miserable living conditions plagued the lives of the early lifeboatmen and masters. Another new broom feared that he was subject to a whispering campaign, telling his employers his correspondence was not safe, there being 'so many enemies about', and his living quarters were such that 'when the wind blows it is almost fit to blow one out'.

Against such a backdrop of suspicion, recrimination and freely waved flintlocks, confrontations with the sea were, if perilous, at least less emotionally taxing. But even here human capriciousness could intrude on the otherwise pure struggle with the elements.

In the 1880s the authorities were alerted to a fad newly prevalent among bored local youths whereby 'the Life Boat Men are frequently called out at night by the exhibition of red lights, flares and rockets, which appear to be signals of distress but which are found upon arriving out to have been exhibited merely for sport by the crews of fishing smacks'. And it was commonplace for captains to refuse assistance (as in the case of the *Industry*) out of misplaced pride, and for crews to drown within the sight of land.

Order and civilisation came to Spurn gradually, in belated step with the march of technological and spiritual progress. In 1839 the lifeboat crew complained of the absence of both church and school, and in the 1850s the local chapter of the Primitive Methodists stole a march on their established rivals by visiting the point each week to conduct a service. In 1867 the wife of a lifeboatman opened a school in her own home. Newfangled paddle steamers brought increasing numbers of day trippers from Cleethorpes and Grimsby. And in 1919 the lifeboat station came under the authority of the Royal National Lifeboat Institution and bestowed upon Spurn its first motor vessel, the *Samuel Oakes*. By all these increments (not least among them the building of an electric telegraph to supersede a mechanical semaphore), Spurn came into the fold of modernity.

There have been sixteen lifeboats since Greathead's nameless vessel, each generation faster, sturdier and more unsinkable than the last. For all the excitement that accompanied its launch, the original Spurn lifeboat of 1810 was a perilous tub compared with its 35-knot, self-righting, 1,200-horsepower counterpart of today. And its coxswain no longer keeps a tavern or has a need to fend off dangerous 'Countrymen'. Andy Gibson introduced me to the man who held that post – Dave Steenvoorden – pushing through a white-painted sprung gate which read NO ENTRY EXCEPT ON RNLI BUSINESS into a sort of temporary structure which was Dave's office and where he was making tea. It was not a busy or cosy interior, but decorated with whiteboards and photographs of lifeboats and the great coxswains of yesterday.

Dave, whose nickname is 'Spanish' on account of a past life as a mate on trawlers sailing out of Cadiz, has hauled corpses from the sea and set out in hurricanes to rescue foundering boats. He was a powerful-looking man, thickset and black-haired, sovereign of the half-dozen modern weatherboarded houses that accommodate his crew and their families. I found it difficult to find the right questions to ask him – what was it that one wanted to know of a lifeboat coxswain? He was not, I could tell, going to regale me with gory tales from the deep. He talked about operational efficiency and 'getting the job done'. On a shelf above his desk I saw in a black plastic folder the *RNLI Guide to Handling the Media*, and I had the sense that he had read it diligently.

Many of the call-outs that the boat attended, he said, were minor and scarcely called for heroism – like taking a doctor out to a ship, or an engineer, or somebody's heart tablets. Once a man had set out for the Netherlands in a rubber dinghy with a road map as his only navigational tool. Another time a dachshund had been undecked by a minor swell. But, he said, theirs was not to reason why; only to rectify wrongs, regardless of whether acts of God or human idiocy were to blame. The most difficult thing, he said, was choosing crew members for the station. It was the kind of role for which 'actually volunteering yourself to do the job ought to be an instant disqualification'.

On Spurn it had become an established tradition that the crew should have families living with them on the point. That, Dave said, was what made it a community, 'to my mind, the last true community in the whole of Britain'. So while he received dozens of applications or more, he discarded all but a handful. Finding a family of ordinary, sociable people prepared to be marooned at the end of a spit of land in anticipation of a cataclysmic event that might see its breadwinner thrust into the middle of the North Sea at its most impolite was, he said, 'challenging'. Further still, the men had to have strategies to deal with their copious downtime. 'Anglers and model makers who don't get seasick with well-behaved children, that's really what we need.'

I had seen the little bicycles and toys scattered outside the houses and could hear the cackle of television despite sturdy walls and double-glazing. What had once been the school was a dark patch in the car park; now the children relied on villages above the point for their education, taken by their mothers in big cars with capacious boots.

The families, said Dave, all got on well. He had to ensure that was the case, and that there were plenty of opportunities for socialising but not too many. Sometimes they'd all be partying hard and there'd be an alert. The men would be in their foul-weather gear and off into the North Sea in minutes – and as often as not back within the hour, having accomplished some impossibly dangerous feat and saved a life or two – and then they'd resume where they left off.

I didn't ask him about 'viragoes . . . a disgrace to their sex', but Dave said that his crew's wives could resent the authority over their men to which he was entitled by his role. 'Ha, yes. Other men's women. Though overall we're best off with them.'

I saw one of his crew, standing in his porch, pyjama clad with cigarette poised at wistful lips as he gazed out in the direction from which the next call to action might come. Perhaps, I thought, he's waiting for some glue to set – or his wife to return from the supermarket.

Away from this outpost Spurn becomes expansive, almost savagely dishevelled, a labyrinth of bunkers hidden in thickets and stitched by overgrown half-paths and the cut and dash of songbirds.

It is in these places that one longs to be a child again, having found the perfect place for adventure and fantastical happenings – like the stranding of a whale.

Jane, the only woman we met up in the pilots' tower, said that a large humpback had been washed up on the sands only weeks ago. Indeed, I had seen it reported in newspapers. In her ribbed serge jumper with epaulettes and white shirt and tie, she scarcely came across as a sentimentalist. Perhaps only thirty, she had mastered oil rig service ships in the North Sea and cruise ships in the Pacific. But, she said, she had found the stranded whale deeply upsetting.

At first there had been attempts to keep it alive. But it's an almost impossible task with an animal of that kind of size. Without the sea to gently enfold it the whale suffocated under its own weight. Vigils were held. People cried as they gazed into its great leviathan eye and cooled its skin with wet towels. I ventured to try to imagine how this must have seemed to the whale, slowly expiring in an alien element, its last impressions of the planet of strange, bereft beings clutching flowers and candles. All hope being lost, a local vet 'destroyed' the whale and the mood changed. For a day and long into the evening people, mostly young men from the surrounding villages and towns but also others from further away drawn by news reports, danced on its corpse, sombre mourning having undergone a kind of bacchanalian pupation.

Little of the North Sea suits big whales; its waters are too shallow, tricky and tidal. Why such reputedly intelligent beasts, with their ancient fugues and chansons imputed to be rich with sea lore and myth, make such basic navigational errors is difficult to fathom, but often the stranded whales are young and thought to have taken a wrong turn in the North Atlantic, or they're risk takers, chasing herring shoals south, miscalculating the chances of a successful exit.

In 1893 a whale 'about 50 foot long, its mouth nine foot wide' was captured trying to leave the Humber – it sold for thirty pounds in the marketplace at Hull the following week. The previous year the coxswain of the Spurn lifeboat, Mr Winson, captured what was reported to be an immense Greenland whale, which 'knocked about violently' before becoming exhausted from loss of blood. The lifeboat crew killed the whale by stopping its blowhole with mud and seaweed. A steam tug towed the cadaver to Cleethorpes Beach, where it became a hit for crowds of sandflies, day trippers and vendors of seaside delights.

And on 3 October 1879 it was reported,

> Seven whales have been caught off Spurn head. Two men, while walking along the shore, noticed a large number of huge fish floundering in shallow water. The men at once obtained a boat and went out, when they found seven whales, three of which were disabled, apparently by gunshot wounds. The other four were easily dispatched, one with a crowbar, and the remainder with a large knife. After some difficulty the monsters were got ashore at Hull where they are being exhibited.

My daughter and I, standing on the sea side of the peninsula, watched and saw no whales, but spotted the leathery black back of a porpoise trawling for bass – to the chagrin of anglers, who themselves were having no luck. We listened for the big ships coming in and out of the river, their rumbling propellers audible a good mile away from the point. And we waited to witness another of Spurn's tricks.

By dint of the narrowness of Spurn, in the last minutes of the day the point itself is reduced to insignificance, a fading sickle curving into the play of light until the moment the sunlight strikes the dunes at an angle so perfectly calibrated that for five heart-stopping minutes its entire length from base to tip shines like a blade of hammered gold, and everything contained within those moments is glorious and hopeful before the sun dips and Spurn fades again.

The autumn after my first visit I felt compelled to return. London had become too urgent and enclosing; Spurn could be the place to draw its venom. There was another reason. I had heard that everything was changing at the lifeboat station. Since my previous trip the road to the mainland had been made impassable by blown sands on at least a half-dozen occasions, and the decision had been made to withdraw the lifeboat families to nearby villages where they would no longer be at the mercy of a possible breach.

Dave wasn't there when I called in; there was a new coxswain, Martin, who was welcoming when I told him about my acquaintance with his predecessor. Martin lacked Dave's saturnine edge and the swarthiness which, I suspect, had contributed to his nickname. He had close-cut hair and wore gold rings in his ears, which he'd acquired in his first calling as a fisherman, beach-launching from one of the small villages just to the north. But the same guide to handling the media sat on the same shelf above the same desk.

The change, he said, was no bad thing. Many of the children were now adolescents. Spurn had been the perfect childhood playground, but as they grew older they had wanted to be less estranged from their peers. A shift system made it easier for the crews, most of whom had stayed in their jobs, although two had left because their wives hadn't liked the change. That afternoon, he said, they'd be taking out a new boy, a former bank clerk. He could see that in the future they might become 'a bit like the French Foreign Legion, where people come to escape the past . . .

We'll have 'em. As long as they can rub along with the crew and they don't get seasick.'

This time I arranged to stay on the point itself, at the bird observatory, a little bungalow hidden in thickets – a sacred space for the cabal of twitchers that descends from October onwards. Spurn is their Mecca because of the migrants that make their first landfall here, exhausted after North Sea crossings. Some of these tiny navigators apparently time their Kierkegaardian leaps with a kind of preternatural understanding of meteorology. Others are caught by forces beyond their control and dumped on Spurn without ceremony, possibly hundreds of miles from where they 'ought' to be. And others still, making their passage south towards Africa, are funnelled down the peninsula before making the leap across the mouth of the Humber.

The observatory – The Warren – is a fug-bound, brown-carpeted common room smelling of old boots and stale men, and a mouldering reliquary of bird-focused images: a decades-old acrylic painting of an eider, identification charts to help distinguish between near-identical species of gulls, a mistle thrush with kapok for innards peering beadily between the cracks of its glass prison, a sofa donated by a well-wisher or recovered from landfill. And the holy of holies: the log of *All Birds Seen At Spurn Since Records Began*.

Its seasoned inhabitants resemble nothing less than a ragtag Chechen militia band, clad in camouflage jackets and woolly hats, clanking with telescopes and cameras and talking about 'getting' rarities known to be in the vicinity – a yellow-browed warbler that by rights ought to be in Andhra Pradesh but finds itself in the East Riding, the bearded tits taking up fleeting residence in a nearby scrape . . .

With a dainty pair of fold-up Zeiss binoculars and wearing mostly navy-coloured clothes, I felt self-consciously dandyish and insufficiently khaki among them. But this is a broad church, many of whose parishioners are misunderstood by their families and peers. Indeed, mutual acceptance is perhaps the greatest part of the attraction of birdwatching. They tell self-deprecating anecdotes, such as that related by a (big burly) panel beater from York concerning a trip to Bridlington, where he and some friends 'were crowded onto beach ogling purple sandpiper –' a bird no less rare in the town than the definite article '– and big burly fishermen looked at us like we was fookin' nootters'.

There's also, and perhaps this applies to most or all of the things that men love best, ambivalence around their fluttering objects of desire. 'Where the fuck are you?' a man demanded of a small flock of meadow pipits which he could hear but not see, though this could hardly be representative of how he felt about birds in general or meadow pipits in particular. His companions believed this red-skinned man, with his thick white bristles and wolfish eyes, to be without peer for his unerring ability to untangle the chaotic twittering of several species simultaneously in song.

At this juncture, he and I and two other men (for to a man, we were men) were stood as we had been standing since the sun had first begun to rise above the North Sea, in the lee of a wooden windbreak, bemoaning a fog which gathered, dispersed and gathered again. Cold, I stamped off into the mist. Other delights had tempered the keenness of ornithological zeal. The sun had risen behind a North Sea mist, or fret, that conferred upon the world a radiant sense of it being on the brink of some wonderful and revelatory moment. I heard the barks of deer and saw their white tails dissolving in the vapour, and from the Humber came the mournful lowing of a ship edging blindly out of harbour. And when the fret began to give way, I saw that the grasses growing up to the cliff-edge path were spangled by dew-bejewelled spider's webs cradled like snowflakes.

Later I strolled towards the beach with my eyes on the lookout for attractive stones. Before leaving Spurn I had a spectacle to see on the Humber side – a great gathering building to a climactic, flickering explosion of feathers and dabbling.

In almost invisible increments, a fleet of shelduck began to emerge. First there was a handful, then scarcely perceptibly more, and soon an armada, waiting out the hour before the ebbing tide disrobed the mudflats. Two – perhaps three – thousand inky black heads were tucked beneath tan wings, the flotilla stretching in a great curve, a mile in length, its little ships not sleeping but saving their energies for the feast of worms that lay wriggling in the yet-to-be-stripped-bare mud.

They were not the only ones biding their time. Hidden in the foreshore vegetation was a division of waders, chucking, dozing, huddling, with more camped out in nearby meres, scrapes and meadows. Each inch-fall of the Humber (sucked back, as it were, into its source) sent a tremor through these anxious armies of birds. The shelducks began to take flight, to jockey and regroup, and the waders to shake off their semi-somnambulant state, and their calls like ululations grew shrill as a kettle rising to the boil.

And then there was just a hand's depth of water, and next a mere knuckle, and the clouds of dunlin, knot and redshank rose from their redoubts in hovering whorls, each bird negotiating landing rights with its neighbours before alighting on the mud to gorge on morsels of protein – lugworm, little crabs and stranded fry.

This was the melee I had come to see and I had feasted. Battalions of birdwatchers were arriving in busloads in their khakis and greens, lugging the optical materiel they used to prosecute their funny kind of love and war upon their prey. The autumn sun shone on them brightly, but the birds seemed unperturbed. With a head full of feathers and pockets rattling with rough agates and pretty pebbles, I took my leave of Spurn, its beach of shapes and shingle and its ceaseless changes.

Last Resorts – Being Beside the Seaside

We cannot compete with Continental resorts for sunshine so it
seems pointless to lay too great a stress on this commodity . . .

English Tourist Board report, 1974

I'm in Whitby in high summer. A rain shower has just passed and
slowly, dutifully, furtively (in case they should be caught out again),
the loosely arranged crowds re-embark upon the beach. The sand
is hard, cold and clammy like drying cement. And the sea is
confrontational, putting up its fists. It growls back at a spaniel that
runs to the edge of the surf offering a bouquet of barks before
retreating.

Towels are spread. Whole families cluster behind candy-striped
windbreaks. This time is precious. It is necessary to take advantage
of even the scantiest break in the cloud.

It is ironic that a regular visitor to the Mediterranean or Bahamas
might consider a summer spent cadging seaside pleasures from a
beach upon the northern coasts of England a kind of ersatz
equivalent of the joys of sun and sea. But, unpredictable and cliché-
pickled as they may be, to these sands every lolling, sun-seeking,
airport-novel-reading, tanned and cavorting pleasure seeker in
Nice, Phuket and Mauritius owes a debt. Regardless of the weather,
a North Sea seaside holiday, *c'est la vrai chose* – a return to the
source.

Some time in the mid-eighteenth century the North Sea sloughed its wholly utilitarian aspect and revelled in its hitherto undisclosed and glamorous possibilities, social, sexual and recuperative. In the late 1600s, as Alain Corbin writes in the masterful *Lure of the Sea*, anything 'vast' was regarded as 'incompatible with beauty because it inspired horror'. The sea represented the antithesis of the Garden of Eden, a place where the pleasant song of birds gives way to the seagulls' harsh cry. To the classically minded and well-ordered citizen of the early 1700s, all that the beach was able to offer was 'the negation of harmony, testifying to the invasion of diluvian chaos' and a 'barren landscape that mankind can neither arrange nor endow with moral significance'.

Two things appear to have happened to that abhorrence. The first was that the sensations of awe, terror and dread evoked by the sea remained but were re-identified as sublime and to be savoured, just as one might come to enjoy the sensation of riding a rollercoaster.

> Thence musing onward to the sounding shore,
> The lone enthusiast oft would take his way,
> Listing with pleasing dread to the deep roar
> Of the wide-weltering waves

wrote James Beattie, describing the progress of his Minstrel, the subject of a long Ossianic poem richly soaked in appreciation of the sublime. The other was that the cult of the spa, assiduously embraced in Cheltenham and Bath and across Europe, migrated to the sea, where it was discovered full immersion in the water was preferable even to the ingestion of foul-tasting 'minerals'.

A bathing machine, a device not unlike a Gypsy caravan but permitting the bather to enter the sea in safety and with a degree of privacy, was first recorded on a beach in Scarborough in 1735. Soon afterwards a Quaker called Benjamin Beale introduced a new, improved machine that became the rage at Lowestoft, Margate and Ostend.

The diametric opposition between the wild beach and the ordered garden that had inspired horror became its very attraction; now the beach represented Eden *before* the Fall, self-knowledge, sexual guilt and fig leaves. In 1813 a *Punch* cartoon showed a giggling gouty gaggle of men a-goggle at the girls sporting in the waves, using every state-of-the-art optical device to magnify their delights. This was, perhaps, a forerunner of the saucy postcard. And by no means was voyeurism solely a male prerogative. In 1840 the following letter was published in *Keble's Gazette*.

> I rode over to Ramsgate and witnessed an astonishing sight. It was nearly high water at midday, and there were at least 30 Bathing machines in the sea, and close to the shore, out of which popped men just as they came into the world, while some hundreds of respectable looking females sat on the beach looking on. I was told that when the experiment was made of moving the machines a little further down from the pier, the chairs and stools of the females kept moving in the same direction as if by magic . . .

The author, gender undisclosed, regarded the phenomenon as a 'blot' on 'an otherwise healthful and pleasant resort'.

For the purposes of leisure there is a multiplicity of seas, the one splintered on the anvil of demography, culture and class. In the United Kingdom a kind of coyness pertains even to the naming of the North Sea. It is as if the very brutishness so conveyed by its northern-ness must remain concealed in order to sustain the pretence that it is just 'the sea', generically indistinguishable from more glamorous, more blue, less coarse and grey seas populated by richer, happier and more deeply tanned holidaymakers. And there are fractions of fractions. When the Tuggses, a family of greengrocers invented by Charles Dickens, find that they have come into some money, they quickly decide that they must 'leave town immediately' as an 'indispensable preliminary to being genteel', but the question arises as to where they should go, and the following conversation ensues.

'Gravesend?' mildly suggested Mr Joseph Tuggs. The idea was unanimously scouted. Gravesend was LOW.

'Margate?' insinuated Mrs Tuggs. Worse and worse – nobody there, but tradespeople.

'Brighton?' Mr Cymon Tuggs opposed an insurmountable objection. All the coaches had been upset, in turn, within the last three weeks; each coach had averaged two passengers killed, and six wounded; and, in every case, the newspapers had distinctly understood that 'no blame whatever was attributable to the coachman.'

'Ramsgate?' ejaculated Mr Cymon, thoughtfully. To be sure; how stupid they must have been, not to have thought of that before! Ramsgate was just the place of all others.

Long before the Tuggses made their fictional excursion to Ramsgate, the respective merits of bathing places inspired considerable discussion – as Alain Corbin describes: 'In 1794, a debate arose between partisans of the Baltic and those of the North Sea. The arguments of the latter . . . included the amplitude of the tides, the power of the waves, the water's saltiness and the fine sand. Defenders of the Baltic vaunted the merits of a more accessible sea that was calmer, with water made warmer by the slighter variation in tides.'

Soon there were already plenty of resorts for the sea junkie to choose from. In 1797 Dr Van Halem founded the resort at

Norderney, on the North Sea coast of Germany. From 1801 the island of Wangerooge became popular. Entrepreneurs soon followed suit with offerings at Cuxhaven, Wyk, Föhr and Heligoland.

'Sea-bathing,' wrote Augustus Bozzi Granville, third son of the postmaster general of the Austrian province of Lombardy, 'I hold to be . . . one of the most powerful means a medical man can wield for the restoration of his patients.' This, he believed, was especially the case at Scarborough, where the arrangements were of the 'most satisfactory kind . . . the almost insensible descent into the deeper water, with the softest bed imaginable for the feet to tread upon . . . and the peculiar transparency and purity of the returning tide . . . render it not only perfectly safe, but accompanied with almost luxurious feelings'.* Thus he describes a sensation that holidaymakers have sought to replicate and improve upon far beyond the shores of the North Sea.

Despite the affordability of Mediterranean and long-haul package holidays and the affectation of distaste for the habits and desires of our ancestors, we yearn to feel the North Sea shingle and cobbles beneath our soft feet, to gorge on greasy and unreconstructed seaside delights and experience the underworld of amusement arcades and to promenade upon the pier. For what such resorts as Scarborough lack in dignity they make up for with an old-fashioned cocktail of tradition, heightened sexuality and home comforts. And so it is that each summer we make our way with the somnambulant inexorability of pilgrims to Whitby, Texel in the Netherlands, *la plage* at Ostend, and to the *Strande* of the German North Sea and Baltic.

---

* But even seawater wasn't infallible. Noted Granville, '[At Scheveningen] in 1836 I beheld invalids who had come from distant parts of Germany for the benefit of sea-water, and who were dying of *ennui*.'

Nor are all the pleasures we discover plebeian or 'low'. On (heavenly) Sylt, which juts out of the land at the point where Germany and Denmark meet, I stepped from a very ordinary bus into an enclave of super-wealth: Bentleys, BMWs and Porsches carelessly parked in the shadow of pristine dunes while their owners, media moguls from Hamburg, Berlin dot-com millionaires and Frankfurt bankers, sported on the pristine beach and refreshed themselves with champagne.

'I had no idea I would find this,' I told a native of Sylt, who was bemoaning the inflationary effect of the presence of such gilded visitors.

'*Everyone* knows about Sylt!' she said. But no one had told me. It was, in effect, a family secret.

Snobbery and the sea have a long and close relationship that's laden with paradox: on the one hand the sea is a place to loosen inhibitions, relax, undress and free oneself from everyday social *mores* and convention. But who would want to do so in the company of the lower classes?

Granville mocked the pretensions of Scarborough visitors: '[They are] the greatest separatists in England, and would as soon think of returning a bow to some "small unknown" to whom they had never been regularly introduced as they would to dance with any one not belonging to their own set. This should be reformed, and the sooner the better.' Today the middle classes that seek out the evocative beaches of North Norfolk at Holkham or Blakeney studiously avoid not-dissimilar shorelines close by. The perfectly respectable place name Skegness means 'headland that juts out like a beard', and the town sits at the end of one of the longest stretches of unbroken sand in Europe. Yet it has become a byword for cheap proletarian thrills, donkey rides, knobbly-knee competitions and orchestrated, institutionalised fun.

That the sea can be so easily socially taxonomised has long been known to tourist boards, who labour to sort us into the appropriate seaside bucket with commendable if patronising and pseudo-scientific diligence. Consider an English Tourist Board paper on the future of English seaside tourism published in 1974 which siloed English resorts into four main categories, lively, distinguished, pleasant and picturesque, thus.

Lively: 'the strength of which is their activity, lots to do, sociability, appeal to children, welcoming informal accommodation, low cost . . . working class image . . . challenge from the Costa Brava'.

Distinguished: 'offer a high quality holiday for older and better off people'.

Pleasant: 'they excel in no characteristic nor are they worse than other English places except in the matter of food. While having no exceptional assets that might be rivalled by other destinations, description equally they have as a group no strong selling points.'

It added a white elephant category too: 'bizarre', which included Whitby, Salcombe and Aldeburgh (and Newquay and Brixham), of which it said, 'It may be necessary to consider whether such places wish to opt in or out of the holiday industry.'

This refractive device put to work in Lincolnshire yielded the following analysis: 'There are three traditional seaside resort towns: Cleethorpes, Mablethorpe and Skegness. According to research findings Cleethorpes and Skegness are regarded as "lively", Mablethorpe is on the arbitrary dividing line between "lively" and so-called "distinguished". Mablethorpe differs markedly . . . in one guidebook was described as a "shanty town".' In a wearied tone the report acknowledged that all this was no more or less than the great British public deserved, noting that while seaside caravan sites are ugly – an attribute all too evident in Lincolnshire, which lacks the valley folds or foliage in which to hide them – this 'obviously fails to deter the people who do spend their holidays at such sites'.

What *was* the future of the English seaside resort in 1974? The board conceded that the weather was much less reliable in Yorkshire, Suffolk and even Cornwall than in Andalusia and Majorca, and that if they were to survive domestic resorts should offer 'a total holiday experience', although it failed to describe what such a holistic solution entailed. Given that even the English Tourist Board appeared so unexcited about the very thing it was paid to promote, how could it inspire anyone else?

Why is it that some resorts prosper and others fall out of favour and slump? Aesthetics must have some role – but not an exclusive one. Most of the Belgian coast is uncompromisingly ugly. At some point in the early 1960s developers began to bulldoze what remained of its former finery, erecting brutalist replacements so overwhelming in their disregard for either man or nature as to elicit a visceral reaction in anyone who chances upon them for the first time. Yet these serried ranks of cubicles promise their seasonal dwellers a covetable view of the North Sea, and in summer Belgium's beaches are unfailingly occupied almost to the point of saturation by mussel-devouring habitués whose annual return is as bankable as that of the swallows.

Meanwhile, once-fashionable, even elegant resorts on the east coast of the United Kingdom have slumped into a kind of all-round dysfunction so complete or near complete as to be comic, the effect exaggerated by their architectural grandiosity so at odds with the listless micro-economy of benefits and burger bars. Other seaside towns possess insufficient merit to warrant any surprise that they have gone downhill, viz. the town of Withernsea on the Holderness coast of Yorkshire, a dull conurbation remarkable for the caravan parks that have spread like psoriasis around its housing estates, for the extraordinarily high rates of teenage pregnancy within them and for its lighthouse museum. As you enter the town, a sign bids you WELCOME TO WITHERNSEA and asks that you PLEASE VISIT OUR LIGHTHOUSE. On exit, another reads, THANK YOU FOR VISITING WITHERNSEA — DID YOU VISIT OUR LIGHTHOUSE? as if the town is collectively anxious that its visitors should take away more than the memory of its muddy beach, brown cliffs and sea, and a kebab.

It is not the fault of Withernsea, which rose on the whim of a local entrepreneur in the 1860s who saw the opportunity that lay in freighting the working class of Hull to the coast by train and providing their accommodation and refreshment. The place has few natural charms or features: not the natural grandeur of Flamborough, the prettiness of Robin Hood's Bay or the endearments of Whitby. But the sea is the sea, and its early patrons were denuded of the choices that their descendants have come to expect.

The town now possesses the menacing air of the spurned, the once-but-no-longer-loved and the fallen-out-of-favour, a place which, like so many others on the coast, has reached the end of the line, its former glories reduced to mildewing relics in a local museum — if lucky enough to boast one.

Perhaps tourism is like a kind of prosthetic limb to stick upon the stump of an amputated 'real economy'. Sometimes the illusion of genuine activity is almost convincing, but more often than not the impostor, with its heritage centres, holiday homes and 'experiences', gnaws on the marrow of the past. Where even tourism has failed, what then for a Withernsea?

I'm not sure that the distinction is between rich and poor towns. On Scotland's Neuk of Fife sits a string of former fishing villages – Ely, Crail, Pittenweem and Cellardykes. Each is exceptionally pretty, with picture-postcard fishermen's cottages, quaysides and drying sheds. But the cottages were long ago vacated by the fishing families, who fled in favour of bungalows with garages, bathrooms, living rooms and gardens well before the death of the fishing industry; thus the quirky little houses have made the inevitable migration from living homes to holiday lets and rich men's playthings, while the only role the sea now plays in the local economy is in luring the golf-mad to the links. It all lends to such places something of the Victorian collector's pickled specimen, essential form preserved but life long departed. The incomers seem embarrassed by their own complicity in the process, buying when the locals, often young adults in search of employment, moved out in search of jobs, 'restoring' the houses to a state of sleek perfection they probably never previously enjoyed, but rendering the villages mute, absent of the weft and warp of everyday comings and goings.

It is a paradox that the sea permits us to be inclusive to the point that we are indistinguishable from the herd, but also to indulge our snobberies and sense of appropriate social distinction. The slogan of the Dutch island of Texel is 'Something for everyone.' Depending on how tightly 'everyone' is to be defined, this is an unashamedly ambitious boast. Texel is known among the world's stock farmers for its eponymous breed of sheep, a stocky unsentimental beast that thrives and produces good wool wherever you care to place it. Twitchers flock to the island in the autumn and spring, when it is rich in migrant birds, and it is also a source of perennial fascination for war buffs, the last shots of World War II in Europe being fired here, allegedly.

Despite the absence of cosmopolitan or topographical attractions, every summer the flat wind-lashed beaches of the island resemble the site of a mass skinning of seals, though thronging with bodies and pleasure. 'Everyone' is Dutch. For there seems to be a (loose) rule about North Sea beaches, that in the main they attract their own nationals. It is mostly Belgians that descend on the sands of Knokke Blankenberg, Germans upon those of Sylt, Amrum and Rügen, and British holidaymakers who head each summer to 'Skeggy', Yarmouth and Filey. A beach holiday within one's own country constitutes a rebaptism in the wellspring of what the Germans call *Heimat* and the British call 'home'. It is a kind of liberation from exoticism, from foreigners, odd food, pushy trinket vendors and the need to board an aeroplane. On a North Sea beach wind-driven knife-sharp shingle may lacerate the calves, but the voices you hear in the breeze are friendly and familial and the body shapes reassuringly like your own. Here there is no shame in celebrating sameness, however banal that may be.

It was the German-Jewish philosopher Hannah Arendt who coined the phrase 'the banality of evil', and in the case of the resort of Borkum it is apposite indeed. Even before the 1800s bathing establishments were springing up across the East Frisians and the Baltic to complement the inland spa resorts of Bavaria and the Black Forest, and in 1844 a Dr Ripking of Hamburg opened a bathing establishment on the island of Borkum, the most south and west of the East Frisians and closest to the Dutch border. Regarded as the most beautiful of its siblings, it gained a reputation for the healing qualities of the sea, the tranquillity of its dunes and its beneficial climate, all attributes which the Borkum tourist board promotes today, along with 'activities and religious festivals for children'.

Borkum provided a welcome summer retreat for the north German bourgeoisie, who patronised its cafés, hotels, boarding houses, sanatoriums and quacks. During the First World War the army transformed Borkum into a military base protecting the entrance to the River Ems. Subsequently, during the Weimar period, it sprang back to life with renewed vigour, the sea providing a balm to forget the agonies of the war. Many of its visitors were drawn from a Jewish population that had throughout the nineteenth century steadily absorbed into mainstream middle-class German society, intermarrying with Gentiles or abandoning the prescripts of their religion (among these, let it be noted, the family of a Dr Ludwig Blass, grandfather of the author).

Jews were inveterate holidaymakers. Partly driven by an eagerness to display the extent of their assimilation but also because they could afford to and desired to, German Jews became a mainstay of the German tourism industry. Whereas before the Great War there had been a tendency to visit relatives in parts of the east which now belonged to Poland, in the 1920s they sought new leisure activities, and were just as enthusiastically courted by the tourism industry – or by much of it at least.

Many Jews dismissed the anti-Semitism they encountered before 1933 as callow and uncouth loutishness – more a nuisance than an existential threat. When it came to holidays, it could be avoided by refusing to patronise the most egregious resorts. And at the beach there was little or nothing to distinguish them. Borkum, with its thirty-six kilometres of tranquil white sands, was and remains one of the most desirable of the East Frisians, but in 1923, almost the height of Weimar liberalism, it declared itself *Judenfrei* and became notorious for the '*Borkum Lied*' (Borkum Song), the last refrain of which proclaimed, 'those who come with flat feet, crooked noses and curly hair (*mit platten Füßen, mit Nasen krumm und Haaren kraus*) must not enjoy the beach, but must be out! be out! Out!' (*der muß hinaus! der muß hinaus! Hinaus!*).

This was a favourite of the local orchestra, and the crowd would join in with such fervour that participating in the singing of the 'Borkum Song' became a defining part of holidaying on the island.

Other resorts, including neighbouring Wangerooge and holiday towns on the Baltic coast, quickly composed their own anti-Semitic ditties so as not to lose market share. When the socialist minister of the interior banned the song the island responded by appointing a local Nazi member of the Reichstag, who enjoyed immunity from arrest, to the post of spa manager. He ordered that the band should continue to play it.

The Jewish lobby wielded considerable influence in Weimar Germany. In response to the growing bullishness of explicit anti-Semitism at North Sea and Baltic resorts – and inland spas – Jewish associations took their own steps. At one resort such an association was successful in having a Nazi propaganda office removed, threatening a boycott by high-spending visitors. Other groups published blacklists of hotels that had treated Jews badly. Some proprietors pleaded not to be placed on the lists and provided testimonies from Jewish guests to the effect that they were treated with every possible civility. Others asked specifically that their establishments be included.

In the years leading up to the burning of the Reichstag the blacklists burgeoned, with many Jews choosing to visit resorts which had particular reputations for being friendly to them, like Norderney – less prestigious and more crowded than its near neighbour Borkum. The ghettoisation, foreshadowing darker successors, of Germany's North Sea holiday resorts had begun, even in the absence of race laws.

Perhaps what happened at Borkum is the extreme of a kind of equivocality that I can't help associating with the beach – disinhibition en masse can lead to terrible things. Doesn't that ambivalence always accompany the determination to seek pleasure in the company of the many? And is not the beach, shot through with ambiguities (it is after all the point at which the land meets the sea, and the earth the sky), the place to find it?

Nowhere else is it possible to engage and disengage from the throng with such swift liquidity, at one moment so comfortably naked among strangers and the next tuned out from the clamour of crowds; from the 'bif-baf-sorry-I-dropped it' of beach games and the jarring cries of happy children, squinting at oblivion, comforted or discomforted by the sublime vastness of everything that lies beyond the shore, and then turning to re-embrace ourselves and our companions, whomsoever we choose them to be.

Mare Frisium, Fris Non Canta

It was in the third decade of the present century, on an
October afternoon . . . when I rode along a North Frisian
dyke in fierce weather. For more than an hour the desolate
marsh, now cleared of all cattle, had been on my left, and on
my right, uncomfortably close, the North Sea tidal flats. The
Halligen and the other islands were normally to be seen from
the dyke; but I now saw nothing but the yellow-grey waves
beating continuously against the dyke as though bellowing
with rage, from time to time spraying dirty spume over my
horse and me, and further out, a bleak half-light in which it
was impossible to tell earth from sky.

Theodor Storm, *The Rider on the White Horse*

When the Romans discovered the North Sea, the Frisian peoples'
gift for seafaring was sufficiently accomplished that the great Pliny
called it the Mare Frisium. He added that 'the Fris don't sing', and
it's true they tend toward the taciturn, as does in its own way the
archipelago of the Frisian Islands, strung out along the Dutch and
German coasts. For the most part the delights of the Frisian Islands
are subtle or heavily disguised. They are flat, expansive, blasted by
winds, and the sands of which they are composed are in a state of
constant rearrangement. But Texel, Terschelling, Ameland, Juist,
Schiermonnikoog, Borkum, Föhr and the others are not without

a subdued, exotic charm. Here are to be found some of the whitest and highest dunes, the bluest seas and even one of the most glamorous holiday resorts in Europe.

There is an elusive quality about Friesland – the word refers both to the islands and to the fringe of mainland historically occupied by the Frisian people. Its seas are so dangerous to the deep-keeled and the unfamiliar, and its landscapes so sunken, that if outsiders know the waters at all it is likely as not on account of a nautical mishap or by association with Erskine Childers's spy yarn, *The Riddle of the Sands*. Set among a labyrinth of shoals and treacherous currents, the novel's reluctant protagonist Carruthers, a bored government clerk, sets out to join a pal for some duck hunting in the German Ocean but discovers an invasion force of landing craft so formidable as to pose an existential threat to Britain and Britishness.

It caused a stir in 1903, for Childers had a reputation as an oracle on such matters. The North Sea had become the silent fulcrum upon which the balance of power between Britain and Germany rested, and the book inspired both imaginations and imitations. In 1910 two British yachtsmen, Lieutenant Vivian Brandon and Captain Trench of the Royal Marines, were arrested in Borkum and Emden respectively. They and their yacht were found to be bristling with photographs of the coastline and its military installations. The German authorities tried them for espionage, the more extreme elements of the German press calling for them to be subjected to 'appropriate mental treatment so that upon their release they may not retain too clear a memory of what they had seen'.

In all probability it was a freelance Boys' Own affair. Childers himself was dismissive of their efforts, noting that if as charged they had been attempting to measure the depth of the water 'while bathing at Amrun', then 'that is within the right of all bathers . . . For my part I should be content to rely for my measurements on the extraordinarily accurate and detailed large-scale charts of the German North Sea coast published by the German Admiralty and obtainable at stationers in London.' Accurate maps notwithstanding, this is a hard landscape and the Frisians are a hard people to read. Some of Friesland's dialects are unintelligible even to each other. Frisian is a kissing cousin of English – as they say, '*Brea, bûter, en griene tsiis is goed Ingelsk en goed Fries*' ('Bread, butter and green cheese is good English and good Frisian'), but only as it was spoken many centuries ago.

I arrived on the island of Schiermonnikoog on a late-summer evening as barnacle geese clucked in the fields and little stirred besides the odd cyclist and heath-hovering owl. Rooks and woodsmoke weaved through the rain, and the crash of the surf was just audible on a distant beach.

Schiermonnikoog means 'island of grey monks', after the sheep-tending friars who, between the twelfth and fourteenth centuries, brought their flocks across from the mainland each summer to graze on its salt marshes. They left nothing of substance behind them but the island's name and a roaring trade in the sale of cowled and tonsured figurines, routinely placed on the windowsills of island houses amid flowerpots and duck decoys. The most desirable of these dwellings are seventeenth- and eighteenth-century cottages with roofs shaped like witches' hats, each one with its own gossiping stool in the porch and a front yard immaculate and tasteful even when the weather is vulgar and foul. And as often as not their inhabitants are wealthy retirees from Amsterdam, Groningen and Rotterdam whose links with the island scarcely extend beyond being able to afford to buy its property.

Arend Maris's house was easily distinguished by its unkempt lawn, peeling paintwork and the jumble of books (lots of Conrad), papers and model ships visible through its front window. Here, among the clutter, he laboured with quotidian regularity on his life's work, a history of the nautical college of Schiermonnikoog, describing how it was established in the late nineteenth century to prepare local boys for careers in seafaring and closed in 1934, by which time steam had made obsolete much of the curriculum.

Arend had also retired and was from the mainland, where he had practised as a forensic psychologist. But he had acquired an islander's tanned face, bright blue eyes and a craggy, friendly smile, wiry hair and a big voice. He was incredulous when I told him about my own project. 'Oh my God!' he said, face conveying pity, elation, avuncular concern in one all-consuming stare. 'It is impossible. There is so much. You will drown in it. Drown in the North Sea. It will be your suicide!'

'Quite possibly,' I said.

He pointed out that his own book, 'a history of one tiny, lousy little navigational school', had already taken him ten years, and he would be surprised if he finished it in his lifetime. 'So let me help you!' he said and made some calls. Unfortunately, everyone he spoke to was indisposed. One man in particular I would have loved to have met had just completed the definitive dictionary of the island's old dialect. But, approaching his hundredth birthday, he had no strength or desire to entertain strangers.

Later, at the end of a long cold walk across the dunes, I rang the doorbell of the lighthouse. A small painted sign relayed the information that it had been built in 1853, was powered by a 200-watt bulb and was usually closed for visitors. I rang anyway. Sometimes saying that you're writing a book opens doors. But not to lighthouses. 'I'm sorry, I'm very busy,' said a crackling voice through the intercom. 'Please go away.'

That night I dined alone at the Hotel van der Werf, a glorious pre-war gem where each exquisitely brewed coffee is served, and steaming bowl of consommé ladled, with a surety of execution that betokens the height of civilisation before 'civilised' Europe destroyed itself so many decades ago. To dine at the Hotel van der Werf is to discover that a thing for which you long since learned not to grieve still lives.

The Prince of the Netherlands was a habitué of the Bernsdorff in the inter-war years, fond of coursing hares on the dunes. Their saddles, smothered in brown sauce and accompanied by claret and sautéed potatoes, would be served up to him each evening. In those halcyon days the café organised seal-hunting sorties for its distinguished guests. And though the sepia tint is blurring to beige, the trophy photographs that line the corridors are still gruesome, piquing one's interest on the way to the sturdy, pompous latrines. Bernsdorff is the kind of place that appears to be single-handedly holding aloft old standards of decorum, a starched napkin draped over its figurative forearm. Here's what I wrote in the bar before supper.

Brown, oak-panelled walls, brown furniture, brown linen tablecloths. A proper Dutch tiled fireplace. A stuffed buzzard (brown) moulders menacingly on the mantelpiece. Little lace curtains hang from a brass rail placed 18 inches above the window sill. The two waiters are comedic in the correctness of their handling of customers and napkins. In 1943, the hotel was hit by a bomb from a Wellington bomber, freezing the entire establishment into a parody of recidivism.

In a dining room that could have seated three hundred princes of the Netherlands I ate steak, creamed spinach and potatoes roasted with bacon and parsnips – prefaced with mushroom soup that arrived in a silver tureen the size of a baby's bath. The potatoes alone would have satisfied a family of six, and somehow the prevalence of brown in all its glorious shades dampened all extraneous sound. Even when the local billiards club met to play in the bar, as it does on Wednesdays, the very occasional *clack* of balls and the screech of moving chairs only underscored the sense of comforting and marmoreal quietness. When I moved on from Schiermonnikoog, taking the cosy ferry with its red banquettes and apple cake slices back to the mainland, and then headed by train towards Germany, I did so contemplatively and with a full stomach.

Half a million people speak Frisian in the Netherlands (confounding Pliny, some sing in it too, like Nynke Laverman, who also sings Portuguese fado, and Elske DeWall, who made her name with a Leonard Cohen cover), but ironically it was in the German state of Schleswig-Holstein, home to only around ten thousand Frisian speakers, that I prised open the lid on the Frisian world a little. It was, of course, of the Schleswig-Holstein Question – which led to two bitterly fought wars in the second half of the 1800s – that Lord Palmerston said, '[It] is so complicated, only three men in Europe have ever understood it. One was Prince Albert, who is dead. The second was a German professor who became mad. I am the third and I have forgotten all about it.'

In Schleswig-Holstein lie the most far flung of the islands, Amrum, Sylt and Pellworm (pronounced 'Pvoorm'). In the midst of these is the still stranger archipelago of half-islands or Halligen. Even on a psycho-political level the area is difficult to locate, for three flags fly over it, those of Germany, the state of Schleswig-Holstein and the province of Nord-Friesland, all demanding some kind of recognition of their respective sovereignty, a situation further complicated by the interplay between the islands' five local languages: Hochdeutsch (High German), Plattdeutsch (Low German), Frisian (in numerous dialects), Danish and Jutish – the latter so derided by all the other language speakers that they tend to call it Potato Danish. People switch between languages according to situation and interlocutor, and there's no exemption for animals:

a man who has bought a horse from a Plattdeutsch speaker might talk to it in Plattdeutsch, but speak Frisian to his cows (which is natural) and use Hochdeutsch – the natural tongue for the giving and receiving of commands – with his dog.

For all this linguistic richness, the train heading north to the heart of German Friesland reveals from its windows a landscape so monotonous and apparently bereft of inhabitants that it accrues a kind of grandeur by virtue of its scale. The train goes on and on, and so does the plain, an unending vista of pastures and dykes, sprinkled with bunched-together livestock fending off the sameness of the all-enclosing fields. Nowhere in Friesland is the terrain much above sea level, so you never know that you're close to the sea until you're right on top of it. But as the plain unfolds, the eye searches out nuances: a singularly ancient farmhouse with a white-painted finial in the shape of a double-necked swan, a harrier levitating above a field, a horse silhouetted against a brooding sky.

While *The Riddle of the Sands* painted the definitive picture of Friesland's fog-bound treacherous islands for the British, Theodor Storm's novel *Schimmelreiter* (*The Rider on the White Horse*) best captures the cultural and emotional contours of Friesland for the Germans. Storm was born in the town of Husum in 1817 and died there in 1888. Through a series of stories within stories the novel tells how a lost traveller riding along a dyke in a deeply rural Frisian backwater of a fearful night encounters a dark figure mounted on a 'high-boned, haggard horse'.

Taking shelter in an inn, the traveller hears how the vision presages the breaking of the dykes and learns the tragic story of the great Hauke Haien, raised in a village held to ransom by the ever-present possibility of being overwhelmed by the sea. The son of a surveyor, Hauke learns Euclidean geometry from an old textbook he finds in a trunk, and being prodigious in every possible way soon stands out as a man of talent and prospects. Once apprenticed to the gluttonous and stupid dyke master he makes himself indispensable, and when the dyke master dies Hauke marries his daughter, the beautiful Elke. Hauke's upward trajectory in the face of local prejudice and jealousy is the triumph of reason over the fug of superstition and conservatism but fails to avert the return of the *Schimmelreiter*, or the tale's heart-breaking conclusion.

The Theodor-Storm-Haus in Husum is one of those quirky little literary museums that smell of mothballs and encourage speaking in whispers. Elegant and writerly, it is tenderly curated with diaries, letters, manuscripts in cabinets with *cartes de visite* and tickets for subscription balls. Storm's own image – bearded and as stern and glowering as his name – is everywhere. But I was impatient both with the ticking long-case English clock in the corner of the dining room and the other visitors, clearly bored and wiling away an afternoon. Storm himself was only polite about Husum, describing it as 'a small ordinary town, my birthplace; it lies on a flat treeless coastal plain and its houses are old and grey. Yet I've always thought of it as a pleasant place.' In a poem called '*Der Stadt*' he described it thus:

> *Am grauen Strand, am grauen Meer*
> *Und seitab liegt die Stadt;*
> *Der Nebel drückt die Dächer schwer,*
> *Und durch die Stille braust das Meer*
> *Eintönig um die Stadt*[*]

---

[*] By the grey shore, by the grey sea,
    And set apart, lies the town;
    The fog lies heavy on the roofs,
    And through the stillness roars the sea,
    Dully around the town

Husum has some well-preserved old houses and a yacht basin but otherwise is as humdrum as Storm left it. Most visitors are only passing through on their way to the islands. And those with the most money are heading to Sylt, a T-bone of sand possessing the reputation of being the Riviera of the North Sea, which is tenuously joined to the mainland by a causeway.

I found little in the British Library about the island of Sylt. W. G. Black, a nineteenth-century chronicler of the Frisian Islands, noted that in Norse days the island was famous for the quality of its lawmakers, and that according to the statutes of the Ancient Thing or law makers' assembly: 'If a maiden or a wife were shamefully assaulted, she must stop the first man she met and tell him how she had been outraged; then together they went to the nearest church, the bell was rung, the neighbours gathered, and with loosened hair the woman demanded the justice of the Thing court.' He continued: 'If her injury was provided against the man accused, then at the third full tide his hands were tied behind his head, a heavy stone tied to his neck and he was flung into the sea or thrown into the current, "that he not do it again".' The sentence of death by drowning – *Quabeldrank* – was, said Black, 'especially exercised upon strangers . . .' Another book, Artur Schultze-Naumburg's *Sylt- The Dream Island* (1966), celebrated the island's naturist potential, hinting that nude volleyball was a must for its local beauties.

Yet there's an unspoken rift unsettling Sylt. Frisians from across northern Germany and even the Netherlands perceive it as a wellspring of their identity, and its dialect, Sol'ring, as the purest incarnation of their language. But tourism discovered its white sands, sweet-smelling marram grasses and rolling dunes in the mid-nineteenth century. By the 1960s it had become a summer playground for Hamburg media barons, industrialists from the Ruhr and Frankfurt bankers. (Ulrike Meinhof, co-founder of the

Baader-Meinhof Group, would holiday on Sylt with her publisher husband Klaus Rainer Rohl.)

That it is a very desirable place is undeniable. My memory of arriving on the landing stage at its southern point is of being bathed in warm evening light and a breeze that sang and zinged with effervescence, pleasant odours and golden smiles. At a place called Kampen in the north of the island, that niceness has been distilled into an enclave of unimaginable wealth. I had headed there for no other reason than that I ignorantly imagined I might find a campsite. Soon, any hope of reasonably priced accommodation had died. Thatched Frisian-style cottages leading to the beginning of the beach turned out to be not the cosy bed and breakfasts and cafés that I'd imagined but retail outlets for luxury goods and jewellery watched over by muscular men in Ray-Bans with sand in the turn-ups of their black trousers. Closer to the sea, a champagne bar, almost a beach shack, rang with the laughter of the sleek cashmere-clad super-rich. I was almost transfixed but couldn't possibly afford to stay.

I hadn't expected to find such wealth in the Frisian Islands, and I expressed my surprise to Hark Martinen on the neighbouring island of Amrum. Hark (pronounced 'Urk') and I had been in touch before I'd set out for the Frisians. He'd said he would show me around and introduce me to everybody, but when I came off the ferry there was a message waiting for me at the quayside. Hark apologised, but it was Ascension Day, which brought with it the national obligation to spend the day drinking, which he was doing, though I could join him if I wanted.

In common with tens of thousands of Amrum men before him, Hark had spent most of his adult life abroad. The habit of emigration had begun around the middle of the nineteenth century (coinciding with the influx of tourists) and continued into the 1960s. Most headed to California and became chicken farmers, or New York, where they ran German-style delis, selling pickles, rye bread and sausage. It isn't unusual for elderly Americans born on the islands to return on vacation for the first time in decades to be able to recal smatterings of Frisian and Plattdeutsch, but no High German.

Now aged seventy ('I've survived; I can do whatever I want'), Hark had taken the ship from Hamburg to New York more than five decades ago. His father had died, leaving Hark with a worthless farm, and there were no jobs on Amrum or even in Hamburg. Decades in the Bronx had taken the edge off his consonants, but he pronounced each slowly and carefully and without a twang. First he had worked as a ship's engineer and then run a delicatessen, and sometimes he had done both, slicing *wurst* one day and sweating in an engine room the next. 'I had citizenship and everything, but then I wanted to come home.'

When I found Hark he was silently sinking large glasses of bright orange sparkling *Apfelwein* with half a dozen friends. He beckoned me to join them, his big noble head sunk between his shoulders like that of a resting vulture. 'This is how we celebrate Father's Day, with a *Herrenpartien*. Today we drink. Tomorrow we talk.'

A maudlin fug enveloped the drinking. For all its poppy sweetness and alarming orange hue, the *Apfelwein* had wrapped its subjects in a wreath of dark and silent thoughtfulness, although some diplomatic mention of football was made on my account. 'Seventy years old. Lucky to be alive.' The company nodded. More *Apfelwein* came. Hark was clearly torn between his innate hospitality and the desire to drink freely and silently, and we settled on meeting the next morning. In between I would head off to explore Amrum by foot, beneath a sun which, I hoped, might dispel the ciderish vapours that clung to my befuddled head.

Like Sylt, Amrum faces the North Sea on its west side, and the Wattenmeer, the inshore waters between the mainland and the islands, on the east. Thus the sun rises over mudflats and sets over a broad white dune-fringed almost untraversable beach called the *Kniepsand*, which resembles more than anything I have ever seen a salt pan. In between there are fields, some forest and a handful of sanatoria, the oldest established as a rest home for Prussian cavalry officers recuperating after the 1871 war with France. Architecturally Amrum's point of interest is not the modern town of Wittdun, where the ferries arrive, but Nebel, halfway up the island on the Wattenmeer side, upon which on high days and holidays visitors converge in a jangle of bicycles and knapsacks.

Nebel exemplifies a kind of Disneyfication of Friesland: a hollow shell of whitewashed thatched cottages, tea rooms, a picture-perfect church with fascinating merchants' gravestones. I felt distinctly uncomfortable and antsy, somehow, for all the cake and coffee on offer. The thrust of my disquiet, I realised as I chewed my way through a *Matjes Brötchen* (a rollmop in a bap), was that Nebel was nothing more than a kind of heartless theatre set, its ghosts − of salty fishermen and whalers and wreckers − long fled, leaving only the bricks-and-mortar skeletons of their former presence encrusted with wisteria and a kind of Tyrolean tweeness. To the island's credit, it has eschewed courting the uber-rich who descend on Sylt, and yet in Nebel there were sufficient Porsches in the driveways of its chocolate-box homes to signify that a week's rent in the season was probably considerable.

On Sylt, Hark had said, property prices were now so inflated that the locals were forced to live on the mainland, commuting each day to service the needs of wealthy outsiders. Nobody wanted to see that happen on Amrum; nonetheless the island was entirely dependent on tourists, producing nothing, no longer engaged with the sea. I asked Hark if there was much social interaction between the local people and the tourists, and he shook his head slowly. 'I don't think so,' he said. 'Not really very much.'

Recently the islands have been portrayed by the German media as backward places where bad things happen. In the past decade a stable of writers has collectively created a new crime genre, *Nordzee Krimi*, using the Frisian Islands (Amrum especially) as the *mis en scène* for a fairly predictable litany of sex crimes and murders, equally predictably solved by a formerly alcoholic divorced detective manqué. The island's candy-striped lighthouse – the *Nordzee Krimi* 'stamp'– adorns the cover of each, reassuring readers that each volume will be much the same as the last. In 2008 German television broadcast a film called *Mörder Auf Amrum*, which the locals took in their stride despite being cast as scarcely intelligible yokels. Not surprisingly, they tend to keep their language to themselves.

When Hark came to meet me the following day he looked glum. The weather was bad; his wife wasn't speaking to him, and his head was sore. We had coffee and drove slowly north, parting the drizzle and family groups of cyclists in rain cloaks. He showed me around the slippery decks of an enormous buoy-laying vessel that he'd worked aboard after returning home from his years in America, and we dropped in on the lifeboat moored alongside it, a beautiful vessel with leather couchettes and French-polished woodwork. By dint of half a dozen years in Cardiff, the skipper spoke English with a German-Welsh accent. He liked to cook Welshcakes, he said, on the beautiful Neff range recently installed on the vessel.

Nebel had looked almost tarty the day before, when the sun had shone. Now, dowdily girdled in rain, all the pernicious thoughts I'd had about it dispersed. Also I sensed that there was something Hark wanted to say, perhaps to apologise for being incapacitated the day before – not that I minded at all.

'Ascension Day is what we call Father's Day,' he said. 'A very special day, of course.'

Hark asked me about my children, and I in turn asked about his. Two, he said, were lawyers, one in California and another in Kiel. (We slowed to let another cyclist past.) 'And then my eldest, my daughter,' he said in his strange, careful, burred way, 'she died. Of cancer. Six years ago.'

And I saw what a terrible day the day before had been for Hark.

Where the road slewed to an end in the wet sand we walked across to where Rainhard Boyens sat in one of the two dozen *Strandkorben* – the all-enveloping carapace-like wicker chairs endemic to Germany's seaside resorts – from which he endeavoured to make a living. Beyond the beach the sea was grey, spumy and unappetising. The few people to brave it weren't lingering. Rainhard had hired out the chairs in the summer season for fifty-two years. His father had been the *Strandkorb* man before him. 'But with this weather,' he said, raising his hands to the unsympathetic skies, 'what's the point.'

He seemed in good humour. He and Hark had been at school together, albeit separated by a year, but whereas Hark had left the island when his father died and the family farm was sold, Rainhard had stayed, supplementing the beach business with odd masonry and carpentry jobs. Years on the *Kniepsand* had tanned his skin to a rich creased acorn brown, through which protruded joyful cobalt eyes. He and Hark spoke in the Amrum dialect, Oomrang, and given that they were two of its 700 remaining speakers I felt privileged to be within earshot of its trills and diphthongs, and generally to be in the company of Hark, erstwhile engineer, keeper of delicatessens and buoy layer, and Rainhard Boyens, a name synonymous with the *Strandkorben* of Amrum.

Later I told Hark that it was touching that they had spent their childhoods together but despite decades of separation had remained friends. 'Yes,' said Hark. 'Yes. I suppose it is. Poor Boyens. He has had his ups and downs.' He left me to wander the dunes on the North Sea side, which I did, trudging the ankle-grinding *Kniepsand* and trying to see in its all-encompassing featurelessness the patterns of my own ups and downs while fretting about needing to check the departure time of the next day's ferry.

Some days later I arrived unannounced at the rather grand-looking Nordfriisk Instituut in Bredstedt (in Frisian, Bräist) and asked if I could spend the day in its archives. Anne Paulsen, the librarian, made tea and plied me with children's books in Oomrang and Sol'ring. She told me about Alastair Walker, a Scottish academic who speaks five dialects of Frisian fluently, and Marron C. Fort, an elderly American who remains the *only* fluent speaker of one of Frisian's rarest strains, Saterfrieschisches, and became its champion, exhorting its natives to preserve their own language.

Anne herself was from Föhr, and thus spoke Fering. Curiously, she said, she was the rare product of a marriage between a man from the island's west and a woman from the east, and so was pretty much fluent in both dialects.

'Are they *very* unalike?' I asked.

'In subtle but important ways,' she said.

To my embarrassment, I told her I had yet to visit Föhr, though I had heard it was very pleasant. She was flattered to hear me say it, and it was a cue for her to ask if I'd heard the island's anthem, '*Leew Eilun Feer*'.

lhuar ik henkem üüb a eerd,
alhü uk het det lun:
at jaft dach man an ian eilun Feer,
det leit mi boowen uun.
An kaam 'k uk hen uun 't lokelkst steed,
huar surgen goor ej wiar,

toocht ik dach äeder an uk leed
am di, min eilun Feer.[*]

I hadn't, I said. It sounded like a very beautiful place.

Föhr, she said, is perhaps the most traditional of the Frisians and, if such a thing was possible, increasingly so. At her First Communion in the 1970s she had been one of only a very few girls to wear the native costume, a black bonnet and waisted jacket, white pleated skirt, large breast piece made of silver filigree. But at her own daughter's recent Confirmation more were wearing costume than weren't. And other old island customs were coming back into currency.

'Like what kind of thing?' I asked.

'Like *Hualarjunkengonger*,' said Anne. The 'dusk walking youth posse' is an old courtship ritual in which young men go in a group with a suitor to the home of the object of his wooing.

'Even now? In the Facebook age?'

'Even now,' she said. 'My sister met her first husband through *Hualarjunkengonger*, and she is very much a part of the Facebook age . . . and divorced,' leaving hanging the question as to whether Facebook or *Hualarjunkengonger* was the culprit for the break-up.

The more Anne extolled the virtues of Föhr, in particular its museum devoted to the works of the artists Emil Nolde and Edvard Munch, the more I felt the pangs of its absence from my itinerary.

---

[*] Wherever I go on this Earth,
   whatever name a land may have
   there's only one Isle of Föhr,
   that in my mind is best.
   If I came upon the happiest place,
   where worries don't exist,
   all the day from dawn till dusk I'd think
   of you, my Isle of Föhr.

But I also knew that the very mention of the island makes some shudder.

Some days earlier a Dutch academic, Herman Vuijsje, had told me about Friedrich Christiansen, a native of Föhr, an air ace in the First World War awarded the Iron Cross for bombing English south coast holiday resorts, who served in the Second as *Wehrmachtsbefehlshaber in den Niederlanden* – supreme commander of the Netherlands. Christiansen was closely associated with German atrocities, Vuijsje told me, but nevertheless in 1951 the inhabitants of Wyk, the capital of Föhr, had named a street after him, a decision that was only revoked thirty years after.

Whether it is or isn't true that the natives of Schleswig-Holstein were particularly well disposed towards Hitler is an open question, but it is well documented that in the early 1930s there was general German Frisian support for the Nazis. While the origins of the Schleswig-Holstein Question were, as Palmerston observed so loftily, obscure and complex, the issue was ultimately whether Denmark or the confederation of states that became Germany in 1871 should possess the area. In 1920 a plebiscite had been held to determine once and for all the Danish–German boundary. The resulting changes traumatised inhabitants on both sides and stranded communities on the wrong side of the line so that even today the border is a terrible muddle of tongues.

So it was no great surprise, as the Nord Friisk Instituut's deputy director Fiete Pingel pointed out to me, that the Nazi slogan '*Ein Volk*' had particular appeal to those in the area who felt themselves to be German. Naively, Schleswig-Holstein's Frisian speakers were convinced that Hitler would encourage the use of Frisian dialects; after all, Nazi ethnological quackery, especially as espoused by some of the more esoterically minded SS bigwigs, had identified the Frisians as being among the purest of the Aryan races. However, the party became paranoiac about the notion of a people speaking a language they couldn't understand, purged the Frisian Nazi associations of potential fifth columnists and flooded the islands with Gestapo spies. Pingel said that when he attempted to research his master's dissertation on the origins of Nazi support in Schleswig-Holstein he met with 'sullen resistance and hostility – it was very difficult'.

In some ways the Schleswig-Holstein Question has yet to be solved, as has the Frisian Question. Perhaps the formulation of the first has been forgotten and that of the second still not properly structured. Some ten thousand people are thought to speak Frisian in Germany, but nobody has counted. And many people consider themselves to be Frisian without speaking it. Frisian is especially rich in dialects, but this also splinters the resources available to preserve it, and nobody thinks it a good idea to create a standard Frisian orthography because such artificiality would be self-defeating. In any event, it would be impossible to reach a consensus on what such a language should look like.

The Frisians have disagreed with each other for more than a century as to whether they should pursue the goal of Frisian nationhood or merely seek greater autonomy and language rights. The potential for internecine bickering is, as Fiete Pingel acknowledged, 'all too real'. Thus the Frisian language, so evocative of the sea, of rich dark brooding landscapes and a kind of collective existential loneliness, may one day disappear under the tide of change. But it is resilient.

Frisian intellectuals have a roll-call of martyrs and heroes at their disposal. There is Albrecht Johanssen, who spent decades researching the definitive North Frisian dictionary (still a work in progress 250 years after commencement); Bende Bendsen, the author of a late-eighteenth-century grammar of Mooring Frisian; of course Theodor Storm, who though he wrote in German captured so completely the dark plains of Frisian fields, landscapes and emotions; and there is Jens Emil Mungard.

Mungard was always stubborn. He wouldn't accept money for his poems, lived most of his life on Sylt in dire poverty and was deeply distrusted by the Nazis, not least for his refusal to allow the translation of his work into German. His verse is simple, symbolic and rich with the fragrance of the dunes, and as I left Bredstedt – or Bräist – for the next stage of my journey I tongue-rolled a one-stanza verse, the easiest to remember for a non-Frisian speaker, no doubt doing it any number of injustices, but enjoying it all the same.

Ströntistel
Ströntistel es min bloom,
Ströntistel neem's uk mi.
Jü gröört üp dünemsön,
Ik üp de leewents-strön
En proter haa wat bið!*

Mungard died of disease at the Sachsenhausen concentration camp, thirty-five kilometres from Berlin, during the war.

Erskine Childers, my introduction to the Frisian Islands, had also died a martyr's death, albeit a long way away and for a different cause.

In awakening the British public to the extent of German naval expansion and suggesting that the militarisation of the German coast was as much for offensive as defensive purposes, Childers was hailed as both a patriot and a prophet. Speaking through Carruthers's

---

* Beach thistle
Beach thistle is my flower,
Beach thistle they call me too.
She grows on the dune-sand,
I on the life beach,
And we both have thorns!

sailing companion Davies, Childers says presciently, "'Here's this huge empire, stretching half over central Europe . . . They've licked the French, and the Austrians, and are the greatest military power in Europe. I wish I knew more about all that, but what I'm concerned about is their sea-power. It's a new thing with them, but it's going strong, and that Emperor of theirs is running it for all it's worth.'" Three years later Britain launched the *Dreadnought*, the largest and most formidable battleship ever to have been built, signalling the beginning of an arms race with Germany.

In May 1910 the *United Services Magazine* had commented, 'Those who have read Mr Childers' brilliant book *The Riddle of the Sands* will not be surprised to learn that one of his predictions has been fulfilled. Germany has strongly fortified the Island of Borkum, ostensibly to guard against invasion but in reality for offence purposes . . . This new development upsets the balance of power in the North Sea, and our own government must meet it by a corresponding increase in our naval strength.'

Childers came from a Protestant Anglo-Irish background and his wife Molly was the daughter of wealthy fervently pro-Irish parents. As a nod to *The Riddle of the Sands* their wedding present to the couple was a yacht, the *Asgard*. By 1914 Erskine and Molly both passionately supported Irish Home Rule, and when it became apparent that guns were being run to the Ulster Protestants in anticipation of a Unionist rebellion against Irish independence, they hatched a plan to level the playing field.

With money raised from equally privileged and committed friends, Childers ordered 1,500 Mauser rifles, old-fashioned but highly effective, and 45,000 rounds of ammunition from a Hamburg arms dealer. It had been a difficult negotiation. The British government had persuaded the Germans to ban the export of weapons to Ireland, and it was only by persuading the dealers, Moritz Magnus, that they were destined for Mexico that an agreement could be reached. The guns were transferred from a German ship off Terschelling on the Dutch coast to *Asgard* and another yacht, and Erskine, Molly and a handful of companions sailed hard and fast across the North Sea, through the Channel and on to the Irish coast, close to the town of Howth, where they unloaded their contribution to the cause of free Ireland. The very next day Archduke Ferdinand was shot in Sarajevo.

Childers spent the war fighting with the Royal Navy in the North Sea and the Dardanelles. Early on he was asked by Churchill to explore the possibility of reversing the premise of *The Riddle of the Sands* for a British landing on the Frisian coast. When the war ended he resumed his involvement in Irish politics. In 1919 Erskine and Molly moved from London to Dublin. By 1921 he had become a Sinn Fein member of the Irish Dáil. Later that year, Childers, whom many had once regarded as the epitome of Britishness, was part of the Irish delegation negotiating the terms of independence from Britain.

However, the man whose alter ego, the amateur yachtsman Carruthers, had two decades earlier paced 'the deck of the Flushing steamer with a ticket for Hamburg' would soon fall foul of the vicious web of Irish politics in which he was entangled. Tried by a hastily convened Irish Free State military tribunal for possession of a Spanish pistol – a token of affection from his one-time friend Michael Collins – Childers was sentenced to be executed by firing squad at the Beggars Bush Barracks in Dublin.

To his wife he wrote, 'It all seems perfectly simple . . . like lying down at the end of a long day's walk.' To the firing squad he joked, 'Take a step or two forward, lads. It'll be easier that way.' And Childers fell dead, his own riddle brutally and prematurely solved by the age of fifty-two.

Myths of Origin – a Land Beneath the Sea

> In the midst of this stillness the earth began to tremble as if she was dying. The mountains opened forth to vomit fire and flames. Some sank into the bosom of the earth, and in other places mountains rose out of the plain. Atland disappeared, and the wild waves rose so high over hill and dale that everything was buried in the sea.
>
> *The Oerla and Linda Chronicles**

One day – or night – towards the end of what has come to be lazily labelled the Mesolithic Period, at a spot twenty-three miles east of where the Norfolk town of King's Lynn is now located, a hunter mislaid a mainstay of his or her livelihood, a spear-like implement with rear-facing barbs carved from the antler of a stag. In all probability, this man or woman was hunting deer, dogs, boar or otters. Once thrown the spear sank beneath fen-like marsh, embedded itself in dense foliage or was simply lost in the forest of ash, elder, birch or oak.

It would, ironically enough, be retrieved by another hunter, this time armed with trawl nets and going by the name of Pilgrim Lockwood, skipper of a steam trawler called the *Colinda*. Lockwood was trawling between two fishing banks, the Leman and the Ower, when the net brought up something which aroused his curiosity.

---

* See http://sacred-texts.com/atl/olb/index.htm

Having carefully broken away a thick encrustation of peat, he found an object which reminded him of a harpoon and, arriving back in port at Lowestoft, handed it to the curator of a local museum. Eight or ten thousand years had elapsed between loss and retrieval. In the intervening period a whole world had disappeared. The harpoon-owning hunter had inhabited an expanse of land that would later become Ireland, Britain and Europe but then made up a contiguous whole, scored by rivers and streams, hatched with thick forests, prowled and grazed by beasts, some suited, others less so, to the soft, gentle hills of today's Norfolk: red deer, hyena, mammoths, archaic kinds of rhinoceros and bears.

Neither this hunter nor his or her kind would bequeath any great civilisation – at least not in the sense of edifices and temples – and archaeologists would chastise Mesolithic folk for their lack of industry and flair. We now consider them to have been civilised, in the sense that they imposed their artistic and technical abilities upon the world they inhabited, though less generously than they might. The harpoon was not the first hint of the North Sea's previous terrestrial existence, but hitherto, when trawlers had hauled the skulls of mammoths from the Dogger Bank, the explanation for their presence was presumed to be either the extravagant animal-keeping proclivities of the Romans or the Great Flood.

There was a particular barrier to further speculation – on the western side of the North Sea especially. What British scholar could, with a clear conscience, denude his race of its island specialness? As late as 1851 the eminent historian Daniel Wilson concluded that 'the first colonist of the British Isles must have been able to construct some kind of boat' and that this was the 'certain starting point' of any investigation of the matter. It was true that a boat was an indispensable tool for navigating a marshy landscape – like that of the Fens of Cambridgeshire before they were drained. But for many thousands of years after the retreat of the great ice sheets the water was brackish and shallow, Britain being part of the great landmass of Europe. The sea came later and gradually. At the point at which Britain and the Continent lost their grip on each other there remained an island the size of Denmark smack in the middle of the North Sea. Possibly it remained inhabited until rising waters and geological forces pushed it below the surface to create the present Dogger Bank.

An autodidact with a sharp grey beard most forcefully captured the vision of the pre-North Sea. In a slim tome called *Submerged Forests* published in 1913 Clement Reid described his investigations into the vegetable life he had found below the present-day tideline, which demonstrated without recourse to biblically derived pseudo-science the existence of a land which had once flourished before inundation. Clues proving his hypothesis were abundant, he said, pointing out that at numerous seaside resorts there were places where fishermen 'will tell you of black peaty earth, with hazel-nuts, and often with tree-stumps still rooted in the soil, seen between tide-marks when the overlying sea-sand has been cleared away . . . if one is fortunate enough to be on the spot when such a patch is uncovered this "submerged forest" is found to extend right down to the level of the lowest tides'. He added, 'These . . . "Noah's Woods" . . . have attracted attention from early times, all the more so owing to the existence of an uneasy feeling that, though like most other geological phenomena they were popularly explained by Noah's deluge, it was difficult thus to account for trees rooted in their original soil, and yet now found well below the level of high tide.'

Reid (and Mrs Reid) dug for days on cold wind-battered foreshores in fear of being so absorbed by their trowelling that they might get caught out by the tide. In so doing he discovered why few shared his passion. The material unearthed was 'particularly dirty to handle or walk upon; so that the archaeologist is inclined to say that they belong to the province of geology, and the geologist remarks that they are too modern to be worth his attention; and both pass on.'

Uncovering how far the forests extended beyond the present shoreline was literally out of Reid's depth, with the exception of Dogger Bank, where, for the preceding fifty years or so an ever more rapacious fishing fleet had been stripping the bank of fish, but also of mammal bones. These were critical and exciting clues to Dogger's past, but their value was diminished by the manner of their collection. Typically they were dredged up by trawler men, who deposited them out of harm's way in deeper waters. And if they did find their way into academic hands, it was without an accurate record of where they had been found.

Mr and Mrs Reid had better luck with the peat — the fishermen called it 'moorlog' — which they boiled in a strong soda solution for up to four days to extract the zoological remains. Their endeavours revealed a strange menagerie of beasts, the bones of which had lain cheek by jowl on the seabed, including 'bear, wolf, hyaena, Irish elk, reindeer, red deer, wild ox, bison, horse, woolly rhinoceros, mammoth, beaver, walrus'.

Reid speculated about the human inhabitants of the world beneath the sea which he had brought to the surface, estimating that its submergence had begun around 3000 BC, at which time, he pointed out, the Egyptian, Babylonian and Minoan civilisations were flourishing, though 'Northern Europe was then probably barbarous and metals had not come into use, but the amber trade of the Baltic was probably in full swing.' Could not, he asked, have rumours of a great disaster, such as the submergence of thousands of square miles of land, been the origin of some of the Great Flood myths?

The harpoon more pointedly brought the world of men into the picture. In 1932 archaeologist Sir Graham Clark suggested that

Reid's forested land must once have afforded an 'easier passage [from the present day British Isles to the Continent] to early settlers than is now the case'. But he dampened any notion that what had been lost was ever more than a glorified causeway between two land masses, as if the making of that final leap was somehow indecorous. Six decades passed before this land was recolonised by an archaeologist from the University of Exeter, Bryony Coles, who suggested that her colleagues should 'instead of focusing on land as bridge . . . focus on land as a place to be'. Daring to christen this new, old world Doggerland (after the Dogger Bank, which must once have been its last outpost), Coles amplified the significance of Reid's research and provided the impetus for archaeologists to trawl deeper for evidence of lives long submerged.

The current explanation for the emergence of the North Sea is that where its southern basin now lies was previously a great plain, free from ice and rich in game, vegetation and rivers, where men and women hunted and fished with tools made of wood, flints and antlers. But as the ice to the north retreated, sea levels rose, flooding the plain until the increasingly slender land bridge remaining between continental Europe and Britain was finally severed.

On the island of Sylt a different myth held until the early nineteenth century: one which attributed the North Sea's creation to the bitter fruits of a soured love. The legend holds that an English queen, Fra Garhoren, was engaged to be married to the King of Denmark, but he broke it off. At that time (according to the myth) England and Europe were united by a sandbank, which Garhoren 'caused to be pierced by the labour of 700 men in seven years with the intention that the waters for the new channel would flood all the territories of the Danish king'. They succeeded, and the tide 'rose suddenly on the North Sea shore and between the Elbe and River Forth a hundred thousand men lost their lives'.

The story was first transcribed in the mid-seventeenth century and is impossible to date. Floods around the North Sea have always been frequent. But if the tale recalls a catastrophic inundation, perhaps it was the Cymbrian Flood, which battered the coast of Jutland and northern Germany around 115 BC, forcing the exodus of the shore-dwelling Celts and Teutons for new lands safer from the sea.

'Atlantis' is an easy word to throw at any settlement which has the misfortune to find itself permanently submerged, and the North Sea's Atlantises are almost innumerable. The entire plain, which over a period of thousand years or so succumbed gradually to meltwater, can be so described — as can in their own singular capacity the towns of Dunwich and Ravenser Odd (once bustling harbour economies premised on fishing, trade and piracy) and the island of Rungholdt. But the bolder claim is that the North Sea is the location not of *any* Atlantis, but *the* Atlantis as described by Plato and typically depicted by images of mouldering columns and arches in an azure wonderland.

In the 1860s a manuscript written in old Frisian surfaced in the Netherlands which was promoted by its supporters as a thirteenth-century text with near-mystic qualities. Its authors were given as the mysterious and genderless Oerla, writing in AD 800 or thereabouts, and a later Linda. Between them they purported to tell first-hand the story of the ancient Frisians, their religion and travails, and a depiction of the destruction of a now-lost world. The subtitle to its 1876 English translation is 'A Purported Chronicle of the Descendants of the Lost Atlantis — of the North Sea'.

The rulers of Oerla and Linda's Atlantis were members of a line of mother-goddesses springing from the loins of the Norse goddess Freya. Some of its inhabitants devoted their lives to the gathering of amber, others to fishing. A nearby country was Britain — a 'land of exiles' whose inhabitants had the letter B tattooed on their foreheads. The great cataclysm came one summer, when

> the sun hid behind the clouds, as if unwilling to look upon the earth. There was perpetual calm, and the damp mist hung like a wet sail over the houses and marshes . . . in the midst of this stillness the earth began to tremble as if she was dying. The mountains opened forth to vomit fire and flames. Some sank into the bosom of the earth, and in other places mountains rose out of the plain. Atland disappeared, and the wild waves rose so high over hill and dale that everything was buried in the sea.

The text was quickly exposed as a fake but as late as the 1930s continued to possess a momentum which attracted a following of cranks and conspiracy theorists, most dangerously of all Heinrich Himmler, for whom the notion of a North Sea ur-civilisation was in serendipitous accord with his own search for Aryan origins. Two decades later the theory was dusted down, dressed up and its more noxious Nazi connotations discarded by a German priest, Jürgen Spanuth, who advanced the theory that a great flood had destroyed a sophisticated civilisation close to the coast of Jutland, whose people had moved south, almost invading Egypt. Spanuth dismissed what he described as the 'quackery' of his predecessors (among others, a member of the Tolstoy clan who set off from Bermuda to discover Atlantis in the Caribbean) but then created his own.

He did at least nod to all the requisite sources on Atlantis – Plato, Marcellus, Xenophon, Pliny, Solon and so on – to concoct his own interpretation of events, a series of natural calamities culminating in the destruction of the Royal Isle Basileia, which he deduced was located upon Heligoland. In 1952 Spanuth visited the rediscovered Atlantis and, armed to the gills with state-of-the-art diving and underwater photographic equipment, set out to uncover its riches. Unfortunately, he reported, the water was far too murky to make the taking of photographs worthwhile.

There are in fact the ruins of a civilisation on Heligoland, for the island was bombed almost out of existence by one of the largest non-nuclear explosions in history in 1947, the shock waves of which still reverberate, as I would discover. And Spanuth's claims have left a legacy, in that the Atlantis industry, alongside duty-free booze and gannet-clad red cliffs, is part of the charm of Heligoland. Every trinket shop on the island sells knick-knacks more obviously suited to Cairo than to a North Sea rock: pharaoh masks, sarcophagus pencil cases and T-shirts that lament, MY BOYFRIEND WENT TO ATLANTIS, AND ALL HE BOUGHT ME WAS THIS LOUSY T-SHIRT. Yet if Spanuth's construction of history proved as damp as the submerged and silt-concealed pillars upon which it rested, the evidence suggests that the North Sea's pre-story is no less fantastical, sophisticated and incredible than the one that he imagined.

Two mornings after my departure from the Humber on the *Longstone* we pulled into the Swedish city of Gothenburg, tucked safely into the mouth of the River Göta, where its harbour cradled a rich dawn light like an old flame. The ship bumped against a quayside and was swiftly attended to by more luminescent men, whose voices – this time – I couldn't understand, though their tenor and pitch matched those of their counterparts in Killingholme.

I had crossed the North Sea, but it had been an uneventful passage, *sans* pirates, storms or other incident – blessings for a sailor if not for a writer. Technology has all but neutered the risks of sea voyages and whittled down ships' crews to a mere handful of men, and increasingly women. The sense of cohesion and mutual reliance that once kept a vessel afloat is no longer required to the same degree, for each crew member's function frequently demands only a small share of their time, the remainder of which is spent alone in their cabin. Ennui is a much greater threat to personal welfare than shipwreck.

Though there was of course Lewis, the Liverpudlian cook. Patrick the mate said that Lewis's under-the-breath comments were reviled as much as his cooking. I understood the latter gripe – with the exception of the big blocks of bread and butter pudding, which seemed to be constantly available, Lewis's concoctions were as revolting as they were archaic. But I had the *Barchester Chronicles* and a notebook, and a pair of binoculars with which to better admire the storm petrels dancing on the waves.

The next stage of my journey was to be by bus to a town called Tanumshede, two hours north of Gothenburg, close to the border with Norway and five miles from the coast. It is not in itself a remarkable place; indeed it is scarcely more than a high street around which is clustered a smattering of dwellings, clapboard red and yellow houses for the most part. The surrounding countryside is composed of rich pastures and quiet fields and solemn forests of ever-so-upright pines which could have been the fruit of Arthur Rackham's pencil. It is in these forests that Tanumshede's splendours are to be found, strange engravings born of imaginations stranger than Rackham's and more beguiling than that of Spanuth, incised into the smooth flanks of great rocks lying beneath the sombre pines. They are easily the most remarkable prehistoric representations in Europe. For the most part they're figures of men, largely in a state of priapism, and some women, and blowers of upward-curving trumpets known as *lures*.

Etched into one rock is the figure of a man who recoils, hands raised in alarm at the approach of a large snake or perhaps at a bolt of lightning. Other images depict goats, deer, oxen, pigs and even a blue whale. But most striking of all are the thousands of outlines of boats, some the size of canoes, some so much larger that they accommodate several dozen people, blowing *lures*, sporting elaborate and extravagant headdresses or wielding axes. In others figures vault over these strange ships, the scenes reminiscent of images from Knossos of Minoan bull-jumping but with boats for bulls. Whoever these people were, boats must have been central to their existence. Some of the engravings appear to represent wedding ceremonies being conducted on the decks of boats.

It was the size of the larger boats — ships even — that scared the archaeologists. If true representations the vessels would have been of enormous length. It was safer to conclude that, like the phalluses, their size had been exaggerated to the point of absurdity, and the boats were figurative, perhaps illustrating some mythical otherworld where boats and men assumed impossible proportions. Further reassurance for that hypothesis lay in the fact that the structure of the boats looked so unorthodox, with two prolongations from the bow, one running out from the keelson, the other extending from the gunwale.

However, in 1921 at Hjortspring on the Danish island of Åls fragments were found of a lime-wood ship, twenty metres in length, buried with an accompanying treasure trove of weapons and shields. The Tanumshede carvings had been dated to the Bronze Age, and the boat fragments to the Iron Age, but the match between them was otherwise close. Evidently, the images ground into the granite slabs in those dark forests represented very much more than aspirational thinking.

Being so unique and such an important clue for the reconstruction of pre-literate Europe, the Hjortspring Boat has been the subject of rigorous forensic examination and fanciful speculation. Several replicas and reconstructions have been made so as to better understand her handling and the purpose to which she would have been put. There is a consensus that she and similar vessels had carried a hundred or so raiders up the creeks and channels of Als for a surprise attack on the island, but that the islanders had repulsed the assault, breaking up the boat and sacrificing its remains by placing it in the bog where it would be found two millennia later. But the origins of her builders remain shrouded in conjecture. All that can be said for certain is that her discovery breathes life into the carvings at Tanumshede and its surrounding forests and fields.

The Vitlycke Museum at Tanumshede (which serves excellent meatballs with mashed potato and lingonberry sauce) has reconstructed a Bronze Age village complete with smoky wattle-and-daub longhouses, pig pens and animal skins. The vision it conjures up of ancient life is convincingly dour, sooty and unhygienic but seems at odds with the lean figures prancing on their boats, apparently unbowed by the assumed miseries of pre-modern life.

Aside from the great chasm of time, the quest for 'authenticity' faces other impediments; for while the dark stillness of the forests feels ancient and unaltered, that impression is misleading. The present coastline is five miles from where it was at the time the carvings were made, when the artists' stones rang out within earshot of the sea. And, for all their solemnity, these forests are relatively recent. In the Bronze Age this part of Europe was enjoying a post-glacial bounce in temperature: where now the trees are evergreen they were then deciduous. It is quite possible that in addition to enjoying a sunnier climate the people were of a sunnier disposition than their modern counterparts. Either way, by failing to divert their attentions toward the creation of a written language, they left little of themselves but their clever flirtatious pictorial extravagances, with which they have taunted us for so many centuries.

A Postcard from Atlantis

> Shrimps are like human beings, sensitive creatures who scuttle
> away into the sand if the water is disturbed by an exploding
> bomb.
>
> > Delegation of German shrimp fishermen
> > writing to the UK authorities, 1952

It juts from the German Bight, out of kilter with the other islands
stretching along the coast from Belgium to Denmark. Appropriately
anomalous and alone, for if the North Sea were to possess a holy
of holies, it would be this former British outpost, rough-cut from
rare red granite and garlanded by shoals, fog and sinewy currents.

Heligoland has connotations of mouldering almanacs and
elephant guns, of a memory hurriedly packed away in a mildewed
sea trunk. Some believe it to be the original Atlantis and claim that
there exists a mysterious connection with the pharaohs. Less
improbably the pagan god Forseti is said to have had his shrine here
until it fell victim to the zeal of a Belgian saint. And the
Heligolanders – in whose veins the North Sea is supposed to
course – still insist there is something special about their island, that
it possesses magical powers like Ayers Rock or Glastonbury Tor.
They also describe themselves as the smallest nation on earth.

Certainly the island is small – just a mile at its longest and a
quarter of a mile at its widest. It is remote for a North Sea island,

thirty miles from the north German coast but well protected by sandbanks and wrecks. Geologically it is one of the strangest features of the North Sea. But it is its story which makes it truly unlike anywhere else. Parchments, ledger books, secret memos and telegrams attest to the island's exaggerated footprint on history, belying the simple truth that it is no more than a heft of rock struggling to support 1,600 people. They're deceptive, these bundled old documents. The island they describe seems lost in time – and provide little help in answering the question, 'What does it mean to be a Heligolander?'

A first trip made in June proved no use. Whatever the island possesses of a soul lay submerged beneath the tramping feet of day-trippers, and the natives were too busy selling ice creams to take time out to talk. But returning in December, ferried across a flat sea alongside half a dozen tourists and a prospective bird ringer, it seemed tongues had been loosened by loneliness and island fever. The old island came a little more into view. Heligoland tucks history beneath its starchy cuffs. As do the islanders, gruff on the surface, true to the Frisian reputation, but warm and engaging beneath.

For the first hour of the outbound leg a pearly fog rubbed up against the bows of the ferry like a lovesick ghost. The captain sounded the foghorn, which wailed mysteriously over the water, and told me that he couldn't talk. It was too dangerous. Then the fog broke and I knocked shyly on the door of the bridge. The fog, he said, was very deceptive. The sea's mood could change in minutes. And he showed me a photograph of his ferry in a sea so heavy two-thirds of her bottom showed as tumultuous crests broke high above the bridge.

Captain Ewald Bebber's unremarkable features (medium height, mousy hair, indeterminate age) belied Heligoland's famous maritime skills, which once gave the island its reputation as the home of the finest pilots. Other North Sea communities could turn their backs on the waves when the land offered richer pickings. The North Sea diet reflects the fecundity of the land as much as that of the sea: fish soup lathered with *Sahne* (cream), sole baked in cream and butter, *Labskaus* – corned beef and herrings and beetroot. But save for a smattering of potatoes, half a dozen cows and some sheep, Heligoland lacks space for grazing or growing. All the islanders collectively possess is their commanding position near the mouths of Germany's great northern rivers and a mastery of the sea.

The day trippers disembark bewildered and a little underwhelmed. The great red cliffs are invisible from the dock, and the only immediately apparent feature is the island's radio mast. Not a single one of the island's clutch of buildings – suburban, two-storey, dark brick, modern – is of architectural interest, and there is no town to speak of, more a village split, as it has always been, between Unterland at dock level and Überland on the plateau, joined by a staircase and an elevator. The whole island can be walked in the space of an hour.

Few outsiders had visited Heligoland before 1807, although the islanders were well known as the 'nomads of the North Sea' for their knowledge of the tides and shoals, their curious dialect of Frisian and their distaste for both meat and warfare. Then the British made a gentlemanly, bloodless conquest at the height of the Napoleonic Wars, and Heligoland was on the map. Despite teething troubles (the first harbour master complained the islanders were 'little short of robbers' and quite probably wreckers) the British came to see it as something of a Shangri-La, a vision of what they wanted their own nation to be but in miniature.

There were no satanic mills on Heligoland, nor scarcely any crime. The first ever travel guide wonders that the jail possessed only one cell, which had lain empty for as long as anyone could remember. No less stirring, its crimson-cloaked maidens were comely and 'went without stays'. And in summer the island buzzed with couples 'walking together about the cliffs or in the corn fields' or dancing 'a curious dance' while their elders looked on drinking beer, tea or an ancient infusion called *Pompompfl*. When the mercury dropped they all came together on the frozen ponds to 'skait most gracefully . . . skimming over a surface smooth as glass, the air crisp and nipping in the strong frost, and the clear blue sky gemmed with innumerable and sparkling stars'.

Heligoland became a resort. Tourists mixed the 'exhilaration of sea-bathing' with the pleasures of an island culture which bordered on the licentious; it was rumoured that the girls took to the waters 'wearing no more than they had on the day they were born'. And it acquired a bohemian edge alongside less cerebral attractions: German writers and activists, including the visionary poet Heinrich Heine, escape the censor. Strindberg came to marry here. The theatre flourished, and periodicals banned in repressive German states could circulate freely.

Much, but not everything, has changed. The grandstand view of a mercurial sea remains sublime. Nothing else in Germany, whose coast is flat and generally unspectacular, compares. Tax-exempt alcohol and tobacco softens the blow of high prices for food and lodging – as it did in 1840, when the British reduced tariffs as an inducement for tourists. And there are the peculiar powers attributed to the island's geology. Asthma sufferers report their symptoms to be entirely alleviated by the pollen-free atmosphere. Others just find it a great place 'to be'.

History has robbed the natives of such existential ease. They are fiercely loyal to the island; it is the one steady thing around which they have been able to construct an identity otherwise chipped away by war, evacuation and economic uncertainty. Given what it's been through, it's curious that anyone still lives here at all. Pilotage has long been in the care of the state; there is little of a living to be made in fishing or lobsters, and tourist numbers are nothing like those in the island's heyday. But somehow they cling on.

I had been in correspondence with Erich-Nummel Krüss for some weeks before my return. He was the curator of the museum and, he said, 'knew a little about the island'. Like Captain Bebber he had begun work on his father's lobster boat before roaming the seas as a ship's captain, returning in later life to become the harbour master. Since retiring he has devoted his time to the collection and assiduous collation of island mementoes, fragments of a glorious past.

He welcomed me into his quiet, neat house, Haus Zanzibar, on the corner by the church and the mini-market. His home office was well ordered and arranged like a captain's cockpit (which he appreciated me noticing), shelves lined with books about the sea, the island, and albums containing a century and a half's worth of photographs. The thronging seafront in 1864. Bathing carriages and bloomered swimmers. Craggy fishermen ferrying tourists to their wicker beach chairs in round-bottomed rowing boats. Tiny fishermen's cottages, fish strung out to dry between them like laundered smalls. The shops, hotels and restaurants were distinguished and well mannered in a hybrid style incorporating municipal German and Home Counties English vernaculars.

Tourists and natives alike were having a very nice time, the former relieving the latter of their reliance on their ancient, noble but dangerous means of subsistence. Revenues from tourism were such that when, in the 1880s, a British visitor asked how the locals occupied themselves in winter he could be truthfully told 'by counting the fortunes made in the summer'. But the British had taken Heligoland for strategic reasons, not as a plaything. By now they were wondering quite what purpose it served, while in Berlin the Kaiser wanted it very much.

Lord Salisbury was recovering from the Russian flu when in a moment of lucidity he saw how, if carefully played, Heligoland could be given up for a larger prize. Salisbury, ponderous, bushy-bearded giant, simultaneously prime minister and foreign secretary, had an astute understanding both of Germany's grievances and of the way to give the impression of alleviating them to his own advantage.

In May 1890 the German empire was new and still finding its feet as one of the great powers, and Kaiser Wilhelm II was anxious to make his mark. Wilhelm had been at loggerheads with Otto Von Bismarck almost from the day of his coronation, and a power struggle between the two led to the Iron Chancellor's resignation. (Wilhelm had accused Bismarck of being trigger-happy in his treatment of socialists and agitators.) As a colonial power Germany lagged way behind France and Britain. It had ambitions in East Africa, but these constantly chafed against the British presence, with the Sultanate of Zanzibar, which lies off the coast of today's Tanzania, a hotbed of intrigue, schemes and mutually held suspicions. Nearer home, Heligoland had become an all-too-visible symbol of Britain's imperial reach. Most painfully of all it threatened to neuter the strategic advantage which would be gained by the planned Kiel Canal, which would link the North and the Baltic Seas and was thought by Germany's admiralty to be essential in the event of a naval war.

Over the course of a long hot summer Salisbury planted the idea of swapping Heligoland for Zanzibar, and did it so adroitly that the German Foreign Ministry became half convinced they had thought of it first. Negotiations – secret and unminuted – took place at Windsor Castle between Salisbury himself and the Kaiser's ambassador, Count Leo of Caprivi. Queen Victoria was not amused when she found out. She had not visited Heligoland but liked the idea of it, the Heligolanders being her only non-British

northern European subjects. She told Salisbury that the transfer
was 'a very serious question which I do not like. The people have
always been very loyal . . . and it is a shame to hand them over to
an unscrupulous despotic government like the German without
first consulting them.' It also set a bad precedent. Salisbury would
next be 'proposing to give up Gibraltar, and soon nothing will be
secure, and all our Colonies will wish to be free. I very much
deprecate it and am anxious not to give my consent unless I hear
that the people's feelings are consulted and their rights are respected.
I think it is a very dangerous proceeding.' In short, the loss of the
tiny island undermined the entire empire.

Difficult questions were asked in Parliament. Opposition MPs
condemned Salisbury's blithe lack of concern for British subjects,
his imperialist horse-trading and the lack of attention to detail –
what, for example, would happen to British fishing rights? Who
would man the lightships? One peer suggested that Britain had
'too good a deal' and it wouldn't take long before the Germans
noticed. But Salisbury argued that at stake was a settlement of the
East Africa question, and thus control of the headwaters of the
Nile. The Nile was the key to Egypt and the Suez Canal, and Suez
was the key to India, which Britain could never give up. When the
MPs finally entered the division lobby, the overwhelming vote was
'Aye.' The official transfer, it was agreed, would happen on 9 August
1890, and the governor of Heligoland was duly ordered to start
packing his things in readiness to go home.

Erich-Nummel Krüss's photograph collection records what
happened next: the governor's wife raising a leg-of-mutton muslin
sleeve to dry a tear as the Union Jack is lowered and the imperial
eagle raised; the first visit of the gloating Kaiser welcoming his new
subjects into the fold of the Fatherland. The images become more
personal from this point: Erich's father and grandfather, chisel-
featured, lean-jawed, sea-forged men among men; his mother as a

child in an island pageant. The family home. And then the submarines and big guns.

During the Great War Heligoland was evacuated of civilians. By 1917 U-boats based in its dock were taking a devastating toll on Allied shipping and threatening to lose the British the war. The islanders were housed in camps on the mainland and suffered discrimination by the German authorities on account both of their recent British links and their Frisian origins. When they returned, they found their island had been transformed into little more than an island-sized gun platform. Their homes, in which the military had been billeted, were for the most part ransacked and despoiled.

The next bout would take a much greater toll. On 18 April 1945 thirteen-year-old Erich sheltered in a bunker deep in the rock as almost a thousand British bombers reduced the island to dust. He and the rest of the islanders emerged into a smouldering moonscape and were whisked back to the mainland, whence not a single one would return to live on the island for seven years. It was what the British did after the war that was extraordinary. 'The bombing in 1945, that was in war. And war is war,' Erich-Nummel Krüss said. 'But there was no war in 1947. And there were still Heligolanders alive who considered themselves British; they even had British passports.' He breathed the sigh of an old man still trying to rid himself of a sense of betrayal.

VE day found Britain once again caught up in the affairs of Heligoland. The terms of the German surrender permitted the British to destroy its defensive structures, in particular the U-boat pens. The force required would have to be on a gargantuan scale and, given the looming Cold War, there was a great deal of interest in everything to do with large explosions. And the Air Ministry was on the scout for a new bombing range. What was codenamed Big Bang saw the bowels of the island packed with some 6,800 tons of explosive (4,000 warheads, 8,971 depth charges, 1,250 tons of TNT, 200 tons of cyclonite, 2,834 beach mines, 51,566 shells of various calibres and 9,400 cartridges). Two years to the day after Erich-Nummel Krüss entered the air-raid shelter in 1945, the explosives were simultaneously detonated, sending a mushroom cloud 8,000 feet into the sky.

Ornithologists had been appalled at the prospect, although some concessions had been made to the birds, including an elaborate warning system to clear them off the cliffs. The Heligolanders themselves were more distraught. They had lobbied Clement Attlee hard and reminded him of their British links. The fact was, they were only accidentally German and they had suffered too during the war. As the Foreign Office debated (internally and interminably) the niceties of international law, entirely unconvinced that the British government had the right to deprive the islanders of their island, the Air Ministry demanded to be allowed to bomb Heligoland for at least another fifteen years even if this meant it 'being rendered uninhabitable for ever', which, the man from the ministry hinted darkly, 'will depend on the use to which it is put for the trial of certain types of weapons likely to be developed during that period'.

Heligoland did not become an H-bomb test site. Britain aligned its nuclear programme with that of the United States and transferred its attentions to the Pacific. By 1950 an Air Ministry apparatchik would confess that he was 'rather ashamed that very little bombing had been done recently on Heligoland', that he had tried to get more done, 'but without success'. Britain would now consider handing Heligoland back – on condition that Germany gave it something else to bomb, which wasn't straightforward. That Britain should still be bombing Germany at all was a cause of great resentment 'stoked up by the Communists', many in the British government believed. Months before the transfer, the high commissioner had received a delegation of shrimp fishermen, who told him their prey were 'like human beings, sensitive creatures who scuttle away into the sand if the water is disturbed by an exploding bomb'.

Eventually the German and British authorities identified a sandbank as the least bad choice for man and prawn alike, which meant the Heligolanders could return – first the men, to build houses (not reproductions of what had been destroyed but modern replacements now universally regretted) and then the women and children. The tourists began to come back too, and with them a semblance of the old way of life.

Erich ordered me to wear a hat as I left his house. It was limb-judderingly cold. Down in the dock dollops of white water came over the quayside, and up in Überland the wind was persistent and strong. There was still time to take the long way around back to my hotel.

In summer the birds had been the main feature of the island, spilling up from the cliff edge like the foam in the quay, but in early December the island was at its most birdless. With the exception of stragglers, the gannets and guillemots which had so animated the cliff tops were wintering in Morocco and Tunisia. (The nests were bereft. So also, in some small measure, was I.) There was another marked change. The grass, which had been abundant and long, now did little to conceal the rubble extruding through the turf like shards of broken bone.

Erich had said the old Heligoland was now dead. Here, underfoot, lay the remnants of his island. A whole way of life had been taken – by emigration, by the loss of traditional livelihoods, 'and by this'. He had pointed to one of the two computers on which he was assembling the island's family tree. 'Nobody even knows their neighbours any more.' Though this last observation I had found difficult to believe.

There is a curious German habit of drinking outside in the winter, keeping the frost at bay with sausages and glühwein. At one such gathering I joined a small knot of hardy souls, mostly women of a certain age. I'd already met Judy, who owned the shoe shop and was the linchpin of a group of eggnog-quaffing friends. At another table stood a grim-looking group of men in dark blue uniforms – not, it turned out, policemen with no crime to fight but bomb-disposal experts. They looked worn out. Earlier in the day they'd uncovered two just waiting to go off. British bombs, one pointed out. He added that he'd send me the bill, which had Judy and her girls in fits.

The next day I ate a slow and potentially limitless *Frühstuck* and watched, safe and warm from behind the window in the breakfast room of the Hotel Panorama, a sea building as white-headed waves galloped towards the island. Then I prepared myself to meet Frank Botter, the *Bürgermeister*, a big man, a busy man, who burst (glancing at his watch, mobile phone hot in hand) into the office where I waited for him. The (Bavarian) director of tourism condescended to act as our makeshift interpreter, and we talked about the difficulties of 'keeping this ship afloat'.

His role, he said, was to cajole, hustle, plead and bully for more funds from the government to make good the shortfall from declining tourist revenues. Tourist spending makes up 90 per cent of the island's revenue, but the interests of the duty-free shops conflict with those of the hoteliers and restaurateurs – the first want short-stay visitors to stock up and go, the others want them to stay, and visitor numbers have dropped anyway, leaving a very small but significant black hole.

'Every year we sell thirty-four million cigarettes,' the Bürgermeister boasted. I quipped that Heligoland might not be such a healthy place to visit after all. He laughed (wheezily) and carried on talking about his plans for extending the tourist season, exploiting the seals and possibly offshore wind power. Perhaps, I suggested, Heligoland could become an offshore banking haven like the British Virgin Islands or the Isle of Man? He pooh-poohed the notion. But he gave greater consideration to the next: what did it mean to be a Heligolander in the twenty-first century?

Bürgermeister Botter exhaled thoughtfully before answering. It was important to understand that a true islander owed his loyalty to Heligoland first. Schleswig-Holstein came a distant second, and the emotional connection with Germany was very weak indeed. He narrowed his watery blue eyes and added, 'To be a Heligolander, it is not sufficient to live on the island for twenty, thirty, forty or even eighty years. You have to be born here.'

Anywhere else in Europe such a statement would have been incendiary. Even on Heligoland it was inflammatory enough to make the director of tourism wince; who, it was rumoured, had his own pretensions to the Bürgermeistership. But then the incumbent hedged his bombshell with a flurry of diplomatic concessions. *Anyone* could even be Bürgermeister if they possessed the right attributes for the job. And only half of the current members of the island's parliament met the criteria he'd just outlined. In any event, Heligoland would probably cease to exist as a separate cultural entity in a century; it would eventually be fully assimilated into Germany. But for the moment, he seemed to be saying, a true islander could feel Heligoland's hurt in his very bones.

Many islanders have left in search of jobs (or driven out by gossip or boredom), but it also has its share of incomers, escaping the city, drawn by the sea, by love, or just because things happen that way. They were keen to talk, even if not openly, as if by explaining their decision to settle they might understand it better.

In Pinkus, a tiny bar just around the corner from the tiny Sparkasse, the tiny supermarket and the Unterland–Überland elevator, I met one such woman. In her late thirties, originally from Essen, she gave a shrug to the question as to why she'd moved to Heligoland, as if she'd hardly ever given it much thought; it had just come to pass. The island was lovely, she said. Everybody had been so friendly. The cliffs . . . the clean air. But she would only respond to questions by writing on the back of a beer mat and then scribbling over it as though erasing a thought crime. Not that anything she said was scandalous or incriminating. I had asked if it was expensive living in Heligoland. How did rental prices compare with Essen? What was the worst thing about the island? '*Neugierig*,' she scribbled. Nosy. People talk.

Possibly she was right to be circumspect, particularly in Pinkus, where, she said, the Bürgermeister hangs out with his Heligolandish-speaking cronies, who keep all the best jobs for themselves and make sure the island runs their way – at least according to those outside the clique of 'true-bloods'.

Walking along the quayside I struck up a conversation with another woman who had moved to Heligoland. Two years ago, she said, she had never even seen the sea, but then fell in love with it and wanted to live as close as was possible. Away from the straining ears of Pinkus she divulged her thoughts freely, without resorting to a biro. Yes, she said, there were gay couples on the island, but not many, and no prostitutes because the men went to Hamburg on the ferry if they needed that kind of thing. The islanders were very close; once they'd accepted you as their own, you had made friends for life.

And yet there was a dark side. The day after she arrived to take up a post in a clinic a man came to say there was no job for her and she would have to find somewhere other to live than the room she thought she was renting. The room and the job were to be given to someone else. 'Who told you this?' I asked.

'I cannot tell you. Someone from government. Pinkus people.' Other bugbears of island life were that the men were in a constant state of sexual arousal, and – she repeated the word I'd seen written the night before – the *neugierig*-ness of everybody. When there's nothing to gossip about, she said, they make up some. 'You go for a drink with a friend and insist you only want a glass. They ply you with more and in the morning people look at you strangely – they've been told you're a dipsomaniac.' It was like living with the KGB.

Why then did she stay? Well, she said, the upside of the nosiness and the cliquishness was that you were never alone, never experienced the alienation which could creep up on you in the city, where nobody knows each other. And there was something special about the place. Never before had she decorated her home with images of the town or city in which she lived. In her old apartment in Stuttgart she had had no images of Stuttgart. But now something compelled her to decorate her tiny studio room with postcards depicting the cliffs, the quay, wicker beach chairs and gannets . . .

My suspicion – that Erich-Nummel Krüss's belief that nobody knows their neighbours reflects the sorrow of the elderly that they are no longer in the thick of things more than it does any real shift – was confirmed. It was surely true that the island was in a state of flux, with new people coming and old families leaving, and the loss of traditional livelihoods had taken its toll on the cohesiveness of society. But people still knew each other and cared, in both good ways and bad. And without stressing the point too much, Forseti and his magical powers were still at large in the imagination of a new era of pilgrims – though many more come for the birds.

Seabirds are almost unique among the avian population in being entirely unconcerned by the prospect of having their bleak, squalid and precarious-looking homes inspected by unwinged interlopers. It is for this that so many visitors come, to look down (not figuratively, but from a height) upon the cacophonous tiers of birdlife huddling on their rocky nests.

Island lore dictates that if an outsider makes a native pregnant and looks as though he's about to hotfoot it to Hamburg, the boats stay in harbour until he has 'done right by her'. This apparently explains the lack of other crimes. Almost everyone will tell you that there hasn't been a murder since 1800 – it is just impossible to make good your escape. It also accounts for one of the earliest (and greatest) books on the migration of birds ever written.

Heinrich Gätke was a wandering ship's painter when he turned up on Heligoland in the 1840s for a brief sojourn, but took to the island, fully embracing its holiday atmosphere – and not to say the future Mrs Gätke. By the time of his death in the early 1900s he was renowned as a great ornithologist and the devisor of the Heligoland trap, neither a chess gambit nor the heading of an early chapter in his own history but a means of catching migrating birds which is still in use today.

Gätke and his assistants diligently observed, shot, netted and described Heligoland's permanent residents, regular migrants and storm-blown oddities for half a century, allowing him to produce a magisterial work of natural history, invaluable to ornithologists measuring shifts in bird populations and plotting migration routes.

In the introduction to *The Birds of Heligoland* Gätke suggests that the island has little to recommend it to most species other than that it offers respite from the sea. It is no more than a pit stop for those birds that need it. Those that have the energy just pass it by. Only, he says, 'those grotesque members of the bird world, the auks and guillemots, find an inapproachable dwelling on its steep and surf-beaten cliff; where on narrow crags and ledges amidst the fury of the storm they hatch their eggs unsheltered by a nest, while their harsh, unmelodious voices mingle in manifold discords with the roar of the never-resting waves'.

Since 1895 things have changed. The guillemots remain but they've literally been pushed down the pecking order by the relatively recent arrival of the gannets, which Gätke had lamented 'unfortunately occurs only in solitary instances'. Now, by dint of sheer muscle and size, they occupy the best spots on the cliff faces, and in the summer are easily the most conspicuous residents, soaring disconcertingly just a few metres above the lip of the cliff on the airstream, their eyes blue and jewel-like and fixed upon your gaze. The guillemots by contrast (which deserve a stanza in Gerard Manley Hopkins's poem 'Pied Beauty') are squashed together like tenement dwellers further down. They are not grotesque, as Gätke says. I expect he didn't really think they were either, but played to a Victorian gallery which valued the sleek and strong over the small and strange.

Gätke's book showcases accretions of knowledge built up in layers. Had it been written on the back of even a decade's or two decades' observations it would have been too slim. 'In the middle of January,' he reports, 'the starlings and skylarks make their appearance . . . [and] present however a very sorry appearance and appear to have but little foreboding of the joys of Spring.' By March 'large swarms of Snow Buntings make their appearance, and depart again after a brief and restless stay'; and later in the same month 'the Fire-crested Wren appears in limited numbers; the Chiff-chaff may be seen in every shrub, and the White Wagtail is found in company with the Pied Wagtail'. And then in May 'arrivals must be classed by preference the three species of Totanus – the Common Sandpiper, the Greenshank and the Spotted Redshank. Of these, crowds of the first frequent the rocky shore of the western coast of the island.'

Then as now the real crowd-pleasers were the raptors, which start to arrive in August, first the Hobby, then 'a week later, young Sparrowhawks, Peregrines, Common Kestrels and Merlins, and young Ospreys, and Honey Buzzards'. Gätke reports that once 'a perfectly white eagle was spotted, but unfortunately not shot', although the island's best 'gunner' Jan Auckens 'had already levelled his gun at it a few paces off, and was in fact in the very act of pulling the trigger' before it rose loftily and disappeared like the mythical beast it may well have been. Jan was one of three Auckens brothers – island legends both for their love and knowledge of birds and their unerring aim. The oldest, Oelrich, was known to everyone as Old Oelk.

Ornithology was different then, involving very much more shooting and stuffing. But while modern ornithologists have a different attitude from their predecessors they're still grateful for the collections left in their wake. His own enabled Gätke to make valuable hypotheses about how, for example, some birds were able to change colour without moulting: 'In regard to the Spotted Redshank, I have, I am sorry to say, only limited material at my command; still, such as I have affords me sufficient proof that in this case also the regeneration of colour is accompanied by a single regeneration of the white triangular marginal spots of the posterior flight feathers.'

For most species he gives the British common name, the Latin name, the German name and the Heligolandish name, revealing both the latter's similarity to English and its archaic, picturesque attractiveness. The Red-Legged Falcon becomes the *Road-futted Falk* in the local tongue, Bonelli's Warbler the *Gru-hoaded Fliegenbitter*, Leach's Petrel the *Storm-swoalk med uttklept stjertt* ('storm swallow with forked tail') and the Osprey the *Fesk-Oadlear* ('fish eagle').

The fact that such a book was possible to research and compile conveys calm and continuity, but by the time Gätke's tome was published Heligoland had become a part of Germany. He had previously been a loyal public servant in the employ of the British administration and in 1890 was private secretary to the governor, Arthur Barkly. Barkly was given less than six weeks' notice of the swap for Zanzibar, and in the best (though not only) tradition of British governorship cared deeply for his staff and subjects. Desperately, and without a great deal of support from the Colonial Office, which had as good as given up on Heligoland, he tried to secure assurances of employment for his staff, including Gatke. And what was to be done with the Union Jack? Bring it back, said the Colonial Office. And the portrait of the Queen? 'Leave it on the island – she is the Kaiser's grandmother after all . . .'

The burst of correspondence which accompanied the swansong of British rule is infused with dark uncertainty. Barkly describes how the islanders 'hope against hope' that the House of Commons will reject the bill; how the Heligolanders are perplexed by the presence of the world's press, which had gathered to report on this remarkable change in the political geography of the North Sea. But with the kind of sigh that might accompany the end of a love affair grown tiresome, Britain disposed of its only North Sea colony with something verging on relief.

Many things have changed. But the youth are still courting, if not in the Spring Hall or on the cliff tops. On my last night in Heligoland Judy's son Sven dragged us to Krebs Disco, a tiny place above a pub with a dance floor the size of a biscuit-tin lid, and the *mise-en-scène* for a drama revolving around Iris, thin-lipped and self-appointed island drama queen, and her long-standing relationship with the son of Klaus the lobster man. This feckless youth of thirty had still not proposed despite them having been together for six years. The fact that 'everybody knew' he was doing exactly what 'everybody knew' his father had done back in the

1970s – Klaus was, it seemed cast from the same mould as Tom Conti's character in the film *Shirley Valentine* – was, one could not help think, because Iris had told them.

Iris's plight had a gravitational force of its own, drawing in others like Sven, Frank and Andreas – who had designs on Iris himself judging by the way he tried to crowd in on her. Frank was a cooler character. With the upright bearing of a nautical man he looked physically tough, not menacing but fit and strong. It was said that when Frank was not managing his bicycle shop in Bremerhaven he was quite possibly the best sailor in the German North Sea. Was this true? I asked Frank. 'Neh, not the best,' he replied, 'but I have the heaviest balls.'

He put his hand in his trouser pocket and rattled them to prove the point. At four in the morning Frank and I were talking about *The Riddle of the Sands*. It was a good book, Frank thought, but not half as good as the book he could write about the sea if only he was able to describe his thoughts. He had been drinking hard but wasn't drunk. At six he would return to his twenty-eight-foot yacht docked in the quay and catch an hour's sleep, and at 7.30 would slip anchor. The glass was falling. Rain was forecast. Frank's assessment of his own worth began to sound like a statement of fact.

My own departure from Heligoland lacked the *Sturm und Drang* of Frank's. I was also returning to Bremerhaven, but on the little Islander twelve-seater plane which comes and goes once a day and is pleasingly like a minibus, and from which, as it bounced up to altitude, the island looked so much less than the sum of its parts, like a remote straggle of godforsaken rock a very long way from anywhere. It seemed improbable that such a place could ever have generated the piles of paperwork I'd seen in the archives, or that upon it had ever hinged the fate of a continent. Yet all this was true. As for my quest to discover what it meant to be a Heligolander, I felt like the woman in the W. H. Auden poem who asks to be told the truth about love, receives many answers but emerges little the wiser.

In Krebs the night before, in a brief intermission from Iris's all-consuming histrionics, Sven and I had discussed the bombing of Heligoland and Germany generally. Fiercely patriotic, he told me that Bomber Harris 'was in the same circle as Goebbels and Himmler and Goering'. I was unsure whether he was saying this as a German or a Heligolander – he is Scottish on his mother's side. He considered this carefully and slowly and sagely wagged an index finger. 'Let me tell you something about Heligoland,' he began. Then his eyes closed and his head swayed on its gimbals. He was out for the count. Outside I could hear the sea thrashing furiously at the cliffs, whittling them into submission. One day, I thought, Heligoland will become Atlantis again; Krebs will be found at the bottom of the sea, with Queen Victoria's portrait and the bombs and the wrecks. But for the moment it contends with Michael Bates's gun turret for the status of the smallest would-be nation in the North Sea.

A North Sea Outrage

I miss those brave young fisher kids, coming home to shore,
Spending all their money, then going back for more.
I even miss Criterion – a very quiet pub –
And a little lass from Subway Street our kid put in the club
Dave Williams, 'Good old Hessle Road'

The Hessle Road district is a working-class suburb of Kingston-upon-Hull built on the banks of the Humber River as it leads out onto the fishing grounds of the North Sea. Two generations ago the Road was synonymous with fishing, and one way or another almost all the inhabitants of its little red-brick terraces had some connection with Hull's deep-water trawlers, as fishermen, or working on the quayside as bobbers unloading the heavy crates of ice-packed fish from the holds of the boats, or in the warehouses or repair yards. And if they didn't, they depended on the custom of the fishing community – big spenders who liked to dazzle.

In the very middle of the district there stands a statue to a fisherman called William Leggett. It isn't a very polished piece of work – he appears clumsily constructed and there is something about the way he holds his binoculars in the air that is jarring but charmingly gauche. But, unlike the obsidian memorials to long-dead generals that blight so much of central London, everybody in

Hessle knows that 'the Fisherman' remembers a curious incident (which has rippled through successive decades) that occurred on the night of 21 October 1904 – the ninety-ninth anniversary of the Battle of Trafalgar.

The Gamecock Fleet – one of Hull's largest, indeed one of the largest in the United Kingdom – of forty-six steam-driven beam trawlers (so named for the way they dragged the trawl from the beam and not the stern) had enjoyed a good two days' fishing since setting out from St Andrew's Dock in Hull on the early tide the day before. It was a box-trawling fleet, utilising a system whereby the boats cruised the grounds together, the fish being packed into boxes transferred each day to a cutter, a fast boat that made the run back to Billingsgate, Hull or Grimsby with the catch and then returned for more. Box trawling allowed the fleet to travel further and to stay out for longer, while delivering a fresher catch. And it relieved all boats bar the cutter of the need to carry space-consuming ice.

That night a forgiving sea and absence of gales allowed for routine maintenance, net-mending and fish-packing to be undertaken at an easy pace, and had put the crews in a relaxed mood. These were highly professional fishermen. The previous year an American zoologist, Dr Benjamin Sharp, had trawled with the same fleet and found them 'a fine set of fishermen . . . all young men and a hardy, jolly lot', who sailed with almost no nautical instruments other than a log, a compass and barometer, and depended on instinct and sea-lore accrued over generations. The captain and mate of the vessel on which he had sailed were no more than twenty-three or twenty-four years of age, and Sharp heard 'no profanity and I do not believe that it was due to the fact that a stranger and an American was among them'. He noted that at all times they adhered to the very highest standards of navigational etiquette, showing the requisite coloured lights to indicate when they were trawling, while at frequent periods the 'admiral' of the fleet would let off flares and rockets to indicate his position and that of the trawls. Quite possibly, it was these rockets that determined what would happen next.

Unknown and of no concern to the fishermen of the Gamecock Fleet, far away in the (even icier) waters of the North Pacific the two nascent modern powers of Russia and Japan were battling for influence and territory in China and Korea, and Russia's Baltic Fleet under the command of Admiral Rozhestvensky had three days previously left the Latvian port of Libau to strengthen naval forces some 18,000 miles distant. Rozhestvensky's fleet was in skittish mood. Rumours of Japanese torpedo boats in the Baltic, and even possibly a minefield, had been dogging it even before departure, and it made progress slowly, zigzagging quixotically to avoid non-existent hazards – its course culminating in an encounter, on the fishing grounds of the Dogger Bank, with the fishermen of Hull.

When the fishermen saw the silhouettes of warships through the mist they thought them to be the Royal Navy's Channel Fleet, and stopped to watch what they presumed to be a set of manoeuvres. What happened next was quite unexpected. Hull's trawler men were accustomed to violence. Sometimes there were spats with fleets from other ports, both British and foreign, over fishing rights or even over whether it was permissible to fish on a Sunday. But now they found themselves caught in an inferno of smoke, deafening noise and shell-churned sea, the whole illuminated by powerful spotlights, in the glare of which they were held by the Russian ships.

The political and strategic temperature of the North Sea had been warming for some years. The effect of *The Riddle of the Sands* on the British public was still palpable. But the prospect of the Dogger Bank becoming, however fleetingly, a theatre of war between two powers fighting in the Pacific Ocean seems, even in hindsight, highly improbable. Although to the Russians it made perfect sense that the Japanese would attempt to prevent them sending reinforcements from the Baltic by ambushing them in the North Sea.

The shelling lasted a terrifying twenty minutes. The trawler men held up fish to demonstrate the harmlessness of their activities, but the Russians stopped only to turn their fire on vessels of their own fleet which they also mistook for Japanese craft. Two trawler men, George Henry Smith (of Flora Street, Hessle) and William Leggett (of Ribble Avenue, a stone's throw from Flora Street), were decapitated by shells. Two others were injured, one losing his hand and the other's thigh smashed open by shrapnel. One of the trawlers, the *Minto*, was sunk, and the remaining vessels limped back to Hull in a state of shock. Word of the events somehow reached home even before the trawlers did, and by the time they were safely inside the Humber the whole community had lined the wharfs to greet them.

Briefly the sense of outrage was so intoxicating that the British Home Fleet was ordered to sea, and the Russian ambassador was summoned to the Foreign Office. In a letter to *The Times* Joseph Conrad described the incident as 'so extraordinary, so amazing, that it passes into the region of fantasy that borders on the incredible'. For the trawling community (whose Promethean struggles inhabited the realm of the fantastic as a matter of course), it was as unforgivable as it was bizarre. But the Russians were bemused – ever so slightly hurt perhaps – by the fact that the affair had caused such outrage. An officer on board one of the warships wrote to his wife, 'As a matter of fact they were to blame themselves. They must have known our fleet was coming, and they must have known the Japanese wished to destroy it. Why did they not cut adrift their nets? The nets could be paid for afterwards.'

On the Hessle Road – Hull's fishing community in spirit even now – the matter has not been forgotten. The Royal Antidiluvian Order of the Buffaloes, to which Leggett belonged, raised a memorial to him in 1907, and thus, in a prominent position on the main Hessle thoroughfare he still stands, cast in white concrete and set upon a red marble plinth. The Russians took their time to put things right. At a centenary event in 2005 a Russian naval attaché laid flowers at Leggett's feet and made a speech apologising for the miscalculations of his former colleagues.

My introduction to Hessle Road was through Hull writer and historian Alec Gill. I was fascinated by the documentary photographs he'd taken in the 1970s and his accounts of the last years of Hessle as a working town, so I tracked him down – not to Hessle but to a terraced Victorian house close to the centre of Hull, where he lives with his poetess girlfriend, Andrey, who writes verses celebrating the North Sea, the city, the river and the low flat fields.

Alec is not a tall man. Born with a congenital curvature of the spine and afflicted by retarded growth, he was sent to a school for the mentally infirm as a child. There he acquired a reputation as a Machiavellian fixer of gang fights, putting his keen intelligence to use in staying out of trouble himself. Now he lectures in psychology and English at Hull University, writes books about the 'old days' and collates photographs of Hull before bombs and maniacal development reduced it to the hodgepodge of theme pubs, outlet malls and university buildings it has become.

'I'm happy to show you around. If you could put a wee bit in the kitty for the petrol, you know . . . I am a Yorkshireman after all.'

Hessle's trawler men once provided Britain with as much as 20 per cent of its protein intake. It lies on the western edge of Hull by the old fish docks, and has the familiar feel of other red-brick northern towns. In the high street, supermarkets have failed to displace a butcher, a bakery selling stotty cakes, several proper fishmongers and a plethora of bookmakers. If Hessle has moved with the times, it is to meet the needs of its growing Eastern European population (it boasts several *Polski Sklep* – Polish food shops) and to provide that ubiquitous and mysterious service, 'mobile phone unlocking'. There are patches of economic gangrene in the form of empty shops and boarded-up pubs, but otherwise it appears almost thriving, at least compared to the glossy soulless retail outlets in the city proper. But as a cohesive, singular community bound together by a common industrial activity Hessle Road is dead.

Behind the high street lies a warren-like cluster of terraces with small front yards. Swathes have been demolished to make way for factories which are now closed, but those remaining are largely unchanged since the days of the Dogger Bank Incident, once allowance has been made for satellite dishes and cars. There have been other alterations. In *The Fishermen*, a 1962 book about the local community, Jeremy Tunstall described the old fish-curing houses 'with their tall kippering ovens [giving] the Hessle Road its distinctive and characteristic skyline, and their black smoke [helping] to thicken the winter fogs', but these are long dismantled and the fogs cleared.

It's too easy to over-endow this community with a kind of continuity that it never quite possessed. Fishing here began with men in small boats trawling the Humber for their own consumption, seldom needing or daring to venture beyond Spurn Point. As an industry it was greatly eclipsed by shipbuilding, whaling and docks. By the mid-nineteenth century southerners had started to settle: fishermen in large, tan-sailed, black-hulled, sharp-bowed smacks from Brixham in Devon and Ramsgate in Kent, who came to mine the Silver Pit, a crater in the North Sea bed which brimmed with quantities of sole that could seemingly scarce be dented.

The extension of the rail network to Hull enabled fish to be transported quickly and more or less hygienically to the insatiable bellies of Leeds and the mill towns, and thus, as the national appetite for fish increased, so did the burgeoning population of bobbers, women to fix the nets, shipwrights, ice makers, gutters and smokers. Expansion accelerated further in the 1880s, when fishing made its sudden, brutal transition from sail to steam, pulling in droves of engineers from the rail industry and sucking the life out of the traditional fishing towns of the north, like Staithes and Robin Hood's Bay, which, though blessed with picturesque winding lanes and cottages, lacked the large deep-water quays the new larger boats required. Hessle Road developed rapidly and acquired a sense of its own apartness, by dint of social lore, proud indifference to the snobbery of outsiders and of course a shared dread reverence for the sea.

It was on Ribble Avenue, one of the low-rise residential streets that turn off Hessle Road (and upon which once lived William Leggett), that we met Betty Cullen, her arms folded on her front gate, chatting to a nonagenarian neighbour with a baby-soft face and hair like the fluff on a dandelion. Both were happy to share their acquaintance with long waits on cobbled docks, often in anticipation of grief. For dozens, even hundreds, of Hull trawlers have been lost since the sinking of the *Minto*.

Betty was the daughter of a trawler man and the wife of a bobber. She was as trim as a stoat and fond of her fags and remembered that the Russian attaché was 'a very handsome man'. But his visit was 'long overdue . . . We've got long memories here on Hessle, very long memories.'

Indeed, she said, waiting was ingrained into the lives of Hessle women. They were always waiting, for good news or bad. 'We'd be at the lock gates waiting for hours to see the lights on the boats as they came up the mouth of the Humber. The news [of the loss of one or more vessels] would come, and the entire community would shudder.'

I couldn't help thinking that Betty was recalling those occasions with mixed emotions – grief but also the togetherness of that shuddering. She said that she thought Leggett's statue now stood not only for what happened on that night in 1904, but for all the mishaps that the Road has endured, which have kept the community strong. Although the fishing has died now. 'Is that a tragedy also?' I asked. She wasn't sure.

Alec told me later that it was now a rare thing to be welcomed into a house, as we were Betty's. It was reached through an alley to a small yard in which grew a clematis. She apologised that the alley had a gate, but the council had put it up after drug addicts had defecated in it. 'That's how things have changed around here . . .'

In the early 1960s Tunstall wrote of houses like Betty's,

Each has two bedrooms and from the front one you can just about spit onto the doorstep of the house opposite . . . The lavatory is outside in a small yard, with a narrow back alley behind. The front door leads straight from the terrace into the front room [but often] the family lives all its communal life in the back room. Here is a table and chairs, a radio and usually a television, a budgerigar in a cage and except in mid-summer a coal-fire burning in the grate. The walls of the house are very thin . . . Intimate sounds come through the walls.

Then, overcrowding was endemic. A family of fifteen in a two-bed house was not unknown, and nor were domestic violence, alcoholism and all the other vices attributed to poverty in industrial towns. Betty, though, was all alone in a house that seemed spacious if a little gloomy. She offered us tea and a biscuit and the news that she was recovering from bowel cancer. Her husband, a former bobber ('Well, they say you marry your father, don't they?'), was in a home. Alec Gill she seemed to regard as both father-confessor figure and favourite son. They hadn't met before but, she said, 'Everyone knows about our Alec.'

While I sipped my tea, soporific on Betty's oversize sofa, the two of them waltzed a soft carousel of shared memories – individuals, incidents – each increasingly iconic with the passage of time. They remembered Rayners, where fishermen from across the North Sea and beyond would meet to drink and fight and pick up whores: 'Not just our boys; Dutch fishermen, Icelanders when we weren't at war . . . The Danes loved our prostitutes. Lovely girls. They'd just sit quietly in the back room, sipping a Coke.' (There were also, although it wasn't Betty or Alec who told me this, other clubs, where fishermen went to meet fishermen.)

Betty was, she said, 'an embodiment of Hessle history'. She laughed through a throaty cough. Her credentials were impeccable: beneath her bed she kept, wrapped in tissue and carefully boxed, the caul in which she was born – a relic believed by superstitious trawler men to confer such extraordinary luck on those who possess one that they are prepared to offer incredible sums to buy them. 'It's my rainy-day fund.' She laughed again, eyeing the Embassy cigarettes on the mantelpiece she was too polite to smoke in our presence.

Some would have you think that superstition was a potent feature of the Hessle Road community, which didn't as a rule give a fish for the Church and used the Bethel (seamen's mission) for pastoral and sometimes financial, but perhaps less frequently spiritual, support. Alec's books are full of Hessle lore: how uttering the word 'rabbit' or for that matter 'pig' or 'cat' was about as unpropitious as anything one might do save drilling a hole in the hull. Or wearing a green jumper at sea.

Superstition wasn't the sole prerogative of the men. Women who practised pyromancy – staring into the grate for augurs of impending doom or the faces of lost fathers and sons – could be identified by the blotches on their fire-chafed shins. And if wives neglected their husband's dirty shirts and underwear once they'd left for the docks (always by taxi – never seen off by their women, which was bad luck), this was less a symptom of slovenliness than of the laws of sympathetic magic, which turn a tumble dryer into a storm at sea – or at least that's what was said.

Betty was glad her husband hadn't been at sea. She had seen how painful the long lonely weeks were for her neighbours before their husbands returned, and how quickly joy could turn to heartache when they did.

The noblest and most distinguishing characteristic of a Hessle Road trawler man (so at odds with the Yorkshire stereotype and the prim East Hullsider in particular) was his profligacy. While their wives drew a living wage from the men's earnings, any bonus related to a share of the catch was for them to spend as they liked. The hoarding of wealth was so frowned upon and setting to sea with money in your pocket was seen as so unlucky that what hadn't been spent on drink, women and threads was thrown into the air from the gangplank for children on the dockside cobbles to scramble for. 'The three-day millionaires, is what they used to call themselves,' said Betty. (Grimsby fishermen, by contrast, possessed a different attitude to money – although famously for a brief period in the boom years of the 1960s more Rolls-Royces were sold there than in any other city in Britain.)

As we spoke and as she reminisced with Alec, Betty shifted easily between planes of time and place. She declared, 'We're hospitable, that's what we are, on the Hessle Road.' But it wasn't the Hessle Road of now to which she referred, but that of the past, which dwarfs it. Moral and other truths danced elusively around each other, at arm's length. 'Was life better then?' I asked. She seemed bemused, made uncomfortable even by the question, and answered with little vignettes of the Hessle Road in its cod-fishing prime which were neither straightforwardly good nor bad.

'You could tell that a boat was due home cos the women would clean their houses for the first time in a fortnight. Slobs they were otherwise.' When the men came home they blew their wages and spent three days drinking and fighting and procreating before heading off to sea again. 'They were wild. But they deserved it. They were heroes. How can you be a hero working in a sticking-plaster factory?' This was a pointed reference to the medical device factory that briefly absorbed surplus labour around Hessle in the late 1980s.

Now, she complained, 'the Poles are drunk and fighting by lunchtime. There are addicts all over the Hessle Road. The girls flaunt themselves in the streets. Those big Norsemen are no more to be seen in Rayners.'

Nor indeed was anyone. For it was closed in 2011 on account of mouse infestation. Today's foreigners, boozers, fighters and tarts are a poor crowd set against yesterday's.

For all her nostalgia Betty knew that fishing was a brutal trade and one that not all men were cut out for. Traditionally, the route in was to go to sea as a deckie learner, a brutal initiation for a sixteen-year-old into a world not only of elemental danger but also often physical and emotional abuse compounded by home-and-sea sickness. 'You'd never push a son to go to sea. You'd never want them to anyway. It's a cruel living,' said Betty. Heroism comes at a price.

For Hessle Roaders, life skirted around the ever-lurking abyss of loss at sea, a term which cruelly euphemises the agony of bursting lungs, exploding engine rooms or the sudden capsize of a vessel made top-heavy with Arctic ice. A third mate or deckie slipping into the murky blackness or being crushed beneath heavy equipment or nets was as good as routine. But the subsequent ripple of sadness could take a generation to dissipate.

Fishing has always been dangerous – up to four times more dangerous than coal mining by some estimates. In the age of sail, smacks sailing close together for comfort in the North Sea would cripple each other inadvertently. The transformation to steam in the 1880s reduced the likelihood of a sinking, steel hulls being more robust than wood, but the new boats voyaged further, kept longer seasons and experienced new perils: larger, colder seas and a greater likelihood of ice. And the risk of misadventure as a result of fatigue or stress or alcohol was increased by longer trips.

Six hundred and seventy-five Hull trawler men were killed during the First World War, and eighty-five during the Second. During the latter in particular, few of the trawlers were fishing; they had been requisitioned by the navy, so the deaths were in effect on active service during a period when the world had become accustomed to death. And then came a flurry of sinkings that disabused Britain of any notion that fishing was just another job. In 1955 two Hull trawlers, the *Roderigo* and the *Lorella*, sheltering from a storm off the coast of north-west Iceland, received a radio message from another vessel, the *Kingston Garnet*, that its propeller had been fouled, and set out to give assistance. In fact the *Garnet* had been able to free herself, but the radio message confirming this was lost in the maelstrom.

The weather deteriorated further, the size of the seas such that any course of action other than meeting each wave head on would sink the boats. Two days after leaving their anchorage the *Lorella* radioed the *Roderigo* to say that the trawler's deck was 'solid with frozen snow. Lads been digging it out since breakfast,' to which the skipper of the *Roderigo* radioed back, 'Same here, George, and the whaleback [the sheltered portion of the forward deck] a solid mass.' The boats had encountered a freak combination of gales and ice, spray from the waves freezing onto their increasingly top-heavy superstructures. *Lorrella* radioed, 'Heeling right over and can't get back,' and that was the last that was heard from her. Some hours later, almost exactly the same message, suffixed with, 'Going over. Going over,' was heard from the *Roderigo*.

For decades acceptance of the perils of fishing and the stoicism, taciturnity and social disadvantage of fishing families shielded those who could have improved fishermen's chances of survival (trawler owners and the government) from blame. But in fun-loving, tie-dyed 1968 a triple tragedy sent a howl of anguish from the north of England to Westminster and beyond, to Harold Wilson's bedroom window.

In early January a vessel called the *St Romanus* left Hull's St Andrew's Dock and disappeared in the North Sea en route to the fishing grounds of Norway. Inexplicably, though the ship sent out a Mayday distress signal on 10 January, it was a fortnight before a search and rescue operation was launched. Nothing was recovered save a semi-inflated life raft off the coast of Cromer. Then, on the 26th, another Hull vessel, the *Kingston Peridot*, sank while attempting to take shelter from an impossible storm off Skagagrunn in Iceland. The same number of crew, twenty, died. And in the same week a third Hull vessel, the *Ross Cleveland*, was knocked sideways while sheltering from a hurricane in an Icelandic fjord. Miraculously (at least that was the word used by the media, by the Icelanders who found him and by his father) a single fisherman named Harry Seddon survived.

A plane full of press arrived in Reykjavik, anxious to understand how, despite being knocked off his sinking vessel, Seddon had been able to climb up a cliff and walk eight miles around the edge of the fjord in drenched and freezing clothes, spending a night in the open before being rescued by a farmer, who warmed him up with mare's milk and whisky. 'What was it like?' 'What did he think might happen to him?' The reporters were demanding that he do what fishermen seldom do even for the benefit of their own families – describe to them his experiences at sea and his fears. In the BBC archive footage he seems bemused by the fuss. The episode was as he had said it had been, no more and no less. What more did they need to know?

To compound the scale of the potential for tragedy, another boat, the *Notts County*, ran aground, and its crew of eighteen would have been lost had the Icelandic gunboat *Odinn*, one of the most aggressively engaged against Hull trawlers during the Cod War, not rescued them.

Once more noises were made in Parliament – an inquiry launched, condolences made – but it took a mouthy no-nonsense Hull fisherman's wife with her hair in a beehive wrapped in a headscarf to force a change. 'Big Lil' Bilocca (her husband was Maltese) came to London with a train-full of Hessle Road wives and a petition. She would, she said, 'camp outside Harold Wilson's window till he does something'. That was sufficient to force the government to require trawlers to carry a radio operator and to close Arctic waters to British fishing boats in the perilous winter season.

A pedestrian subway once ran from Hessle Road beneath a railway line to the clamour and stink of St Andrew's Fish Dock. The railway is now the A2381 dual carriageway, flanked with the sub-architectural blight of out-of-town retail. Subway Road (notorious in the good old days as the locus of regeneration) remains, but the underpass is blocked, and the dock has been filled. Where trawlers once jostled gunwale to gunwale scarlet poppies nod on waste-strewn scrub bounded by bollards and capstans. The nearest parking is in the lot of a curious standalone Chinese restaurant, reputedly much frequented by one-time deputy prime minister, John 'Two Jags' Prescott.

In 1904 Dr Sharp, his stomach no doubt churning as he set out on his first North Sea trawl, recalled coming to the lock gates, 'where a crowd had gathered to see us pass out. The gates opened and soon we were moving on the broad, muddy waters of the Humber.' Those same gates, which counted in and counted out the great fishing fleets heading to the hunting grounds of the northern seas, have been left to rust in a fly-tipped wasteland given to dubious crepuscular pleasures. Sharp had reported of the dock itself that it was

> entirely given up to steam-trawlers. Here we may see them tied up two or three deep along the stone sides of the dock with their trawls triced up in the rigging to dry and the great 'otter boards' hanging from the davits at their bows. Some are taking in coal and ice, the latter chopped fine and sent into the ice hold on a chute, others are being repaired and painted. If we are early enough in the morning we may see the 'single-boaters' from the North Sea and Iceland unloading their fish and shovelling the old ice overboard. Along the north side of the dock, a long shed has been erected, where the fish is landed in baskets. Cod, coalfish, haddock, ling, gurnards, plaices, witches and soles. On the cement floor may be seen great halibut and skate the size of barn-doors dressed and auctioned off to the highest bidder . . .

The only part of that description that still rings true is that the waters of the Humber, tapping impatiently against the quay, remain muddy and broad.

As in the case of the murder of Cock Robin, any number of antagonists could own up to being responsible for the death of Hessle's fishing community. In the immediate aftermath of the Second World War the fisheries boomed. Not only was there an insatiable appetite for protein, but the fishing grounds of both the North Sea and much of the North Atlantic had mostly lain fallow for five years or more, and the trawler-owning companies made record profits. But the boom turned into a bust. Having invested heavily in new capacity, the boat owners found that the catches weren't sustainable. With the end of rationing, cod and haddock competed with battery-farmed chickens and New Zealand lamb for the nation's appetite.

Geopolitics also wielded a big stick. Since before the Second World War British trawlers had been searching for larger and more reliable fish stocks beyond the North Sea, particularly around Iceland and Norway. But as those countries looked to the seas to fuel their own economic development, conflict became inevitable. What British trawler fleets had come to regard as an unassailable right established by custom was challenged. The first Cod War broke out in 1956 and resulted in an uneasy truce – as did the second in the 1960s. But it was the third chapter in the 1970s which scuppered Hessle Road. This time Iceland played its trump card, its fortuitous position in the North Atlantic between the United States and Russia. The United States had a key airbase in the Icelandic town of Keflavik from which it spied on Russian air defences; and ultimately it was the politics of NATO that did for Hull's long-distance fleet.

I have heard it said that Henry Kissinger's arrival at Humberside Airport sealed Hessle's fate (though it isn't an episode that his many biographers have dwelt on), the story being that during the course of a Grimsby Town home game, he told the foreign secretary and local MP for Grimsby Anthony Crosland that, in the interests of the Western alliance, Britain should back down and respect Iceland's unilaterally imposed 200 nautical mile exclusion zone. But it would be too neat to point the finger of blame wholly at Kissinger's corpulent frame. Britain had negotiated greedily, indeed clumsily, with the wily Icelanders, refusing a generous quota offer which should have more than sufficed, given that fishing, like all heavy industry in Britain, was on the wane as the country sought more sophisticated, value-added livelihoods in keeping with the aspirations of the 'white heat' generation. Fish processing came into such a category, slicing and filleting and freezing, coating in breadcrumbs and putting into fancy boxes – which is what Betty found herself doing for much of the 1960s and 1970s, supplementing her husband's bobber's wage, and enjoying the camaraderie and economic emancipation that came with her own income. Even during the Cod Wars much of the fish she worked with came from Iceland, arriving in heavy crates lined with polystyrene.

'Do you know,' she said as Alec Gill and I were about to take our leave of her nut-brown parlour, with its photographs of her son, who works on an oilfield support vessel on the North Sea, and her daughter, an occupational psychologist, 'sometimes we'd find stuff written inside the crates. Rude stuff. Once they wrote "F— off, Britishers." But another time they'd stuck a five-pound note in there, and written, "Buy yourselves something nice, girls." They was funny times. Very up and down. It's all gone now, of course.'

Alec and I went to take stock and say our own goodbyes in a fish-and-chip shop within view of the Leggett memorial. I had a small cod and chips and he the 'Senior Citizen's Discount Meal'. We started talking about Russia – which he knew quite well, it turned out – and about the Incident, and how things had changed and how they hadn't. I said I'd settle up and asked for the bill, but when it arrived the girl from behind the counter asked Alec if he'd sign it. There were almost tears in her eyes as she did so.

To me she turned and said (as Betty had), 'Everyone knows our Alec. He helps us remember what we used to be.'

In the *Halligen* or an Axolotl in the Almost-Islands

[T]his was no magic island but a Hallig of old North Friesland which had been rent into these smaller islands by the great flood of five hundred years ago; the white birds were herring gulls which glided along the shore above their nesting grounds.

Theodor Storm, 'Eine Halligfahrt'
(Journey to the Halligen)

I first came across the Halligen in a few column inches of newsprint, part of an article about places that might, courtesy of global warming and an attendant rise in sea level, have disappeared within four or five generations. I asked a German friend whether he had heard of them. 'Are they a small mountain range close to the Swiss border?'

'No,' I said, 'they're an archipelago of half-islands in Schleswig-Holstein, north of Heligoland and south of Sylt and Amrun.'

'They are unknown to me,' he said, and then tittered. 'They must be very low profile.'

The article was accompanied by a photograph – taken from the air – in which the Halligen resembled green blisters bursting through a grey-blue epidermis. Rooftops were visible as well as landing stages

and roads. They looked like the remotest places in the North Sea –
and give or take a Shetland Isle or two, I think they might be.

The boat for Langeness, the *Hilligenlei*, leaves not from the
harbour at Husum but from an out-of-the-way landing stage at a
place called Schlüttsiel. As the vessel threads its way as if on cat's
paws through the channels, the cook ladles out big bowls of a rich
pea soup, the centrepiece of which is a frankfurter, and proudly
displays his trademark trays of *Apfelkuchen*.

Theodor Storm said of his first approach to an un-named Hallig,
'In front of us a grey dot now appeared on the horizon, gradually
broadening and finally rising up as a small green island before us.
A winged guard appeared to surround it; as far as the eye could see
along the shore, the air was swarming with great white birds rising
and falling through each other in ceaseless silent turmoil . . . It was
almost like a fairy tale.'

Formally speaking, Halligness is reinforced by introducing the
word before the name of the Hallig; thus Hallig Hooge, Hallig
Langeness, Hallig Hamburg, Hallig Grode. Fewer than a hundred
people live on Langeness, but it is the most populous Hallig. Some
are entirely uninhabited. The full-time population of Grode, all of
them members of a family called Momsen, is seven, one of whom
is the Bürgermeister.

But a Hallig is not an island – of this their inhabitants (who call
themselves Halligers), are uncompromisingly certain. Unlike islands
proper, they point out, the Halligen have no rocky core but are
merely the remnants of old polders, the rest of which were washed
away by the Great Mandrenke of 1362, which killed 6, 000 people,
ten times as many cattle, and destroyed the city of Rungholt, the
church bells of which (so they say, as do Suffolk people of Dunwich)
can still be heard by ships passing on still nights.

What sets the Halligen further apart is that to protect themselves
from floods their inhabitants still adhere to an ancient form of

defence, their houses being built on mounds of earth called *Warften*, which rise some six or eight metres above the level of the fields, like the *terpen* built by their ancestors millennia ago in the Netherlands. If struck by a *Sturmflut*, or storm-flood, a combination of low pressure, high tides and strong winds, the Halligen are subsumed beneath the North Sea, and their inhabitants both human and animal crowd into the houses and barns on the Warften, each of which becomes an island unto itself until the flood subsides. Forsaking the frankfurter soup, I stayed on deck as the ferry crept out into the Wattenmeer channel. A weak sun pushed through a muslin sky and rippled on the surface of the sea like moonlight. At the edge of the channel, which was marked by nothing more than uprooted saplings orphaned in the ooze, a dozen spoonbills, the first I'd ever seen, took hunched, probing strides in close step with each other, ivory white against the silvered mud. I saw no garland of herring gulls, but a swarm of arctic terns and early swallows, two species whose utterly different trajectories (the one from pole to pole, the other from Europe to Africa) just happen to cross over the North Sea, the swallows dipping for insects, the terns scanning the surface and dropping. And then came a blast of an ancient tongue, the door to the bridge opening, the captain and his mate cracking jokes in guttural smokers' Frisian.

The passage to Langeness was tortuously slow, the chain-smoking captain picking his way delicately over the barely submerged flats. As the *Hilligenlei* approached the landing stage it did so with the tremulous surety of a very ancient tortoise moving towards its mate. Then the clanking, jangling consummation, the climactic reversal of the ship's engine, the lowering of the gangplank, and vessel and land were coupled.

Only a dozen people disembarked, I hesitating briefly, watching with a strange kind of pleasure a handful of reunions: a sister clasping a younger sibling, some paternal patting, maternal embraces, the significance of these encounters heightened perhaps by the need for a sea crossing to be realised. I had only the strange bareness of the Hallig to meet me.

The people of Langeness are distributed between sixteen Warften. Each is anywhere between one half and two kilometres from its nearest neighbour, rises around eight metres above the fields and is home to between one and five houses, including cowsheds and sheep pens. It is said – or at least I heard one person say – that the ancients determined the location of the Warften according to where the Druids divined that they wouldn't be struck by lightning – and no one could remember a lightning strike in living memory. The church and school, with its sixteen pupils, share one Warft. On another is the Hilligenlei pub (I'm unsure as to whether it gave its name to the ferry or the other way round or neither), and on another again the island's tiny shop.

The first interior impression is a kind of deflation. From the sea Langeness was visible only as a low-lying silhouette. But once disembarked it was the horizontal-ness of it that was almost overwhelming, a soft green plane of scudding scents (cow smells, sea smells, clover) and whistling birds and breezes, and in early May great herds of brent geese nibbling and chuckling in every field. And there were cows, Welsh blacks owned by the man who owned the pub and the six Highland cattle brought to the island by the Kaufmann family, who ran the store. I met the Kaufmanns because they occupied Hunnenswarf, an amble of a mile or so from Neuwarf, where I was staying with Mrs Nissen and her husband Fiede, who was both Bürgermeister and 'boat postman'.

Language skills are not strong on Langeness. As I walked up the slope to the Warft I passed an old man in a captain's hat, a giant pair of ship's binoculars around his neck like the pair possessed by Chris, whom I had met in the Essex marshes. We tried some words but beyond the ubiquitous north German greeting 'Moin' found nothing mutually intelligible to say. Still he carried on talking, pointing his stick to the expanse of fields, the skies, the ditch-twinned goose-pocked thread of a road running from one end of the Hallig to the other and beyond to a sparkling ribbon of sea just visible beyond the furthest meadows. And he went on his way, and I went mine.

There was no immediately obvious sign of life on Hunnenswarf itself. The small shop was closed up. I stood on the lip of the Warft watching an angry squall venting its rage on the east of the island, while in the west the clouds had given way to vigorous blue. It seemed fine just to stay and wait for somebody to show up, and before long a figure emerged from between two farm buildings. Being, I guessed, eighteen or twenty, I thought that he might speak a little English. But we found ourselves enjoying the same conversation as the one I had just had with the elderly man, though with less pointing and fewer words. And then, just as I was beginning to feel quite far from home, less in space than in time, a young woman asked, in silk-steel Home Counties tones, if she might be of help.

Absolutely, I said. I was writing about the islands but hadn't bargained on a deficit of spoken English, Germans tending to be obliging in that respect. She said that it was for that reason she had come to work as an au pair on Langeness prior to reading German at Oxford. It had for the most part been a total immersion, with the added benefit of a heavy dose of Plattdeutsch.

Largish boned, heavily tanned and with a thick head of black hair, Angela (as I think she said she was called) ventured beyond a small gate into a garden strewn with children's toys, opened the door to the house beyond with its dark thatch like a fringe drooping below the eyes and shouted into the darkness of a corridor. I picked up an odour that was domestic, rural, old-fashioned. There was some shouting back, and she told me to come back at five o'clock; the Kaufmanns would see me then.

Nobody knows exactly how ancient the Warften are. By some guesses, enhanced with a little archaeological conjecture, the oldest could be over two thousand years. Even the doughtiest houses are much more recent, dating back to the early 1700s, a period representing an economic springboard for the Halligers. It was a fortuitous boom. The King of France having placed a veto on Basques working in the Dutch whaling industry, Amsterdam looked to Frisians to man its boats, and the call to harpoon was eagerly taken up by the Halligers. They subsequently returned from Arctic seas with cash, cosmopolitanism and crates of Delft tiles, with which they set about building convincingly bourgeois houses on their Warften.

The habit of travelling beyond the islands for employment endured long after the whales had been as good as hunted out. In the early 1920s W. M. Davis wrote in the *Geographical Journal*, 'It has long been the custom . . . for those who intended to become sailors to gather at a town on one of the larger islands in the early spring and sail thence to Holland, especially to Amsterdam, where they hire out for summer cruises; but they habitually return for winter. The returning sailors seek wives from among their own people, and a moderate excess of feeble-minded offspring appears to result from close intermarriage.'

I returned at five. Neither Irina Kaufmann nor Angela was visible, but the same not-so-bright youth with whom I had not successfully conversed earlier was leaning without obvious purpose against some relic of farm machinery, watching a small glinting grey car, which he managed to convey to me belonged to Mrs Kaufmann. It traversed the Hallig, went past the Warft and back again, having no hills or corners to disappear around or beyond.

Davis again: 'It may well be imagined that life on a Hallig consists of a simple round of duties. The women are good housewives and keep the living rooms clean and neat in spite of their being under the same roof with the cow stable and sheep pen. The days of summer are busy; many of the men being then at sea, the home members of the family must gather the hay crop and tend the cattle.'

Gradually the car snaked back, crept up the slope and came to a stop. Mrs Kaufmann opened the door and said, 'You might think,' as if paraphrasing Davis, 'that it is simple living here. But we are always busy. Especially in the summer.' That afternoon, she said, she had picked up her son from school, driven her daughter to the Hilligenlei pub, where she worked shifts behind the bar, delivered some straw to a neighbouring Warft, where a cow was in labour, and taken delivery of some stores for the shop.

From somewhere her husband Hanni emerged. Perhaps in his mid-forties, he wore an islander's unkempt beard and a little woollen cap. In Plattdeutsch he said, 'I'm not going to stay to talk. I'm the rudest man in the world. I'm very busy, and I've got a pain in my gut,' and turned and left. Irina watched him fondly as he ambled towards the fields clutching his belly.

Now we sat at a small garden table in the dappled shade of a rare tree. Angela joined us with coffee and *Apfelkuchen* and some children tumbled about on the lawn. Irina, who was originally from Stuttgart, understood English well but turned to Angela to help her with speaking. Angela had been with the Kaufmann family for almost nine months; her English was getting rusty, she said. I saw that there was a strong bond between the two women, who spoke to each other easily and with evident affection. Both of them, and Hanni and the tumbling children, looked extraordinarily healthy, which Irina ascribed to unstinting exposure to the sky and their outdoors life. 'When people come here from the city they always look so . . . so . . . *blass* . . .'

Blass means pale – possibly deficient in exposure to the sun.

Coming from the Swabian heartlands, she'd had to adjust not only to the semi-unintelligible Plattdeutsch, but to a wholly different regional character. 'Everything else was easy.' She said that, unlike Swabians, Halligers aren't talkers but tend to be morose and lack a sense of humour. (Davis: 'They have no games, no songs. Indeed, among the elders singing is seen as a sign of tipsiness.') On the other hand, she said, Swabians are hardly relaxed, always fretting about money and domestic order. 'I know when a Swabian has been staying because the room is tidier than it was before they arrived.'

Irina had been on Langeness long enough not to feel like an incomer. In some ways, things had been turned on their heads. For the island's men the local government provided work maintaining the stone sea defences, which didn't prevent flooding but did stop the Hallig being washed away. But for women there was nothing to do, bar the kind of activities Davis had outlined ninety years ago. Typically, after attending college on the mainland they sought their fortunes elsewhere in Schleswig-Holstein or even beyond. This meant that the men who stayed to maintain their jobs and property needed to look further afield for wives – to Swabia for example.

In the early years of their marriage Hanni and Irina had lived with his grandmother, who had known Langeness long before the introduction of mains water and electricity. Hanni's grandmother was formidable but had imparted to Irina a kind of understanding as to what kind of travails an islander ought to be capable of facing. In her girlhood, for example, before the road was built, getting from one part of the Hallig to the other was so laborious that community ties beyond the closest of the Warften were not as strong – you were less likely to know the people living at the other end of Langeness than you were now. Nor, given the previous reliance of each Warft on its inhabitants' ability to collect rainwater, could the old lady abide the sight of anybody wasting it. Indeed, it exercised her almost as much as hearing that one of her neighbours had failed to be diligent in their persecution of water voles.

'Why should they kill the water voles?' I asked.

'Because the voles dig into the banks of the Warften and damage them, making them weaker each time the *Sturmflut* comes.'

Irina had taken over that particular baton. She pointed to the nearest Warft, Peterswarft, where I could make out a man tending his lawn. He was a perfectly nice man, she said, but a weekender who might not execute his duties as a Halliger, or kill the voles, as diligently as he ought.

What, I asked her, about the *Sturmflut* and *Landunter* (literally, 'Land under'): wasn't it a terrifying experience, coming so close to drowning on a regular basis?

'No!' she said. 'It's wonderful!' And described the excitement and anticipation of watching the approach of a storm flood, stocking up on supplies, bringing the livestock up onto the Warft, checking its banks for vole holes. 'It's kind of like Christmas.'

While the Warften settlements look like houses on hummocks, their construction is finely calibrated to deal with the onslaught of a flood. The incline of the banks is such that it weakens the assault of the waves, absorbing its force, much in the manner of Hauke Haien's dyke as described by Theodor Storm. The walls of the houses are strongest on the west, facing the sea, for it is from the west that the storm rails the strongest, while posts within the houses hold up the roofs, in case the waves should succeed in battering down the walls. In effect the houses play a kind of architectural brinkmanship with the waters of the North Sea, which often come to within half a metre or less of the lip of the bank. From the great flood of 1962, during which 6,000 buildings were destroyed and 347 people drowned, Langeness emerged almost in splinters, but unbowed.

Usually, the waters subside after a couple of days. But it isn't unknown for the conditions to be so bad that the ferry can't dock, 'and of course, the *Löre* is submerged. Have you seen our *Löre* yet?' Not yet, I said. I was looking forward to it. I would do so before I left for Hooge the next day . . . The conversation paused to give me time to gather my thoughts and gobble down some apple cake. Irina reflected a little further: 'Of course,' she said, 'Christmas is only once a year, which is a godsend.'

To see the *Löre* was almost worth the visit to Langeness in itself. At the eastern end of the Hallig there begins a narrow-gauge rail track, which tapers into the sea, although its first stop is the tiny single-Warft Hallig of Oland a few kilometres distant. There is no rail service per se, rather each family owns a Lilliputian carriage, the length of a saloon car and propelled by a petrol-driven engine. These are fantasy vehicles, sides and interior furnishings built of scrap plywood and old cushions according to whim.

I watched one family cram in five children, some sleeping bags and a dog. They were off on a holiday, they said, and I promised myself not to tell my son about their carriage on my return home because it would make him insanely jealous. It was navy blue with three white-framed windows like portholes. The engine started up, and the *Löre* trundled off into the blurring distance.

Whether the Hallig will boast a *Löre* in a decade's time is uncertain. Some predict it will become one of the first victims of *Landunter*, which until recently was sufficiently infrequent to retain a kind of specialness, occurring perhaps only three or four times between the equinoctial autumn storms and turbulent early spring. But in the past year alone it had happened thirty times, more often than in any other recorded twelve-month period. No one I spoke to dared mention climate change by name. The climate was evidently changing, but whether this was because of global carbon emissions, who knew?

Most of the Wattenmeer, and the Halligen, are protected as a UNESCO world heritage site because of the area's environmental importance as 'one of the last remaining natural, large-scale, intertidal ecosystems where natural processes continue to function largely undisturbed'. It is the single largest nursery in the North Sea for fish, the scientists say, and there is said to be as much biodiversity in its shoals, dunes, mussel beds, tidal channels and estuaries as exists in the Amazon rainforest. So the area's human inhabitants receive economic sweeteners from the local government, and also from powerful NGOs such as UNESCO and the WWF, to persuade them not to undertake activities thought to be damaging to the ecosystem and to take up positive and sustainable methods in their stead. Thus, the complex interplay of land and sea is mirrored in the almost equally intricate relations between natives and outsiders.

On Langeness, for example, few of the locals own cows any longer but lease their fields to farmers on the mainland: the cows arrive around April and return on the *Hilligenlei* in October. Cattle are essential to keep the habitat in a fit state for the myriad birds spending winters and summers on the Halligen. They compete with the omnipresent brent geese, but the farmers receive compensation for the pasture that the geese are estimated to devour.

There are on each of the Halligen and on the other islands in the Wattenmeer information centres extolling the virtues of UNESCO's stewardship, with detailed diagrams explaining tidal cycles and the impact of floods. Invariably there's a fish tank replete with starfish, hermit crabs, blennies and other local denizens. These centres have become part of the landscape. They also provide a year of opportunity for the school leavers who run them, living in dormitories and generally having an extremely enjoyable time at the German taxpayers' expense.

Relations with the locals can be brittle, for the Halligers perceive the impertinent mooncalves as emissaries from the world of pontificating experts, who periodically arrive from elsewhere – sometimes abroad – and tell them how to run their Hallig and generally live their lives. Hanni's grandmother would not be best pleased. Not all the experts from abroad leave. Indeed I soon felt that were I to stay longer than a week or so, the siren song of wind, birds and an uninterrupted view, even if of nothing in particular, would conspire against my ever boarding the *Hilligenlei* again.

Connoisseurs of the Halligen like to say that no one is like another. Like Texel's boast of being 'Something for everyone' this is perhaps far-fetched. They are uniformly flat and their houses are all built in the heavy-roofed Frisian style. But the meat of the claim, I suppose, lies in nuance: each is ever so slightly different, and the merest change in detail becomes hugely exaggerated by big skies and the sprawling presence of the sea.

Hooge is less elongated than Langeness and its population only eighty. But by contrast a couple of its Warften are almost sizeable: on Backenswarft there are four cafés, two museums, a fish-and-chip shop and a town hall clustered around the *Fething*, an ancient rainwater repository now reduced to a duck pond. The entire Warft probably occupies an area comparable to that of three tennis courts cheek by jowl.

My first evening on Hooge, knowing no one, I had been contemplating a return to my hostel-like room in a converted farmhouse to read my book and listen to the melancholy night sounds of snuffling ducks and lowing cows. But I received an invitation to an amateur production of a play to be performed wholly in Plattdeutsch. In other circumstances this might not have been so alluring, but as it was I half-ran the two kilometres to Backenswarft, where at 8.30 prompt the curtains opened before an audience of two dozen mostly uncomprehending tourists in the basement of what I took to be the town hall.

It was unclear as to whether the play was or wasn't funny. I understood that it was a comic tale of insurrection set in an old people's home, a point of convergence between *One Flew Over the*

Cuckoo's Nest and *One Foot in the Grave*. But few people laughed very much, perhaps on account of not being able to understand the dialect. The real spectacle came with walking back through the velvet night, and though I was happy with my own company, the expanse of dark fields, scarcely punctured by the intrusion of distant Warften, was achingly lonely. A slender band of sickly crimson interceded between the horizon and heavy dark cloud. The welt of an afterthought of sun hung in the west, and the sky, untrimmed by trees, had the stage to itself.

It turned out that most of the big personages on Hooge were outsiders one way or another. After the curtains had closed on the play I introduced myself to the middle-aged man who had played the part of a sex-obsessed geriatric. He scrutinised me through professorial half-moon glasses. 'Please,' he said, 'come and visit me at the school tomorrow; it would be my pleasure . . .'

By the morning I had acquired one of the bicycles that are strewn around Hooge among the geese, and I thought of heading to the church, which sits amid old graves, surrounded by ditches and meadows and cows, and is reputedly the prettiest and oldest in the Halligen and beyond, famed for its painted carved wood panelling and Prussian reds and blues. A clanking bell, admonishing and beckoning, rang out across the fields, turning the ears of a number of appropriately placed sheep and lambs.

I took a seat near the back. Candles were lit at the aisle end of each row of pews and in a candelabra above the pulpit. The other pews were filled for the most part with families which I guessed from the bright snap of their holiday clothes to be tourists. Presently the pastor arrived replete with pointed beard, black gown and fork-tongued collar. He cast a benevolent gaze at his flock, folded hands across his chest and asked the congregation to say where they had come from: 'And who is from Berlin?' (A show of hands.) 'And who is from Kiel?' (A smaller show of hands.) In English, he

added, 'I think we even have a visitor from abroad!' His eyes
narrowed and concentrated their Lutheran gravitas upon where I
sat at the back of the church.

It was a long service, during which he accompanied himself
enthusiastically on the guitar for the hymns before mounting the
colourful pulpit and delivering a sermon, which I felt, though
understanding little of it, was hectoring and bullying. He gave
meaningful looks to three teenage girls in the row of seats in
front of me and said things about Facebook which elicited
anxious titters, and proceeded to tell the fable of the fox and the
wolf.

Once the service had drawn to a conclusion, for which I was
truly thankful, we chatted in the carved doorway, half in and half
out of the sun. I asked the pastor about his sermon, and he said that
it was about the need to take Jesus into one's heart, and how the
simplicities of Hooge – the sun, wind and sea – should be seen as
a parable about good living and the avoidance of temptation and
sin. He had taken much longer to make his point while thundering
from the pulpit.

I asked whether many of the congregation were from Hooge.
None, it turned out. He himself was visiting from Kiel, where he
lectured in theology, and he was not a native Frisian, having come
north from Bavaria to take up his position. ('We have a place on
Sylt – only a tiny caravan, of course . . .') 'But,' he insisted, 'the
Church means a great deal to the Hallig people. In their own way
they are devout. In the summer it is difficult for them to attend
because [and he reiterated a leitmotif that was becoming familiar]
they are very busy.'

We talked a little about the 'Frisian mentality'. 'Have you read
Storm?' he asked, and I said that I had read what I could find that
had been translated into English. What, I asked, did he take to be
the significance of the climax of *Schimmelreiter*?

The pastor looked uncomfortable. During his lifetime Storm had been a bête noire for the Church. On the one hand he was a paragon not only of literary talent but also, as a highly respected magistrate and lawyer, of probity and ethics. But on the other hand he consistently rejected organised religion, and when his stomach cancer got the better of him shortly after the completion of *Schimmelreiter* he refused the last rites, much to the chagrin of those who had prayed for a deathbed conversion.

In the closing stages of the book, when Hauke Haien, who has hitherto disdained the Church, is on the verge of losing his beloved wife to a fever, he calls for divine assistance but is overheard crying to God, 'I know you cannot change everything that happens, even if you wanted to,' thus denying God's omnipotence and provoking his neighbours' suspicion that he is an atheist or satanist or both. 'I think,' said the pastor, 'that *Schimmelreiter* proves that Storm was coming to Jesus. The flood is the divine power that Storm had tried so much to reject.'

Or perhaps, said Uwe Jessel, the flood was just a flood.

Jessel was the teacher who had played the Viagra-charged geriatric in the Plattdeutsch play. After leaving the pastor I cycled to the Warft where he had his school. It was Sunday, but he'd be in his classroom attending to chores, he had said, and later two of his pupils – 40 per cent of the total school complement – would be turning up to help. When I found him, he was squinting at a maths workbook, listening to Mozart and brewing a cup of lapsang souchong tea. School, class and home were all one.

I never found out what brought Uwe Jessel to Hooge. It wasn't that he was evasive about it so much as that whatever the reason it had long ago dissipated. He and his wife were here and would probably not leave. It was, he said, a unique challenge having a school of five pupils, especially given the diversity of their ages: the youngest was six and the oldest seventeen. And so, he said, far from having it easy, he was *very busy* ensuring that each of his charges was learning a curriculum suited to their age and ability.

The classroom was crammed with books, photographs, a fish tank, a stuffed guillemot and things found on the Hallig's shores. I thought of the old school on Spurn Point, long since disappeared, and about how in between thrashings the teachers would take their charges collecting on the dunes.

Uwe said the thing about Storm was that his writing could lend itself to so many different interpretations; that was what kept it alive. Often you felt – and I could see exactly what he meant – that he was less presenting a riddle than exploring something dark, encountering shades of light on the way (but as if for the first time), and taking you, the reader, with him. And then of course you needed always to be on guard against over-interpretation. Take the flood. This school where we now were was built in 1968, on the site of the old school which had been utterly destroyed in the flood of 1962, when for the first time in generations the *Landunter* had been so vicious that it breached the Warft, and many buildings, including the school, needed to be pulled down. In Hamburg dozens had died. He took a sip of lapsang souchong and then, cup poised by his lips as if the thought had just occurred to him, said, 'That was a flood. Not a metaphor.'

I asked Uwe what he thought the best and worst things were about attending such a small island school. The worst, he said, was that the oldest child missed the company of his peers – it was 'sort of embarrassing for him' to be in a class with a six-year-old. But contrariwise, he said, this meant that the oldest became sensitive to the younger children's needs and developed a keen sense of empathy, while the younger ones didn't get lost in the crowd but could each receive as much attention as they needed.

Breaking a long silence, two boys knocked on the door and came into the room. The purpose of their extra-curricular visit, Uwe explained, was to renovate an old fish tank in preparation for the arrival of *der Axolotl*, a curious amphibian from Mexico which a naturalist would be bringing from Bredstedt. The old glass had been taken out of the frame and the putty scraped out, but now the challenge was to squeeze in the new panels, which were a little too big.

The boys stood by while Uwe pulled and pondered to the accompaniment of a horn concerto. 'Probably best you leave us to it,' said Uwe and added, 'Just think, tomorrow when you step aboard the *Hilligenlei* just as the other passengers are disembarking, you'll be crossing paths with the first axolotl to live on Hooge.'

Uwe Jessel pointed me towards the next but one Warft, from which a strong headwind bowled unimpeded over baize-green fields. It was a struggle to cycle against it – like running up a downward escalator – and I was sweating and breathless when I arrived at the house of the Bürgermeister, Matthias Piepgras. For some minutes after he greeted me I could scarcely speak, but he took sympathetic puffs on a meerschaum and beckoned me indoors. Among his clutter of papers and half-finished projects I felt quite at home – more so hearing something approaching music coming from his sitting room. Leonard Cohen was just grinding to a croaking close (not in Frisian), and the Bürgermeister's girlfriend Christiane Lenemann was making strong coffee.

Craggy but not austere, Piepgras was immediately likeable. Like Uwe, he wasn't a son of the Hallig, but had been a 'teacher for slower children' on the mainland before he had had a 'life crisis' and felt a desperate need to be somewhere like Hooge, surrounded by nothing but the balm of sea and fields and clouds, where he could recover his confidence and strength.

Christiane came in with the coffee, and steam and pipe smoke curled around each other in the sharp light thrown by the dusty windows.

Being mayor, he said, had neither been thrust upon him, nor had he actively sought it. 'But things were run so badly, they needed a . . . how do you say?'

'Outside perspective?' I ventured.

'Yes! *Genau!* Exactly!' And so, he said, he had interfered so much and made so much noise that he found he had acquired the job.

Christiane was not a Halliger either, although I guessed that she had endeared herself to most of the locals when she gave me a copy of her book *Halligluud*, a large red tome with photographs that I'd seen for sale at every possible outlet on the coast of Schleswig-Holstein. I told them that I had met a Bürgermeister before, Frank Botter on Heligoland.

'Ha!!' said Matthias. 'Botter! Yes, big man, like a bull! Nice guy. I met him one year at the Schleswig-Holstein Island Bürgermeister Annual Conference.' For some reason to meet someone who had also met Botter struck me as hilarious. I told Matthias that I couldn't imagine Botter listening to Leonard Cohen. 'Yes, maybe not,' he said. And then I remembered all the things he had said about being a 'real' Heligolander. Did Matthias encounter issues on account of not being native?

A quick exchange of nervous glances flicked between him and Christiane, and he tamped his pipe before explaining that on a place as small as Hooge there were bound to be issues. Were he to be the Bürgermeister of, say, Husum or Bredstedt, his life would be easier. As it was, there was so much to do and he had only a skeleton staff, so he was arguing for more money with the government of Schleswig-Holstein and taking responsibility for decisions made in the interests of Hooge which sometimes clashed with the individual desires of its inhabitants.

'Let's put it like this,' he said, 'I have my political enemies.'

I asked jokingly whether he felt in physical danger.

'Not yet. But three of my cars have been destroyed outside my house.'

'Did you ever expect when you were teaching special needs on the mainland that you would become the Bürgermeister of an island of ninety souls?'

'No. That I never expected. I never expected that at all. Not at all.'

I was embarrassed that our conversation had taken on an interrogational slant and sensed that despite his amiability Matthias was wary of me being there, and wanted to be left alone with Christiane (which I could understand), Leonard Cohen and his pipe. And, thinking about his cars, for a few spiky moments I saw how of a night you might feel exposed on the Warft. You might be safe from lightning, I thought, but were vulnerable to flood, unwelcome thoughts and memories, and hooliganism. And I thought about the fate that had claimed Hauke Haien, which led me, irrationally perhaps by dint of too much coffee and exertion on the pedals, to fear a little for Matthias Piepgras.

When I left the sun still shone but disobligingly the wind had performed a volte-face, and no matter how hard I cycled, my destination – coffee with Fiede – seemed resolutely distant. I tried to remember the words to 'Suzanne', and by the time I had recalled half of them, I'd arrived.

The next day I woke early to catch the ferry back to Schlüttsiel, where I had been staying on a farm in what as far as I could tell was a barn converted to take school parties. The institutional odour of cheap cleaning products and clipboards pervaded its cluttered corridors and showers. I'd seen my hostess fleetingly, but Patricia, the wan, anxious-looking, friendly 'help' from Krakow, was more visible and engaging.

She said that with the exception of her employer she had scarcely spoken to a single Hooge native since arriving three months before. She wasn't too lonely because there was another Pole, Peter, who also worked on the farm, helping out with the cows and the bicycle rental business. But didn't that seem surprising given that everyone was squeezed together on the Warft? She didn't mind so much, she said.

Last year she had worked in Madrid – which she'd loved – and before that in Toronto, which was *excellent*, and she had chosen to come to Hooge because she was intrigued by a place so remote and quiet. 'I can't complain really,' she said. 'And in August I'm leaving Germany to work in a care home in Surrey, near London. Do you know Surrey? I'm really looking forward to it. Will it be good, do you think?'

I gave a dissembling reply and felt sad anger for Patricia's plight and at the Hooge inhabitants' truculent lack of interest in her presence on their island. Across from the *Fething*, I watched a handful of farmers manoeuvring a cow into a stall. They were big men in blue overalls with Old Testament beards, and I could have been looking across a chasm of centuries, not just a duck pond – and perhaps they couldn't look back. I remembered something that Arend Maris had said about islanders not really believing the rest of the world existed even when it stared them in the face.

The morning, its all-too-fitting drizzle beneath which both sea and meadows sulked, was ripe for lugubrious thoughts. I'd been on Hooge and Langeness long enough to want to leave and not to. The world of buildings three storeys tall and more, and ordinary high streets with their promises and compromises was already intimidating. Silence was impossible in the Halligen, banished by the wind, lisping sea, clamouring birds. But the sense of apartness that Matthias Piepgras had perhaps discovered before he became entrenched in the affairs of Hooge's good or not-so-good inhabitants had bitten deep. Maybe if you stayed too long it resulted in a sternness of soul, a tendency to scowl and suspect that singing was tantamount to levity.

The *Hilligenlei* picked its way towards where I and a handful of others stood shivering on the quay; the swallows and terns, oblivious to the change in the weather, continued their aerobatics unabated. Soon there would be coffee and frankfurter soup and apple cake, note-writing and wondering what and where was next. Quite without warning I played host to an abrupt and violent sensation that the pastor was wrong about the *Schimmelreiter*, that the bursting of the dam, Hauke galloping along the dyke as it collapses, the terrible tragedy that unfolds, stands not for a dying man's plea for forgiveness but as a broadside against pettiness and piety – even, I thought, against the low burble of soft rock music that seemed to fill every public space in Germany, even aboard a ferry.

I drank my coffee and ate the soup and the cake. Had I passed a man with an axolotl? It was hard to know, but I knew that strange Mexican amphibian manqué, thriving as it does on adaptation not confrontation, would find a home on a half-island where the natives are kind to strangers – at least most of the time.

Where Two Seas Meet

The streets are lined with ropes, behind which are small potato plots or patches of corn, espaliers of dried fish outside the houses, ship's timbers used for these, here and there a little shed, the roof of which is the hull of a boat. The street deep in sand, the town infinitely long, with dunes, potato plots and corn fields, and children asleep in the sand.

Hans Christian Andersen, Diary entry, 18 August 1859

I came to Skagen for the reason that the Danes come to Skagen: Skagen (the 'g' is silent – the name rhymes with 'Dane') carries a kind of aura of wonder with it, conjuring a golden age of artistic brilliance, one long summer stretching into an ethereal twilight. It lies at the very northern tip of Jutland, or Jylland, where the North Sea meets the Baltic amid wild beaches and dunes. It is also the epitome, for the Danes, of all that is best about their country: unkempt and evocative shores, stylish design and cinnamon buns.

One painting above all others captures the reputation of Skagen: two young women are strolling arm in arm along the foreshore. In long white dresses belted by pale sashes, heads turned conspiratorially towards each other, they're deep in a long-lost conversation. Artist and viewer tail the couple from a dozen yards behind – not directly but offset a little. The sun has gone, and dark lapis sea and sky have merged, as they do in the first minutes of twilight. But the women themselves, and the beach upon which they walk, glow in the residual light. It is the most valuable Danish painting ever, and has borne the weight of countless reproductions and homages. (Arguably too many. Were they less commonplace the keen sense of nostalgia it evokes might be sharpened. Less saccharine but more piquant.)

The artist was the husband of the darker haired of the women. He was Peder Severin Krøyer, and his wife Marie was once described as the most beautiful woman in Copenhagen. She, also, was a brilliant artist, as was her companion in the painting, Anna Ancher, who was married to another painter, Michael. These two couples were the nucleus of the colony known as the Skagen artists, who fell in love with each other and with Skagen, putting both an inaccessible corner of Jutland and themselves on the map with their beauty and intrigues and natural gifts. That was all some time ago, but something of them still lingers in that blade-like Scandinavian light and in the tourist shops and museums their legacy bequeathed.

Most of Skagen sits on the Baltic side of the Skagen Odde peninsula, which pokes from the top of Jutland like a fruit knife. The rest of it, a sort of appendage connected by a thread of road, faces the North Sea side. Maybe Skagen is the only town that fronts two seas in this way.

Before the artists' discovery of Skagen there was little there at all. A fishing community and the open boats which, at the end of each fishing trip, were hauled up upon the beaches, the town having no harbour. It was far from anywhere that wasn't itself far from anywhere, and notwithstanding the train that runs up via Frederikshaven from Aarhus, in the centre of Jutland, it still is, by the standards of a small country endowed with a state-of-the-art transport system.

I took that train which lumbers through the bunched and compact fields and forests. Then for the last twenty minutes of the journey we were rumbling through a sea of heathland, the contours frozen, dark, cropped grasses trembling, and though my companions in the carriage were mostly high-school students in bright colours fixated on their iPhones, the ground across which we travelled was for me reminiscent of a handful of watercolours my great-grandfather, a Scot who married a Dane, had painted more or less contemporaneously with the Skagen set – of which he must have known but to which he did not belong.

This man, John Connell, painted dark shallow-roofed cottages nestling in the folds of that same landscape. The handful of his paintings that remain have darkened with age but they still coincided with the colours I now saw, the ochres and sombre greens and the saturated blues above. And he painted the tan-sailed fishing boats that plied the Jutland coast.

The little train pulled into Skagen, and I followed my nose past low-rise office buildings (the Danish Fishermen's Association, a firm of marine architects) to a small apartment set back from the pedestrianised main road, along which a handful of tourists ambled, gazing desultorily in the windows of clothes shops, apparently unable to find what they were searching for or unsure as to what that might be.

Of Skagen the town, its most obvious feature was that almost without exception the houses, municipal buildings and church are painted mustard yellow, and their roofs tiled in red. Custard and rhubarb, mustard and beef. This, I thought, might have worked had it not been that the paint finish was immaculate, not an ounce of weathering apparently permitted. Looking harder at the buildings, I concluded that the logic had run along the following lines. Many, but not all of them date to the mid-nineteenth century and have enormous value as examples of vernacular architecture. The newer buildings deviate, but it is difficult to impose 'heritage' on a modern building; far easier to repaint an old one. So all of them have been 'aged' by making them all new.

Yet the scale was pleasing. I took lunch from a hot-dog stand, the vendor generous with the mustard and ketchup.

That the greater part of Skagen is turned over to a marine industrial zone was also a pleasant surprise – it would mean I wouldn't spend the entirety of my time in museums or dawdling on beaches. Also I was encouraged to find a town maintaining links with the sea that transcended the picturesque. But with its grey and blue corrugated rectangles and chimneys and fork-lift trucks, it looked difficult to crack. I carried no letter of introduction to the men in hard hats and blue boiler suits cycling urgently from one noisy shed to another. Lorries flew by on the quayside road. And where were the women in muslin dresses with gauzy veils and charming smiles, the palette-dabbing artists on the dunes?

I slept well in my apartment opposite a lingerie shop. On the outside the building was no less custard and rhubarb than the rest; inside it was light and airy but warm, and its geometry possessed a pleasant, dignified and quiet demeanour.

Freud said that when two people make love there are four involved. Where the two big seas, the Baltic and the North, clash it also gets a little complicated. The eastern part of the North Sea where it becomes the corridor that takes it to the Baltic is called the Skagerrak. East of a line that starts at the tip of Jutland and runs north to the Swedish–Norwegian border, this then becomes the Kattegat. Whether these smaller, more local, rich-in-consonant waters represent distinct seas in their own right is a subject upon which even the dictionary is confused, seas not being as easily taxonomised as birds or insects:

> The Skagerrak is a strait running between the southeast coast of Norway, the southwest coast of Sweden, and the Jutland peninsula of Denmark, connecting the North Sea and the Kattegat sea area, which leads to the Baltic Sea. The Kattegat is a continuation of the Skagerrak and may be seen as either a bay of the Baltic Sea, a bay of the North Sea, or, in traditional Scandinavian usage, neither of these.

For mariners, the point itself, Grenen, a couple of miles northeast of Skagen, is one of the black spots of the North Sea. Kattegat translates as something like 'cat gap', implying that its straits and shallows are so narrow that only such a slender beast could pass through them. In the age of sail literally thousands of vessels were torn apart by the currents here.

During the American Civil War a North Carolina ship was wrecked upon the point and its crew rescued by local fishermen, the ship's captain recuperating at the home of Ole Christian Lund, commissioner of sand drifts, who at the time was planting grasses to secure the dunes against erosion and prevent the land from slipping away. In jest he told the captain that he could 'do with a slave' to help him with this task. Some months after the captain returned home, a ship anchored close to Skagen, a jolly boat came ashore, and Jan, a Carolinian slave, made nervous landfall accompanied by instructions to whip him every day to ensure productivity. The letter also promised a wife for Jan on request, so that Skagen might start its own slave colony – which the commissioner wrote to say would not be required. Jan may have been delivered from slavery, but his was still a far from happy lot. The locals, few of whom possessed the worldly wisdom of the commissioner of sand drifts, clustered around him, prodding, poking and disbelieving. Only a handful had even heard of the existence of black people.

Jan was not whipped, and he was paid a servant's salary for his labour, but he was lonely and not readily accepted into this community of fair-skinned, rough-bearded fishermen, except, apparently, when he ventured to buy a round of drinks. It is debated in Skagen whether, after Jan's death, he was buried in the consecrated churchyard or alone in the dunes with his pet monkey, Jocko, another stranger shipwrecked in a strange land.

Maria Groes, whom I met at the tourist office by the harbour, gently besieged me with statistics proving that Grenen had become an internationally known attraction. I can't remember quite how many tens of thousands of visitors arrived every year, and how they broke down by age, nationality, long or short stay, but to my mild annoyance it was apparent that even at the end of the holiday season, when I had a holiday apartment at a knock-down price, many of those whom she was paid to encourage to visit were doing so at the same time as me.

Close to the place where the seas (whether two, three or four) meet, the road stops at a large car park with a gift shop, toilets and information stand, before a path continues through the dunes towards the actual point, which is not very far, perhaps a kilometre or so, the Baltic on the right to the east and the North Sea to the west. I thought I would have Grenen to myself; Spurn Head, another anvil between two bodies of water, had been very obliging in that way. But in mid-September this short tongue of sand was a gangway for a thin but persistent trickle of visitors, for the most part teenage school groups, the girls linking arms and singing in some malevolent approximation of harmony and the boys trying to distract them, and which, when it reached the very end, bunched up like a swarm of flies caught in a bottle.

Social anthropologists like to divide the process of the *rite de passage* into three stages. First comes the preliminal – the build-up and anticipation; second, the act itself, whether wearing special clothes or being confined to a mud hut; third is the postliminal stage, in which the subject emerges with a new name, a sore and abbreviated penis or some other change in status and identity. But it is the second stage that is most important, for it is in this liminal zone that the act of transformation, however cursory or brief, occurs. Like crossing the equator (which counts) it is irreversible. This is the ritual at Grenen, to take a few yards into the foaming water while your partner, friends, parents or children (or a solitary writer) photograph your double baptism, one foot in each sea. It appears to make its participants happy, for they beam and giggle beneath the strong Scandinavian sun.

I also dabbled in the surging surf, another quest fulfilled, but it was a different experience for me. I'd intended to come to Skagen for as long as I'd intended to write this book. I saw it as one of the three frontiers of the North Sea, and so different from the first that I had visited, Kingsdown on the coast of Kent, where the drama of the Channel cliffs gives way to the gloomy flats of Thanet but no ceremony or beacon marks the change.

I had noticed something as I joined the throng of pilgrims. Where the point tapers (coming to a head, as it were) both seas were within vision but also earshot. They sounded different: the grey, more easterly sea murmured contentedly while the deep blue waves of the North Sea announced their arrival from great distances with something like a quiet, triumphal roar. It was comforting to see that the distinction was more than a cartographer's abstraction. Where the two meet they rush past each other myopically in their exuberance. Meanwhile, out in the Baltic, large numbers of freight ships sat glumly in the distance, waiting for pilots to take them into Frederikshaven a dozen miles down the coast.

After *my* irreversible passage, I walked back along the North Sea side of the point. Whereas the Baltic shore was clean, the tide scarcely noticeable at all, the North Sea had brought gifts of kelp and strands of bright green seaweed, broken crabs, cods' heads, half a dozen gloves (none matching), strewn out within a dozen yards of each other, the usual beer cans, but most pleasingly three dolphin vertebrae, almost clean of flesh but still odorous, which I stuffed into a bag before winding my way randomly through the dunes, almost tripping over the grave of a poet, Holger Drachmann, and moseying around the bunkers built by the Germans during their wartime occupation of Denmark.

I'm as wary of museums as I am of all forms of taxidermy, but Skagen possesses a handful of some of the finest in Europe, not by dint of their size but through their ability to sustain the flickering light of the past, so easily killed off by digital trickery and ambitious curatorship. At the (custard-coloured) house of Michael and Anna Ancher I paid my kroner, and a woman of a certain age, long greying hair tied in a loose ponytail, handed me a pair of the felt slippers that the Russians call *valenki* that I might not disturb the ghosts or scuff the wooden floors.

Of all the Skagen set, Anna was the only one born there, the daughter of Erik Brondum, keeper of the inn named after him. Painters had been visiting Skagen for decades, but in 1874 art students Michael Ancher and Karl Madsen visited for the summer and fell in with the teenage Anna and her cousins Martha and Henriette Moller. The next year they returned with a friend, Viggo Johansen, and a few weeks of radiant Scandinavian summer fun yielded three engagements: Michael Ancher to the innkeeper's daughter, Karl Madsen to Henriette, and Viggo Johansen to Martha. All six went to live in Copenhagen, but hurried back for holidays, attracting an ever-growing coterie of other artists, among them P. S. Krøyer and Marie Triepcke. They had first met in Paris and came to Skagen after marrying in Copenhagen in 1889.

The Skagen set painted each other to an extent that verged on the incestuous, almost as if in the grip of a need to create a myth of themselves not only as artists but as a realisation of an idyll. Krøyer painted Marie almost obsessively and with ecstatic reverence: Marie in the garden with her beloved chocolate Labrador, by the seashore with their daughter Vibecke, smiling, in repose. Marie's portraits of herself are very much darker.

Vain they may have been, but the artists were not oblivious to Skagen's other inhabitants, in particular the fishermen, whom they depicted both on the beach, hauling in boats or nets, and in less heroic moments, gossiping at the shop or the inn. Or in death. *The Drowned Man* depicts a fisherman laid out on a table, only his face and the torso of his yellow oilskin illuminated by frail sunlight through a small window. His wife clutches a lifeless hand, and sea-booted friends look on from the shadows with quiet, grim pity. Artists and fishermen held each other in mutual respect and were of necessity close. The fishermen depicted in the paintings, with precursive echoes of the socialist realism that would emerge from the Soviet Union in forthcoming decades, were identifiable individuals, not generic proletarian heroes.

Many of these paintings are now kept in Michael and Anna's house, which is more or less intact after being bequeathed to the town by their daughter in the 1930s. It is an elegant lived-in building, in which it feels akin to burglary to wander among such intimate belongings and effects. I was mortified when my mobile phone began to ring (though there was no one to hear it) as I stood before a portrait of Anna Ancher, her nose distinctively hooked as a consequence of a teenage fall from a hayrick in the year that she met her husband-to-be.

Close by is the Skagens Museum, the erstwhile Brondums Hotel. It is more obviously a museum than the house, with its shop and galleries. It also houses the famous picture of Marie and Anna on the beach at dusk – but only by the skin of its teeth. Three years after its completion *Summer Evening at Skagen Sonderstrand* was bought by a German actress, Lilli Lehmann-Kalisch, and lost to the world until it reappeared in a Danish auction house in 1978 with an estimated sale price of 173,000 kroner (£13,700). Skagens Museum raised double that sum but was still outbid by the German media baron Axel Springer. The hammer had fallen at 520,000 kroner, the highest sum ever paid for a Danish painting. The Danish art world was shocked by the prospect of this masterpiece, only recently recovered, leaving the country. However, two days later Springer called the museum to say that he would donate the painting, but wanted to have it in his home until his death, an event which occurred six years after the auction.

Close by is a painting of Marie alone: a three-quarter-length portrait, she stands gazing out at the waves with her Labrador by her side. Also nearby is the picture of a midsummer-eve bonfire on the beach, around which, smiles blazing in the reflected light of its flames, stand the great and good of Skagen, their children sitting on the sand. To the innocent eye, the theme is wholesome communality, but in the background, eyes shining with love, Marie stands arm in arm with another man, not Krøyer, her husband and the author of the painting, who by the time it was complete had already lost her to her companion at the bonfire.

Around the height of Skagen's incarnation as the playground of the Danish art world, a British travel writer, Charles Edwardes, author of *Sardinia and the Sardes*, visited Skagen by bicycle, having pedalled through a sodden afternoon along the seashore. When Edwardes arrived in Skagen, the only hotel was Brondums. Arriving, dripping, at the door, he was soon 'puddling up a clean, broad pine-wood staircase and into a bedchamber of metropolitan luxury', and after the 'angelic visitation of a white-capped maid', who brought him warm water, he looked out on to the red roofs, much sand, a lighthouse 'and a strip of sea in as pretty a state of leaden perturbation as ever evoked anxiety in the heart of a fisherman's wife'.

He was intrigued by the hotel's inhabitants, many of whom were 'men of the brush and pencil', its dining room already a 'bright picture gallery . . . Here a girl's head; next the damsel a seascape, all green and white and blue; then a fleet of Cattegat fishing-boats, cloud studies, face studies and much else.' Edwardes's fellow guests included 'Swedes from Goteburg, smoking and drinking, and a portly lady in red velvet . . . who might have been a real queen or a stage princess, but was probably only a burgher's wife.' Chestnut-coloured boys in blue jackets, he observed, sold the guests shells and starfish and sniggered when their backs were turned.

Edwardes also made the pilgrimage to the point at Grenen, but the weather was formidable. Sand was thrust in his face 'with a blinding slap', and many of the women of the party, incommoded by their skirts, vanished into the sandhills to recover from their exertions. In the evening he attended the St Hans Day celebrations with which he had timed his arrival to coincide. Excited young people made bonfires in the teeth of the wind and dared each other to jump over them. 'One evoked great admiration by running this gauntlet on his hands and knees . . . until a tub-shabed dame slid from a sand-heap towards the fire and got him by the neck.' Later a thousand people gathered in the screaming wind as the bonfire grew ever larger, before retreating to eat strawberries and cream, 'a dream of epicurean deliciousness', and drink sherry. 'I have no idea, even now, who St Hans was,' he reported, 'but he must have been a very worthy gentleman.'

It is almost inevitable, given the year of his visit, that the Skagen set were present at the bonfire, but they, their dramas and still unfolding passions were unknown to the English cyclist.

By this time Kroyer's mental health was deteriorating and his marriage to Marie under strain. Moreover, the colony in its entirety was riven with rivalries and smouldering feuds. Soon Marie went to Sicily to escape Krøyer's dark moods and met the Swedish composer Hugo Alfven, who had long been in love with her, having seen her husband's depiction of Marie with her dog. It was Marie who seduced Alfven, coming to his room one morning wearing a red satin nightdress, bringing a basket of red roses.

Learning of the affair from Marie, Kroyer invited Alfven to Skagen, where he stayed in an apartment. Kroyer reasoned that familiarity would exhaust his wife's passion for the composer, but it was a doomed strategy, and it was Alfven that he painted arm in arm with Marie at the bonfire, a painful acknowledgement that she was lost to him. When she had a child by Alfven, they divorced. Kroyer fell into despair and died in 1909. Marie moved to Sweden, marrying Alfven, who would later leave her for a mistress, and she died in Stockholm in 1940, by which time the artists' colony had long since disappeared.

I woke at six, on the morning after my arrival, to commence my assault on the harbour, beginning with the fish auction, which takes place each morning at seven and ten. I had expected disappointment. The great fish auctions of the past, with rows and rows of gargantuan cod, halibut, turbot, tuna, conger eel and haddock, and terrier-like fish merchants with their language of arcane gesturings, are all but gone. And in an arching, hangar-like space, half a dozen men haggled over half a dozen crates of mackerel and a tub of prawns. The whole business was quickly over, the men dispersed, the fish dispatched, and I found myself alone with the sad thought that these might have been the very last of the North Sea. But that wasn't, or isn't, the case.

Courtesy of Maria Groes, I had the telephone number of Willy B. Hansen, the port director of Skagen Harbour. He was, I knew, important, and this was reflected in the size of his office in the harbour control tower, to which I cycled gingerly in anticipation of our meeting. Willy offered coffee, and I offered an apology for the short notice of my request to meet. But he was professionally gracious and, he said, anxious to share the 'good news' about Skagen's development.

Willy was a short stocky man possessing the apparent agelessness of the managerial caste. He had served in the Danish merchant navy, been a fisheries patrol officer, and headed search and rescue missions in Greenland. Then he had changed sides, joining the Danish Royal Navy and qualifying as a submarine commander. He had served in the Iraq War and later led surveillance operations against al-Qaeda in the Arabian Gulf. 'My God,' I said. 'I never thought Danish submarines might be spying on al-Qaeda in the Gulf.'

'Oh yes,' he said. 'We did it quite a lot, actually. It was very exciting.'

His current remit, he said, was even more 'exciting', responsible as he was for increasing the profitability of Skagen and ensuring that the two shipbuilding yards, the fish-processing factory at Skagerrak Pelagics and all the secondary businesses remained competitive and fit for purpose. He talked about investments in the tens of millions of euros and targets that had been met ahead of schedule. Two of his priorities were to ensure that the harbour could accommodate ever-larger fishing vessels and to reduce turnaround times so that the boats could unload their fish more quickly ('Yes, most of it will be ground into fishmeal') before setting out to sea again for more. He was also building a cruise-liner terminal to increase visitor numbers and he pointed out of the window at a dredger, busy scouring channels to allow deeper-draughted vessels to enter the harbour.

Many North Sea and Baltic harbours had simply not understood the need to adapt, and had atrophied. They should have taken a more entrepreneurial approach, he said. That wasn't universally the case. Peterhead in Scotland was also doing 'big things' to maximise its own advantages. Sometimes he went across to keep a eye on developments.

'Spying?' I asked.

'Of a sort. Yes.'

'Do you go in a submarine?'

'No.'

Willy's Skagen, I saw, was not the Skagen of dead artists and dune grasses singing in the breeze; it was the Skagen of economic progress. I asked Willy whether there was any conflict between boosting fishmeal production and harbour dredging and the aims of environmentalists, the tourist industry and those who loved Skagen for its quietness and isolation. He answered with polished tact.

'In the old days,' he said, by which I took him to mean before he took the post of port director, 'issues sometimes arose. But the important thing is communication. As long as we – all those who have an interest in Skagen and have it to heart – can share and understand each other's concerns these kinds of thing can be avoided.'

I had lunch at one of the wine-coloured wooden shacks in the harbour where, sitting on an outside bench, you can eat delicious *fiskefrikadellen* (cod hamburgers) and other piscatorial delights. September is when Skagen tries to keep tourist numbers from slumping by celebrating the 'blue time', the late evenings when the light possesses its most haunting qualities – which the Skagen artists endeavoured to capture in their landscape paintings and portrayals of fishermen.

Perhaps the tourist board oversells the blue time, encouraging shops to mount blue window displays, promoting 'blue markets' and blues nights in the wine bars. Nature's subtlest gifts die, a little, in the throats of the public into which they have been rammed. Still (and the day had yet to sufficiently decline that the effect was at its peak) there was no denying the extraordinary quality of the light, absent of haze and beneath which the water of the harbour basin was as reflective as highly polished glass.

Emboldened by Willy and the cod burgers, I put in a call to Tage Rishøj, managing director of Carstensens Shipyard. I could see its main building across the harbour, and in its dock was a ship. Willy thought Carstensens one of Skagen's greatest assets. Mr Rishøj would see me too. Without ado he bade me don a hard hat. From a shelf in the lobby we tried to find the smallest. Still, my head rattled inside it like a walnut.

Carstensens employs 250 people and generates any number of secondary jobs and contracts for local businesses. It is one of only a few shipyards left in Denmark, but it was booming. It specialises in building for the pelagic fishing industry, boats catching the species that swim close to the surface of the water, particularly herring and mackerel. Each year the boats become bigger, more technically advanced and luxurious. Carstensens's clients, both trawler-owning companies and skipper-owners, come from all over northern Europe: Norway, Ireland, the Shetlands and the Scottish ports.

In the harbour shipyard sat two brand-new boats days away from delivery, and we squeezed past workmen busying up and down gangplanks with the urgency that attends a project nearly finished. Tage nodded towards a man very ordinary in appearance – youngish, not obviously rich or brawny but wholly anonymous, no tattoos visible. 'He will be the skipper. And the owner.' I asked if it would be OK for me to introduce myself. 'Bad timing,' Tage said. 'He's just about to sign the final paperwork.' And transfer the final instalment of some twenty million euros into Carstensens's bank account. It was probably best that he wasn't put off his stroke.

A distinctive smell of 'new-ness' pervaded the bridge. The teak was immaculate, the instruments shiny, many of them still sheathed in protective plastic. An L-shaped leather sofa faced a wide-screen television that disappeared into a sideboard at the flick of a switch. Almost every aspect of the fishing operation could be handled from a tiny console at the rear of the bridge: the nets lifted, emptied, fish pumped into cool water to keep them in optimum condition. Down below Tage showed me the crew cabins. Not large, but not shared and equipped with built-in TVs, Internet access and en-suite showers. 'It's been like this for twenty years. Fishermen don't have to rough it anymore.'

Environmentalists rage against these extraordinary machines, which pillage the North Sea and beyond, but perhaps their greatest victims are the fishing communities. This boat, said Tage, had the capacity of the entire fleet of 300 boats that decades ago sat in Skagen harbour. On the other hand, the boats are more adaptable: they can switch between trawling, purse-seining and drifting at the flick of a switch, and many of the old evils of fishing – young novices cooped up with alcoholic old-timers in unsavoury conditions and bearing the brunt of big seas armed with little more than a set of oilskins – have been thankfully erased.

In the harbour there remained, picture perfect in that honest but hallucinatory light, a dozen or so traditional Danish trawlers, among the world's most enduring and endearing vessels, their rounded sterns and baby-blue hulls archetypally recognisable. Some are half a century old, but still, if in ever-decreasing numbers, continue to plough their foredecks into the North Sea regardless of weather. Only aboard one of these sea-scarred warrior boats was anyone home: Jacob Hammer, a large man, dark-haired, broad-chested, moustached, standing at the door of his tiny bridge with one foot on the gunwale, shooting the breeze and drinking beer with a few friends who seemed to arrive by foot, bicycle and mobility scooter. I sidled up sheepishly on my rented sit-up-and-beg, like a schoolboy trying to join the gang. 'Have a beer!' said Jacob, and he handed me a can of Slots Classic. Like that new boy, I beamed with the glow of acceptance.

Jacob's accent was as distinctly un-Danish as any I'd ever heard. Danish friends had warned me that the way the inhabitants of northern Jutland spoke was incomprehensible: 'They sort of gobble up the end of their words.' But this wasn't that.

'You're not Danish?' I asked.

'Not *really*. I came from Torshavn in the Faroes in 1968.' And yet his voice had a certain twang, on account of which, had he said he'd arrived from Central America I would have been less surprised.

Jacob had done well out of fishing. He pointed to an enormous vessel standing proudly out of its element in the dry dock. He'd owned a half-share in that once and sold it profitably. Now he was devoted to *Sarah*, the prettiest and smallest boat in Skagen. Most days, weather permitting, he set out to trawl for sole.

'It's a funny thing,' he said. 'The last few years the sole fishing has been no good. No fish at all. And now they're back. Millions of them. It's almost taken the fun out of it. I just go out, throw out the nets, haul them in. A few tonnes of sole. The trouble is, the price of sole is nothing. That's always how it is.' He laughed. 'Difficult to get everything exactly right: lots of fish and good prices. Sometimes it happens.' He crushed his empty Slots Classic tin in a hand like a giant starfish and handed himself a full one.

I hung around with my new friends for a while, nodding sagely as old fishermen swapped stories in a language of which I had not the slightest grasp. They came and went, these sea dogs, enjoying their Slots. 'Aah,' said Jacob. 'Life is *gooood*.'

Presently we were joined by a man whose brow appeared more furrowed. Tall and thin, white-bearded and grave, he looked like, the perfect foil to Jacob. Hooked onto the handlebars of his bicycle was a plastic bag containing a cardboard box. It smelt fine. And soon Jacob and Jens invited me to join them for lunch in Jacob's boatshed. This was a large airy building crammed with boat tackle, but more surprisingly paintings of the harbour and fishing boats adorned its walls, executed with craftsmanlike and meticulous precision.

'He's like Leonardo, eh?' said Jacob, and he nodded towards Jens.

'You did these?' I asked.

'Yes,' he said. 'I like to paint. When I have some time.'

Jens hadn't retired – couldn't afford to, he said, although he was past seventy. He kept busy as a carpenter and decorator, but like Willy the port director had spent much of his working life in Greenland during the boom of the 1970s and 80s, when builders had been in demand. He had even taught at the territory's only navigational school, although, he said, that had been a bit of a disaster – the literacy and numeracy of the Greenlanders were so poor it was fruitless to try to use them as bedrock for training in the art of using sextant, chart and protractor. But still. It was an experience, and it had inspired him. Had I heard of the MS *Hans Hedtoft*, the 'Danish *Titanic*'?

Slowly and between mouthfuls of breaded plaice, Jens told me the story of how, in late January 1959, the *Hedtoft* had set out from

Julianehaab in Greenland for Copenhagen with a cargo of frozen fish and a complement of forty crew and fifty-five passengers. She was of the very latest design, and the outward trip to Greenland had been her maiden voyage.

'On 30 January,' said Jens, 'she issued a distress call to say that she had hit an iceberg sixty kilometres south of Greenland. Two German trawlers responded to the call and headed towards her location. Two hours later she radioed that she was sinking. But the weather was bad, and rescue planes were unable to fly. For a week ships and planes searched for the *Hedtoft*, but there was nothing to be seen, no wreckage. Nothing. The only clue ever to emerge was a lifebelt washed ashore almost a year later.'

We pushed aside our paper plates and contemplated the awfulness of all those deaths at sea, the waiting for assistance, the slow lurching beneath the cold waves, the inevitability of drowning.

'But –' Jens broke the silence almost brightly '– I think I now know where she sank. I have done the calculations – remember I used to be a navigational instructor – and I am certain that I know where the *Hedtoft* can be found.' On the other hand, he added gloomily, nobody, these days, was bothered enough to look for it.

I spent the next morning walking and cycling on the Baltic side, past the royal villa which is now a retreat for 'artists and scholars' built in the year that the Great War began and painted in the town's colours. For Skagen, where most things appear approachable, it looked forbidding. There were signs: NO ADMITTANCE and PRIVATE. I could see no scholars or artists. They were indoors, I surmised, rendering the landscape in pen or paint. But a French window had been left tantalisingly ajar, and on the sill of a first-storey window stood a bottle of wine.

I had a useless stab at sketching the coast myself, and later a woman with a Labrador (like Marie Krøyer's, I thought, though of course it wasn't her) asked whether I had been painting. 'Just

dreadful drawing,' I said. She, she said, had been collecting stones –
the pieces of flint with holes that the Danes so prize, call cow
stones and hang on wires or string to decorate their summer
houses.

I headed back to Jacob's shed to join him and Jens for another
lunch. 'Have a Slots!' said Jacob, and a paper plate of plaice and
prawns was pushed in my direction. The subject for discussion was
the future of fishing and how it had all been taken over by big
business.

What was happening was madness, said Jens. For anyone now to
make money out of the sea, it was necessary to borrow eighty to a
hundred million euros: twenty million to buy the boat and the
remainder to buy up the quotas necessary to fill it. There was no
future for anyone who lacked big corporate backing.

'Whose sea is it anyway? Does the bank now own all the fish?
How can you capitalise nature, fish, like that? Not only does it
make no economic sense, but it's immoral. And unsustainable.
Everyone knows that the fish could just disappear overnight,
leaving the trawler owners with huge unpaid debts and useless
boats.'

Everything Jens said made sense to me. Did he think there was
a parallel, I asked, with the recent financial crisis, in which the
banks had over-stoked the market with sub-prime mortgages?

'Yes,' he said, 'and it's driven by the same thing: everyone is
trying to make money without working. It's just speculation.'

Jens seemed disappointed and uncertain and let down by the
world, not for his sake but for its own. The natural cycle of things
had been disrupted, he argued. A generation used to mean twenty-
five years, but now it had been stretched to forty because everyone
started their families so much later. Nobody was serious about
anything any more, and everything was postponed as people shirked
their responsibilities for as long as they possibly could.

Jacob appeared less dispirited by the state of the world, and was pottering and tinkering with things in his shed. I knew that he knew I wanted to go fishing. He'd yet to decide, it seemed, and was busying about happily, sort of singing – 'Da da daa da da daa' – while in the kitchenette a radio played a song about being in the mood to dance, romance and take chances by an Irish girl band called The Nolans. I myself was in the mood for fishing, and was hoping that Jacob would take a final weather check, announce that the wind wasn't so bad after all and point me in the direction of some sea boots. But it was not to be.

We walked out onto the quayside, where the wind was picking up, bashing the stays against the masts of the fishing boats and playing kick-the-can on the cobbles with an abandoned can of Slots. Standing on a bollard, a herring gull appeared to be choking to death on a large cod's head. 'I think,' said Jacob, 'that it isn't going to happen today. *Sarah*'s just a little boat. It's going to be a pre-e-etty uncomfortable ride on a day like this.'

Jacob was a kind man. To soften the blow he told me about another writer, an Australian woman whom he had taken fishing, but who had vomited without cessation for a whole day. And he walked over to the bucket of ice where he kept the Slots and pulled out some sole, which he handed me, advising me just to dredge them in flour and fry in butter and oil and serve with fresh lemon and pepper. But there it was. 'Next time, maybe,' said Jacob with a kind of avuncular concern that I appreciated. 'Hey – maybe you'll find someone to help you eat all those fishes!'

If the weather was too bad for fishing, the obvious thing to do was to return to the Grenen to see the meeting of the seas in one of its darker moods. The wind was growling now, and in the distance the white horses were leaping higher. Despite the weather, tourists were heading off determinedly, hoods and coat-tails flapping, shouting at each other against the wind, arms raised against the flying sand.

On the way out I saw a man in a black suit and tie loitering by a big bunker, part of the Atlantic Wall, upon which some wag had daubed the words ZIMMER FREI. It was a curious vision – like a scene from a Jack Vettriano painting gone awry – or perhaps, I thought, he was the first to arrive at a gathering of crypto-fascists or a fashion shoot, if there's much difference between the two.

Up at the tip I met three Chinese girls. The night before, in a pizza joint, I had amused them by trying to speak Mandarin, so we spoke a little more. Learning I was from London (they had recently arrived in Denmark from Beijing and were studying business administration in Aarhus), they wanted to know whether I had ever met Dr Who. 'He is so cooool!' they shrilled. I took their pictures, and they took mine with my battered Leica, bemused by the fact that it was impossible to review the image once the shutter was fired. I left them to flirt with the white horses and wandered back towards my bicycle by way of the old bunker.

Now it was actually cold, though there were few clouds, and the sky kept its enamelled sheen. It came to me that the men in suits (the first had been joined by others, and young women in nice dresses, all stoically gripping flutes of champagne) made up a wedding party. Had they been here only yesterday they could have recreated something of the romance of the old days – toasting the bride as she tiptoed on the shore of the Baltic, bowered by blue and serenaded by gentle waves that snored like children as they crept back and forth upon the sun-warmed sands. But they huddled against the concrete, looking cramped and uncomfortable.

I stole glances at them as I carried on, labouring against the wind and, reclaiming my bicycle, took a different path back into

Skagen, one which took me by chance along the Sonderstrand, the beach upon which P. S. Krøyer painted Marie and Anna. Looking north, it was unchanged from its depiction in scores of paintings by the Skagen set – broad, peaceable, other-worldly – but at its other end abbreviated by a giant fishmeal factory, the smell of which is like that of cat biscuits, diluting the breeze that rolls across the marram grasses.

Skagen, I thought, is the place where not only two seas but also two Denmarks meet, sometimes but not always without rancour. I held my nose and let my gaze rest on the kindly blues of the Baltic.

The Fishing Game

'Just as when you're doing well, and hoping for a throw that will land you on top of the board, damned if you don't hit a snake, and come down to the bottom, and have to start all over again; while the chap who's missed every ladder, and hit almost every snake, lands home.'

'Marney' in Leo Walmsley's *Three Fevers*

Fish are political beasts. They can make or break a man, a town or even a nation in a way no other animal can. And they do so with scarcely a thought.

The office of the last trawler fleet in Grimsby is located at the southern end of the town's old fishing quarter, long known as the Casbah, reflected the bustle of its oriental-esque labyrinths and booths. A plain-fronted 1920-something building, even the interior has changed little in decades. Coffee-coloured tiles line the passages to waist height. The first-floor landing meets visitors with a white hatch, above which is written the word RECEPTION, and before this I waited, hesitating to knock.

My own tentative steps up the ill-lit uncarpeted staircase were followed by those of a real-life trawler man clad in oilskins and boots. He barked loudly to announce his arrival. The noise – guttural, unintelligible (at least to me) – elicited the opening of the hatch and revealed a pretty girl in a white blouse. She smiled. The man handed over a plastic bag. 'There you go, love,' he said. 'Nice bit of cod for your tea. And a bit for Andy.'

The hatch closed on the smile, and the heavy tread descended the stairs. A few minutes later, Andy Allard, chief executive of the Jubilee Fishing Company, last trawler owner in Grimsby, greeted me with a firm handshake. A large sandy-haired and clear-eyed man in a smart cream suit and white shirt, he didn't look like the anachronism I was expecting to meet. His was a hereditary role, one that he might not have willingly sought out, though it looked as though he'd grown into it comfortably, if wistfully.

Andy's office was panelled in oak. A large map of the North Sea showing the fishing grounds, hazards, lightships and channels and the approximate positions of his vessels at any given time hung behind his desk. Elsewhere, the walls were hung with grainy photographs of members of the fishing dynasty of which he is a scion, and the boats that made it wealthy.

There were concessions to modernity: a 1970s gas fire, in front of which slumped a pair of old sea boots like hounds worn out from the hunt, and of course there was a computer on the desk separating us, the trawler owner and the writer.

'Now then,' he said, 'let's see what we can do for you. OK?'

There was only so much that Andy Allard needed to say; his office window overlooked the fishing-dock basin, which was as good as empty. He handed me a photograph of the dock in the glory days. At least one hundred trawlers, berthed like sardines in a tin, where now there was only one. Back then, like St Andrew's Dock at Hull, Grimsby's great rival, the Casbah had rattled and groaned with smoking and curing, boat repairing and outfitting, bobbing and lumping, filleting, packing and crating. Today it's like a North Sea Pompeii, sufficiently well preserved to allow some glimpse of what it once was, but its residents, bar ghosts, are now on a permanent leave of absence – almost.

The trade is still important to Grimsby. There is a daily market, fish arrive by both truck and boat to be bought by the local merchants, who send it on to Billingsgate and restaurants around the country. They make judgement calls on the quality of the fish based on what they know about the trawlers, how long they've been at sea, how and where in the hold the fish was packed. Each trader has its market niche. CCS Fish Company specialises in dogfish – a fine eating fish, cooked quickly in batter or baked. Others look for less-than-premium fish for the fish-and-chip trade. Next door to CCS, Peter Guest & Sons sells Danish foods, and not just fish but also cookies and packet soup. Grim, founder of Grimsby, was himself a Dane. Trawler-loads settled in the war. There's a lot of Danishness on the Lincolnshire coast.

And there is a handful of smokeries, slow-smoking haddock against the headwind of a changing national palate. Even Richard Enderby of the Enderby Smoke House seemed to have lost his taste for it. 'To be frank with you, Tom,' he said, having shown me ranks of spatchcocked haddock laid out on ancient racks in his 'heritage' smokery, its walls bubbling with decades of tar, 'I'm a bit fed up of the whole thing really. The price of haddock is up because the Icelanders are keeping it to themselves. The EU quotas are tightening. And people aren't eating smoked haddock like they used to.'

It might be, he said, because they don't know how to cook it properly. Bring a pan to a boil, literally put it in and take it out, then pop an egg in to poach, put it on the haddock and tuck in. Or it might be because, in a Britain agog with exotic taste sensations, haddock and egg isn't the teatime treat it was once.

Grimsby is in limbo, a fading damsel waiting for a second chance. Energy from wind is the 'next big thing', but even the 'renewables' strongest proponents don't deny that it'll never restore the town's fortunes. All the while the Victorian dock buildings are crumbling into the most delicious state of dilapidation. The most magnificent of all of them, the gargantuan red-brick ice factory, is being willed to death by its owner, Associated British Ports, which cannot think quite what to do with it, lacking both the money to fix it and the stomach for a fight with the heritage lobby. And Richard Enderby would really like to chuck it all in to take photographs of the Wolds.

Over 230 species of fish live in the North Sea. Cod and herring are the most economically important – certainly on account of their tastiness, but also, in the case of cod, the ease with which it can be dried and thus preserved, and in that of herring brined or pickled and its longevity equally well assured. Haddock, plaice and sole arguably constitute the other members of the North Sea 'big five', and then of course there are turbot, whiting, tope, pollock and bream, not to mention the blue-mouthed redfish, the very poisonous weaver fish, the delicious but easily bruised saithe, the hooknose, the witch, the scaldfish, bullrout and megrim.

Few other fauna have been as meticulously investigated as those with fins. Since pre-scientific days men have strived to anticipate their movements. When and where would shoals appear? Why would they disappear just as suddenly? When they went, where did they go? Stubbornly they still refuse to be understood. Rays and sharks prefer the east coast of England to the continental coast but no one knows why, just as biologists puzzle over what it is that causes Ray's bream, a grumpy-looking little fish that wears a permanent frown, to throw itself plentifully onto the beaches of Yorkshire in some years and fail to show up at all in others?

Making sense of the North Sea ecosystem is difficult because there are so many variables. Taking large quantities of a predator species (and most fish are both predator and prey) increases the numbers of smaller fish – and perhaps some of their other predators, given that extra prey are released. Closing down a herring fishery can result in a spike in the numbers of cod, because herring eat cod spawn. And catching fewer cod has a similar effect on herring, because cod eat herring. Yet no one is certain as to how the mechanisms function because so many other considerations play a role. Fish swim within a column of water which is forever moving, driven by tides and currents. Unusual currents and incursions from the Atlantic can do extraordinary things to populations. And there are the great unknowns: some years fish fail to show at all, killing communities with economies premised on their regularity.

There are also mysteries as to how the first North Sea peoples engaged with fish. These early inhabitants of the shore appear to have had little need to venture far out to sea to profit from it. The most enduring archaeological evidence of human seaside snacking is in the form of middens or piles of opened mussel and oyster shells. As the Neolithic appetite for *fruits de mer* became more cosmopolitan, people began to exploit the tides and the forces of rivers, building fish traps and weirs, erecting walls of stones on beaches which trapped fish when the sea retreated. The evidence is quite scanty, not least because the Ice Age altered the coast so substantially, but there are beguiling glimpses: the incised depiction of a fish on a Neolithic pig bone, traces of hazel and dogwood fish traps and sinker weights.

Archaeologist Robert Van de Noort has described the homes of such seashore dwellers : 'a habitation area with hearths immediately above the shore, with refuse and the odd damaged log-boat on the water front, and wicker fences with basketry fish traps running out from the shoreline'.

In our minds land and sea exist as opposites, but around the edges of the heavily tidal North Sea space changes identity every six and a half hours, existing in a permanent state of in between, the ebb tide revealing acres of rich mud or sand traversable by foot until the flood. Spring and neap interfere with what can seem like a kind of wilful arbitrariness. And in places – though their extent is much reduced by drainage and the cutting of reed beds – the North Sea imposes itself on land, in the pockets of the English fens that lie beyond the Wash or the islands of the German coast. In these wetlands, so archaeologists believe, early man travelled as much by log boat as on foot, just as the Iraqi Marsh Arabs used reed boats before the vindictive draining of their environment by Saddam Hussein.

The rock engravings at Tanumshede tell us that by the Bronze Age fisher-people were voyaging far from the coast with line and hook. Mummified piles of fish heads and tails uncovered in Friesland add that the fish were being dried, smoked or otherwise cured and transported elsewhere. Pliny said disparaging things about the 'fish-eating' Chauci who inhabited the area – perhaps because his own more 'civilised' kind (though otherwise Catholic in tastes) appears to have never acquired a taste for North Sea fish. The Romans settling in Gaul and Britain imported *garum* (fermented fish sauce) by the amphora-full and salted Spanish mackerel, but never took to turbot, ling and skate.

By the Middle Ages, fish had literally gained new currency. 'Sterling' is a corruption of 'easterling' – herring from the Baltic or the 'Eastern' sea. Ecclesiastical institutions demanded tithes and other taxes to be paid in herring. The self-same fish sustained not only coastal communities but settlements deep inland whose inhabitants might never set eyes upon the sea themselves. A large shoal of herring can be made up of three or four billion individual fish and a cubic mile or more of sea. 'Herring' itself comes from an old German word meaning 'army' – apposite given their ability to tool the destinies of nations.

The greatest, most dazzling accomplishment of the herring is the financing of the golden age of the Dutch Republic and is thus responsible, it could be said, not only for magnificent art but also for the liberal ideas that emerged from the Netherlands and have nourished civilisation ever since.

But each cause must have a cause. In this case it was a quirk, what the writer Charles Wilson called 'a mysterious change in the habits of the Gulf Stream' in the early 1400s that precipitated a shift in the habits of the herring, displacing a tranche of their shoaling from the Baltic to the southern basin of the North Sea.

To their credit, the Dutch seized the opportunity more enthusiastically than other North Sea nations, perfecting methods of catching the slippery armies swarming in their waters, devising techniques for curing and marketing the fish, and trading the surplus. In 1488 a Dutch official wrote that the Netherlands was 'unable to acquire anything good, profitable or useful except through the agency and intermediary of the sea', a magnanimous observation, given the efforts expended on the existential battle with the self-same benefactor over the course of the past millennium or so.

The Dutch developed new craft: 'well-boats', with a live-well that enabled the fish to be kept alive once caught, 'busses' for catching large numbers of fish far from the coast, and herring-chasers to transport the catch to market quickly and so for the best price. A circle of virtue was created. A highly proficient fishing fleet, naval excellence and dominance of trade routes were the mutually reinforcing instruments of Dutch power underwritten by what Adriaen Coenen called in his *Visboek* of 1578 Holland's 'golden mountain' of herring.

By the 1600s fishing had become the cause of political rivalry between North Sea states. In 1633 Sir John Burroughs wrote a treatise, *The Sovereignty of the British Seas* (long before any delimitation of maritime boundaries was even conceived), in which he lamented the plunder of fish from English waters by the Dutch. In part it was lambast against the rapaciousness of the Dutch, but it also bemoaned the indolence of the author's own country, which had robbed it of the ability to compete. Glory and profit were there for the taking, he said. Recently, he observed, a fleet of colliers returning from Newcastle had encountered a shoal of cod, ling and herring of such enormity that 'with certain Sheep-hooks and other like instruments' it was possible to draw up such numbers of fish as to out-value the holds full of coal.

But the 'Hollanders' had the sea stitched up. 'Besides Seven hundred Strand-boats, Four hundred Evars, and Four hundred Sullits, Drivers and Tod-boats . . . every one of these imploying another Ship to fetch Salt . . . being in all Three Thousand Sail, Maintaining and Setting on Work at least Forty Thousand Persons, Fishers, Tradesmen and Women and Children . . .' they possessed 'some 700 Pincks and Well-boats, and in the herring season, 1,600 hundred busses, each of which made work for three other vessels'. The maintenance of this fleet required the labour of untold numbers of spinners, hemp winders, packers, tollers, dressers, block and bowl makers, tanners, keel men, sawyers, boatmen, brewers 'and a number of others, whereof many are maymed persons and unfit to be otherwise employed'.

Holland, though smaller than a single English shire, had increased its 'number of shipping' to 10,000 vessels – more than the fleets of most of its rivals combined – and almost half of this fleet was sustained by fish caught off British coasts. 'The number of [Dutch] ships fishing on our coasts being eight thousand four hundred, If we allow but 20 persons per ship, one with another, the total

Mariners and Fishers amounted to One Hundred Sixty Eight Thousand: out of which Number they daily furnish their longer voyages.' Another Dutch advantage was the construction of their ships, their busses being 'Great and Strong, and able to Brook Foul Weather', while the English boats 'being small and thin-sided, are easily swallowed up by a rough Sea; not daring to adventure far in fair weather, by reason of their weakness for fear of Stormes'. The Dutch were trading British fish for 'oyles, Wines, Prunes, Honey, Wools . . . Velvets, Sattins . . . Alloms, Iron, Steel, Copper, Button-plates for armour, pitch, tar, Hungary Gilders' and the British were missing out.

Part of the blame lay with something approaching a national malaise – complacency, lack of effort – whereas the Dutch were organised and thrifty and fished hard the whole season, ranging far in search of new stocks. British fishermen by contrast stayed put 'till the Herring come home to our Road-Steads, and sometimes suffer them to pass by, our Herring fishing containing only Seven weeks at the most, and theirs Twenty'. And the Hollanders were 'industrious . . . no sooner are discharged of their landing than presently put forth for more'; the English brought back their catch and refused to set out again until they'd spent the money. (Even as late as the early twentieth century a typical Dutch rota would be a six-week trip followed by a two-day home break before setting out again.)

Other nations would in time catch up with the Dutch – a golden age will inevitably lose its shine – and by the end of the nineteenth century Germany, Britain, Belgium and the Netherlands each boasted large steam trawler fleets chasing the ever more precious and hard-pressed fish of the North Sea. It seems counter-intuitive that such great claims should be made for the right to access resources that are as wild, robustly resilient to husbandry, as transient and wilfully disrespectful of borders as fish.

For that matter, so is the notion of sovereignty over the sea, an element over which we clearly *do not* possess anything other than fictional dominion.

By the end of the Second World War the industry had dwindled to an echo of its former self, partly on account of the danger of mines and U-boats, but also through the mass recruitment of boats and fishermen for war service. In Britain trawlers had been requisitioned in great numbers by the Royal Naval Patrol Service, often into the perilous business of minesweeping, and were also used as spy boats. The *Fishing Times* frequently ran news stories of 'heroic actions' – of how, for instance, the cook of the Grimsby trawler *Warren* 'manned the machine-gun' against a Heinkel bomber though sprayed with shrapnel, but went on to put the tea on for the boys while near-identical stories featured in the German trade press; and stoically, silently, fishermen were killed in even greater numbers than they were in peacetime.

Peace brought reparation in the form of a North Sea brimming with fish, but the dividend would only last so long. From 1958 the Icelandic government extended the boundaries of its territorial waters, locking other nations' fleets out of the rich grounds that they had come to rely on. In 1975 the Reykjavik government enlarged its exclusive economic zone to 200 miles. By this time inshore North Sea fisheries were already feeling the impact of EEC Common Fisheries Policy, which greatly degraded native fishermen's rights to exclusivity in what they had traditionally regarded as home waters. Though the economic and political forces behind the decline in fishing and other European heavy industries (mining, steel, shipbuilding and so forth) might not be the same, they're comparable. Even if the workers themselves strived to cling on to their livelihoods, the nations had become weary of their heft, grime and proletarian clumsiness, so out of kilter with modernity. Many of the old players sold up their quotas and took the decommissioning money, watched their good boats being scrapped and turned away from the sea with ne'er a glance.

Though fewer in number than once they were, trawlers still scour the North Sea. But fishing has become a furious, infuriating game, demanding submission to a web of bureaucracy and acronyms. Quotas, usually obtained through historical fishing rights, or purchased, are extraordinarily expensive, even dwarfing the cost of equipping a trawler. EU rules determine how much of a given stock can be caught and for how many days a vessel can remain at sea. And fishermen are bemused by scientific evidence that appears to contradict their own observations, or feel hectored by NGOs, policymakers, celebrity chefs and scare-mongering journalists whose understanding of the reality of fishing is mostly informed by people like themselves.

From the distance of the shore it's still tempting to imagine fishermen to be bound by a single invisible thread, loosely stitching together their lives through oceans and ages with the sinew of the cold and the constancy of slime and scales. Fishermen seldom boast or indeed talk of the sea when on the land, but gently consent to the chronicling of their exploits by outsiders. A noted cod historian wrote, 'The illiteracy of the fishermen is the reverse side of the literacy of the diplomat. The fisherman is intensely individualistic and suspicious,' adding that those who fish for eel are much worse in this respect.

Even in the Mersea estuary the oyster fishermen are wary of being photographed lest their secrets be given away. Just like poker players, they watch for 'tells' – small signals like wind shifts and surface ripples – and attempt to exert some influence over the essentially unknowable by the use of mascots, the avoidance of dangerous words and colours. Superstitions can be rooted in practicality: until even the early twentieth century it was almost a distinguishing mark of a fisherman that he couldn't swim. Here a brutal logic applied: given the slim chances of a man overboard being rescued, it was more merciful to die a quick death by drowning than a prolonged one. Other taboos are harder to explain: the prohibition of words like 'pig' and 'rabbit' more closely resemble symptoms of a collective obsessive compulsive disorder.

For any other sailor the purpose of going to sea is to reach an intended destination in the minimum possible period of time. But fishermen linger and drift, roughing out the worst weather even if safe harbours beckon. It's a different kind of relationship with the sea. And again like gamblers, they stand to win either nothing at all (or even to lose everything) or unquantifiable rewards entirely disproportionate to their efforts.

Perhaps this is all landlubbers' fantasy. Fishermen no more adhere to the stereotype than do urbanites, country dwellers or office workers. But by being taciturn, they have allowed others to speak about them or on their behalf, if sometimes with dubious authority. A reputation for hard drinking, womanising and profligacy has blighted the industry for ever. In 1888 the governments of Britain, Germany, Belgium, France and the Netherlands, 'having recognised the necessity of remedying the abuses arising from the traffic in spirituous liquors among the fishermen in the North Sea outside territorial waters', signed the Convention Respecting the Liquor Traffic in the North Sea, prohibiting the sale of booze by 'any person on board or belonging to a British vessel' within 'the North Sea limits but outside territorial waters' to anyone belonging to a fishing boat. Over a century later a sociologist published a paper suggesting that up to 40 per cent of fatalities on Norwegian fishing boats could be attributed in some measure to alcohol. More recent studies have uncovered heroin use among some trawler crews.

Victorian Britain wagged its finger at the rough ways of fishermen but portrayed them as flawed heroes in torrents of books that, though clunky, convey something more than dull tables of fish landing weights ever can. In one of the best-read collections of North Sea stories, Walter Wood's *Tales of the Dogger Bank*, several sea-brutalised skippers meet their end, though not before undergoing some kind of last-minute epiphany. 'The Atonement of the *Vanguard*'s Skipper' sets the tone. Its growling godless whisky-sodden protagonist sets out to sea in the face of an imminent storm, driving his boat with a kind of diabolical fury. 'It's goin' to be a snarly night,' he tells his crew, 'an' there'll be some mischief done afore the sun shines again. But if it blew six times as 'ard as it's going to, I'd carry every rag I've got. This breeze is too fair to let any of it be missed.'

The boat is swamped, killing the first mate and sweeping the crew overboard. The wise and cautious mate had long warned the captain that his impetuous nature would be the death of all of them, his dying words being, 'You was a bit too rash for once, an' would carry on too long. We should ha' been close-reefed two hours since. Yes, I'm done for, an I've a wife an' child at 'ome.'

Only the captain and the cabin boy – whom he'd previously beaten with a belaying pin – are left on board the *Vanguard* until finally somewhere off the Norfolk coast they are spotted from the shore and, wishing to finally atone for his arrogance and pride, the skipper ensures that the cabin boy is saved before facing his own fate: 'The deadly liquid wall advancing – the last mad charge of his relentless foe. He had seen too many hills of death like that to misconstrue its meaning. He rose to his full height, majestic in his last stand, and steadied himself against the jagged mast.' '"Tell 'em ashore to give the insurance money to the widders, and the ten pun in the bank to the boy,"' he cries before the sea 'broke in a towering cloud, and crumbled around the dissolving smack. The strained timbers were rent asunder once and for all, and the skipper was carried into deep water.'

If Wood's fishermen are redeemed by God, in the Danish novel *Fiskerne* by Hans Kirk the best characters are saved *from* their piety through gradual humanisation and tolerance. *Fiskerne* (*The Fishermen*) was based on the migration in the last years of the nineteenth century of a community of fishermen who abandoned their village on the isthmus of Harboøre after successive years of storms had all but pushed it into the sea. The villagers, members of a revivalist and puritanical Protestant sect, resettle on the eastern side of the isthmus by the protected banks of the inshore Limfjord but struggle to adapt to the hedonist mores of their new neighbours. With sympathy but not unsparingly, the villagers are depicted as struggling to escape the parochialism, dogma and intolerance that has, like some hard carapace, sheltered them for so long from the wind, the sea and the privations of poverty.

If some North Sea fishermen stayed firmly within sight of their home shores, so others have been nomadic. From the late nineteenth century Scottish herring boats would sail south to chase the 'silver darlings', migrating with their prey past the Yorkshire coast and on to the East Anglian ports of Yarmouth and Lowestoft. The presence of women was a major social component of great migrations; the herring gutters and packers of Aberdeen, Fraserburgh, Lerwick and Anstruther would travel down by train, putting up in lodgings or sheds, each bringing with her a sea-kist – a chest of cloths, towels, boots, a gutting knife and an oilskin coat.

Nobody worked like the herring lasses. A good gutter could get through sixty in a minute; if the catch demanded that they stay at their farlans (troughs) beyond midnight, so it was. But this annual trek was also enormously enjoyable – a release from the strictures of home and an occasion for courting and dancing. For almost a century the ritual was as certain as the herring themselves. Slackening off during the First and Second World Wars, the fishery was vigorous again by the end of the 1940s, with over a thousand curers working in Yarmouth each summer. But within five years there were virtually none, and by 1969 the silver darling party was over, the Fishing Board of Scotland reporting, 'No boats made the voyage to East Anglia this year.'

One explanation was that as European prosperity burgeoned, its population could afford to diversify its sources of protein. A German dish called *labskaus* consists of mashed herring, hashed beef and beetroot in proportions which traditionally vary depending not only on the taste and discretion of the cook but also on the respective fecundity of the sea, the dairy and the fields. Invariably, a good year meant less herring and more beef.

Fishing communities around the North Sea share traits and experiences, but have always diverged in the social structures underpinning them. In 1913 the men of a German fleet went on strike in an unsuccessful attempt to obtain free food while aboard the boats. Crewmen possessed little security, their skippers owing no obligation to employ them on subsequent trips, and obliging them to buy what they ate at sea was another source of profit for the owners. In Denmark the tendency was for ships to be communally owned, profits and risks shared among all aboard. In the Hull and Grimsby fleets the boats tended to be owned by companies employing both crew and skipper and hierarchies both ashore and at sea to be rigid, though frequently the cause of conflict, although the Shetland whitefish boats – perhaps following the Danish model – were staunchly democratic, camaraderie usurping coercion as the tool for success.

There are few accounts of women fishing though it has created opportunities for women to 'fill the gaps' while the men were away, running businesses in order to compensate for their husbands' low or erratic income. During the period of the Dutch Republic such women enjoyed higher status than their peers by dint of a system of power of attorney that gave them licence to set up their own businesses and arrange their husband's and father's business affairs – perhaps another instance of fishing's contribution to the Dutch golden age.

We overlook fishermen. And fish too are mostly out of sight. Conceptually shoaling with money, seldom seen in the raw state, reduced to numberless abstraction, future stocks loaned against, capitalised, securitised and speculated upon. Fitting, then, that close to the capital (or to *a* capital, London) a fishery thrives on the island of Mersea, a roughly diamond-shaped morsel of fields protruding just shy of the mud of the Blackwater estuary.

My friend the fishing lawyer Daniel Owen arranged an introduction to Richard Haward. We met in a lay-by just beyond the causeway, a narrow road suspended a few feet above the mud which would be beneath the water soon, given the high autumn tide. A neatly lettered sign warned: PRIVATE MARSH – SAMPHIRE GATHERERS WILL BE PROSECUTED.* Richard, hair and beard luxuriantly creamy-grey, was friendlier, though I had arrived late and disrupted his schedule. 'The green dory will

---

* My favourite North Sea sign to date: SAY NO TO THE SEA-EAGLES (Pin Mill near Ipswich, 2010).

take you out to the oyster boat. Don't take photos of anyone else oysterin'. They don't like it.'

I followed Richard's orders, walking out past a row of freshly painted beach huts to a hammerheaded spit of shingle beyond which skulked a typical estuary vista. Not fog per se but the sea and air still washed-out and drab. The dory came to meet me, drawing up on the shingle with a *crunch*, and we headed out to the little dredger, twenty-five feet of her, shelter-less bar a tiny fo'c'sle the size of a Portaloo. I met Richard's son Bram, the captain, a young man called Sam and sixteen-year-old Bubby, the hand. Later I asked Richard where his son's name came from. 'Abraham Stoker, Bramwell Booth, Bram whoever you want him to be.'

We motored into the ash-white void – in reality just half a mile around the coast. There was less than a twitch of wind but still it was achingly cold. The boat was heading out to a thick patch of rock oysters that Bram had recently spotted. Soon half a dozen boats were in the same vicinity. Bubby waved to a blue one 300 yards away and pointed to other boats at various points of the compass. 'That's me daad an' uncle,' he said, the old Essex accent still very strong. Remarkable, I thought, considering the 1934 observation of a man called Hugh Edward Cranmer-Byng, who decried the 'swamping' of the native accent 'by a polyglot population whose affinities to Essex are actually as remote as Mesopotamia'. Almost all of the crews were related to each other – these were friends and family, not deadly rivals.

'Who are you all hiding the oysters from, Bram? It looks like a very open secret,' I said.

He nodded out towards the mouth of the estuary, whence, he said, 'Other boats – outsiders – might come. It's best to keep it among the Mersea men.' The Mersea men have long been known for their oystering.

We set to work – or at least Bubby and Sam set to work while I nursed a cup of tea in my fast-cooling hands and tried to strike up a conversation with Bram, who also seemed to have few obligations other than to keep the boat in the right place.

An oyster dredge is a big purse made of steel rings. It scrapes the bed and is raised above a shelf at the stern of the boat, where it is opened, releasing the oysters with a clatter like a sudden hailstorm. On the seabed the oysters form into thick muddy clumps of dozens of shells, and after each haul Sam and Bubby chipped away at these with miniature pickaxes, putting the separated oysters into crates and stacking them amidships until the shelf was cleared. It was hard, monotonous work and precluded conversation. And so we carried on all day. Dredge, chisel, crate. Dredge, chisel, crate. On the other boats a single man manoeuvred the vessel, worked the dredge, opened the purse, chiselled the clumps, crated the oysters. It seemed unenviable. And yet, said Bram, 'I wouldn't have it any other ways.'

In sentences broken by long glances out into the grey, Bram described the complexities of the oyster fishery: how his mum owned the boat; Richard owned the purification plant; his sister was his employer; Richard bought the oysters. Bram didn't really understand it, but the fishing was straightforward. 'We just catch 'em. Just go out there and catch 'em.' And that was it.

Later in the day Bubby offered to take me back in the dory. In the dredger he'd been very quiet, but now that Sam and Bram weren't around he became almost talkative. Perhaps he hadn't yet acquired the fisherman's knack of being tight-lipped. He'd left school as soon as he could, he said, and no one complained when he did because he kept getting into trouble. He wanted a living from the sea, and there wasn't much school learning that stood you in good stead on the boats. But, he added, he was bored of oysters – gill-netting, that was the life for him. And he revved up the little outboard, carving deep furrows in the still waters and leaving a straight wake behind.

Radiant Star of Shetland

I inquired what they generally had for breakfast. They answered, 'Piltocks.'

What for dinner? 'Piltocks and cabbage.'

What for supper? 'Piltocks.'

Some of them declared that they had not tasted oatmeal or bread for four months.

Patrick Neill, 'A Tour Through Some of the Islands of
Orkney and Shetland', 1862

On a Kentish beach in the village of Kingsdown a pub called the Zetland Arms graces the gravelly shore. Kingsdown is right where the North Sea becomes the English Channel, and from it you can see, if mist or cloud have deigned not to intervene, the French coast as a thin chalk line laid lightly on the horizon. I like the pub's nod across eight hundred miles to the North Sea's opposite extreme, Shetland, erstwhile Zetland, the northern tip of which shares a latitude with Nanortalik in Greenland. The cliffs of Shetland face the Faroes, Norway, Orkney and Iceland, and though none of these are within eyeshot, there is a sense that it is to this exotic maritime world, long slipped out of the mainstream of Europe's cultural tidal flow, that Shetland belongs.

Its hundred or so islands are scattered like batter-splats, craggy and intricate, slipping and ripping through the grey waters of the seas that embrace them, the Atlantic on the west and its strange orphan, the northern North Sea, to the east. At low tide the archipelago possesses 1,700 miles of indented coast. In places auburn sand sweeps the shore. Elsewhere black cliffs thrust out of a white spuming froth of sea. The islands are deeply notched by clefts, or geos, natural tunnels and caves. Voes and wicks, deep, cold, lake-like bays, elide the distinction between the elements, mirroring the heather-topped hills in their glassy gaze. There are few villages of any size. Settlements as often as not are little more than a quayside, school and kirk, and a shop with a petrol pump which might or might not be open, depending on an obscure and unwritten almanac known only to the islanders.

The Shetlanders have always had need to spread out to work their land with any hope of success. Even now the population inclines towards crofting – a small flock of Shetland sheep (famed for their wool, miserable to eat), a cow or four or a little posse of pigs, or those eponymous waist-high ponies. These living crofts with their white walls and twists of smoke humanise the bare hills. Those that are crumbling, roofless and derelict are reminders of how hard it was to eke an existence here when sea and disease, uncaring lairds and the allure of emigration even to the ends of the earth always threatened to suck the music from the islands. On a summer walking tour, Betjeman wrote, 'All over Shetland one sees ruined crofts, with rushes invading the once tilled strips and kingcups in the garden. "Gone to New Zealand" is a good name for such a scene, because that is where many Shetlanders go, and there are, I am told, two streets in Wellington almost wholly Shetland.'

In winter, the kingcups long dead, the croft corpses are more mournful still, though there's succour for the sheep, sheltering from the wind in the lee of long-deserted byres. But for all that, Shetland is a bright star in the North Sea firmament, drawing in people, money and investment, exhaling music, fish and oil and a distinctively un-insular mindset for an island.

Shetland's apartness is more a sense of distance than difference, underscored by that long ferry journey, ploughing north from Aberdeen over twelve hours and 250 miles of swelling sea. Forty years ago James Nicolson wrote,

> The vague concept of a Shetland way of life is difficult to define. Some people maintain that Shetland is basically a Scottish county with an unusual history now largely forgotten, but there are still fundamental differences between Shetland and Scotland, some difficult to pinpoint. There is no regret in Shetland for the passing of Norse rule, and no antagonism towards Scotland for the mistakes of 300 years ago, but there is still a feeling of separateness that is stressed quietly in innumerable ways. For instance, the Shetlanders consider themselves British rather than Scottish, and refuse to participate in the friendly rivalry between Scots and English.

It all still holds true. In the run-up to the 2014 Independence referendum, many Shetlanders warned that were the Scots to win independence, Edinburgh would attempt to exert greater control over Shetland than Westminster ever has. The Scottish National Party is presented by some as a Soviet-style centralist group bent on bringing the islands into the Holyrood fold, and the Shetland flag (officially adopted by the Shetland Islands Council in 2006) turns St Andrew's saltire through forty-five degrees, pushing the vertical bar off centre to give it a 'Nordic' twist. There was even, in recent memory, a vandalistic craze for scratching out the thistle sign that points the way to Scottish, sites of tourist interest. The SIC (Shetland Islands Council) argued that it should be replaced by a Viking ship, though this was rejected. Perhaps, squaring up to its own aspirations of independence, Scotland fear losing ground. Meanwhile in the Shetlands shortbread, tartans and collectors' sets of miniature whisky bottles are refreshingly absent. A preoccupation with longships and horned-helmet motifs fills the void.

'This bloody Viking obsession – so annoying,' a man called Danus Skene, a columnist for the *Shetland Times*, told me in Lerwick. 'It would be over the top in Denmark or Norway.' Danus though regards Britain as a construction as artificial as the Shetlanders' Viking past, indeed, he says that the consolidation of Scots rule over Shetland and the Act of Union in 1707 were almost simultaneous and part of the same process of the aggrandisement of Britain. Most Shetlanders owe their lineage to the Scots, he points out, and Shetland couldn't survive on its own. In truth, the appetite for an independent Shetland is weak. Still, Shetlanders have sewn together truths and half-truths in the creation of their own myths.

And it *is* a mysterious story. In the eighth and ninth centuries Norsemen settled and displaced or absorbed the mysterious Picts, of whom little is known or left bar their brochs, the squat cylindrical forts or towers that dot the islands, and a handful of twig-like runic scratchings. Whether the Picts were slaughtered, assimilated or fled is uncertain. Quite possibly they metamorphosed over time into the mysterious *trowies* or 'little people' who inhabited the Shetland imagination well into the nineteenth century. Then the Scandinavians imposed their own social geography on the heather-clad hills, lochs and peat bogs, and introduced the Law of the Thing – the custom by which great councils would meet at an appointed place to dispense justice and settle disputes.

For six long centuries Shetland was, indeed, a Nordic country. The spoken language was a variant of Old Norse, Norn, and with it every rock, stone, cliff and tarn was christened (and what strange names – Unst, Muckle Roe, Whalsay, Balta, Fetlar, the Skerries, Hascosay, Uyea, Haaf Gruney, Clubbi Shuns, Tonga Water, Maddle Swankie . . .). The old gods were worshipped, the old tunes danced to, and old songs sung. There being so few trees, the Shetlanders imported boats in flat packs from Scandinavia until even the early nineteenth century. When the islanders began to make their own they did so after the old model, and *yoals* and *sixareens*, their longboat genes so evident, are still to be found on the hard or at the quay of every Shetland harbour.

It took an unpaid debt to drop the gale-knocked Shetland Islands into the lap of the Scots. In 1469 King Christian I of Norway betrothed his daughter Margaret to James III of Scotland, a dynastic manoeuvre intended to shore up his hold on the Danish–Norwegian union, but the dowry was dearer than Christian could pay in one sum and he pledged the Shetlands as security. Margaret died on the voyage to Scotland and the dowry was never paid. Some say British sovereignty is only de facto, and that were the florins handed over (adjusted for inflation) the debt would be redeemed. But long before that non-marriage the Scots were sizing up Shetland, arriving in waves to scratch a living from farms in the bare hills. And then came the Stewart earls – still a byword for despotism in Shetland – and the lairds, who obliged their tenant crofters, benighted in the winter months and scarce able to sleep in the surfeit of summer light, to fish for them in return for the right to work the bare and often blighted land.

The mix is even more cosmopolitan than that. Shetland was firmly on the Hanseatic trade routes, and for generations merchants from Bergen, Bremen and Hamburg brought not only cloth, beer and butter (so difficult to churn from the thin island milk), but links to mainland Europe, which must have seemed so much more real and vital than either Scotland or the notion of

Britain. When the Act of Union was signed in 1707 and tax imposed on the Hanseatic trade, Shetland was plunged into depression, earning assistance from neither Edinburgh nor London. But soon came the Dutch in great numbers, both to fish for the herring that could be hauled from the rich Shetland waters and to trade, setting up booths on the quayside by which exotic luxuries could be exchanged for wool, piltocks and mutton.

'We're no less Dutch than we are Vikings,' said Danus Skene, who is himself only a Shetlander by dint of a tenuous family link.

There are no tourist-thrilling puffins in the dark bone-chilling Shetland winters and no midnight sun. That I heard the footsteps of my own fear softly keeping step with my travels owed nothing to the kind, friendly islanders, but everything to a storm, the early inklings of which made landfall a few hours after I disembarked from the Aberdeen ferry before sunrise in dark and solemn Lerwick. Perhaps bad weather is a traditional greeting for writers. When the medical student Edward Charlton arrived in Lerwick in 1832, his ship was refused berth for six days on account of a rumour that one of its seasick passengers had cholera. That first night, as Edward ministered to the needs of the condemned unfortunate, a 'grit gale' bore down upon the islands, tearing off roofs and scattering the fishing boats.

If the ship snapped her cable as she threatened to, Charlton wondered, would the worse part of shipwreck be the dashing upon the rocks or 'receiving very much rough usage at the hands of the terrified inhabitants, so much [does] the fear of the cholera overpower all other considerations'. In the morning, hungry and pining for dry land, Charlton learned from a Dutch herring buss that sixty Shetland six-oared open boats were missing. One was later discovered, its crew only half alive, washed up on the shore of Norway.

I first caught wind of the storm eavesdropping in a small quayside café with green-painted walls and pinewood booths. 'What kind of storm?' I asked the waitress as she handed me a doorstep sandwich. Blizzards, she said, and very, very strong winds. The roads would be blocked; there'd be 'nae ferries runnin'' and, she added, 'Aye, it'll be the old ones that feel the force of it. It always is . . .'

'De saving grace,' said her colleague, 'is that you'll ha' nae bodder wid fallin' trees. Nae' bodder at all.'

From a hilltop that evening I watched a steady procession of boats seek the safety of the Bressa Sound, and by eight o'clock Scots, Danish and Norwegian fishing boats were all safely hitched to the Lerwick quayside, their crews playing video games and watching DVDs. The supermarkets were busy – there was a near run on milk and booze. Shetland was battening down.

That night I stayed at the croft of a friend an hour's drive from Lerwick, the road unfolding like the pages of a book of magnificent screen-prints, land, sea, lochs and islands overlapping in patterns both profound and simple, but now gouged and scoured by wind-driven snow, the storm's imminent arrival trumpeted by a prolonged lupine moan rolling down the frosted slopes. Even the crows and ravens were struggling.

It wasn't until the early hours that the real guts of the storm seemed to suck up the house and spit it out. Bounded but formless, escalating, compressing, it seemed to steal the air from the room in which I lay shrinking beneath the covers in anticipation of some awful blow. It drew tighter and closer and roared until, for several seconds, the very stones of the croft shook and trembled. And then it passed on, witch-like, into the dark hills. Shetland lost no *sixareens* or *yoals* that night, but power and telephone lines were down, gardens ravaged, and all flights, both from Sumburgh to Aberdeen and the inter-island service from Tingwall, were cancelled, and would be, foreseeably, for days.

I headed north towards the oil terminal at Sullom Voe, at which hundreds of thousands of barrels of ancient forest rendered black, viscous and valuable by the passing of millennia arrive each day by pipeline and tanker. At night the terminal sits beneath the flickering reflection of its lights and flares. By day it is almost invisible, tucked behind barricades and fences.

In the early 1970s the prospect of becoming a hub for the North Sea oil industry hung over Shetland like a cleaver. Islanders feared a descent into hell. The Church of Scotland declared that the Shetlands were being 'called upon to make an unjustified sacrifice to preserve and protect a society with an insatiable appetite for energy'; in a House of Commons debate a Labour MP said that the islands' 'simple gentle people' would be outwitted by the 'land-grabbing Mafia of Edinburgh and Texas'. Oil would bring the curses that it had inflicted on so much of the world: corruption, rentierism, the death of traditional industries, prostitutes and drugs. It would destroy fishing grounds and ancient places. Beaches would become accustomed to the floundering of birds, more tarred than feathered in the wake of the inevitable and catastrophic spills.

Crofters close to areas slated for development feared the compulsory purchase of their smallholdings and fought hard to preserve the tough life they had perfected. Outsiders would come, not for any love of Shetland, but to earn as much money as they could in as short a time as possible. Worse, the islands would be reduced to assets on the books of oil companies in Houston or Dallas. And like the lairds who had had the crofters in their grip for so many hundreds of years, those shiny-suited money men would squeeze and squeeze.

And the islands didn't need the money. By the 1950s and 1960s Shetlanders had become well off compared to their forebears. Many had earned good money whaling in the South Atlantic, and after near-extinction made the industry unprofitable, the Leith-based whaling company Christian Salvesen provided grants for ex-whalers to buy knitting machines. The islands' fishing fleet was making a fortune from the seas around Shetland and a fish-processing industry developed. Oil was seen as surplus to the requirements of a place that had become, like an impecunious aunt rescued by a windfall, accidentally rich.

So, realising that oil needed Shetland more than Shetland needed oil, the local county council led by a Plymouth Brethren accountant called Ian Clark sponsored an act of Parliament, the Zetland County Council Act of 1974, affirming Shetland jurisdiction over the site chosen for the oil terminal, and establishing a reserve fund to smooth the transition once the oil ran dry. After the act was passed it was presented as a David-versus-Goliath success for the islands, though that interpretation isn't universally shared: in 'Natural Causes, Essays in Ecological Marxism', for example, the writer James O'Connor describes it as a cover myth for 'the last of Britain's imperialist ventures' and maintains that many decisions are made directly 'by the British civil service and imposed on the people of Shetland on the grounds that they are merely technical-administrative matters and not political questions at all'.

Yet the oil has enabled Shetlanders to enjoy at least parity in living standards with much of the rest of the country, while the outflow of young adults has been stemmed by new jobs and secondary industries. Oil money has allowed Shetlanders a breathing space to appreciate their own talent for music. And that there are more swimming pools per person on Shetland than anywhere else in Europe is, thanks to an exuberant, possibly misplaced council initiative, all on account of oil.

A few miles along the cusp of the brooding Voe sprawls the settlement of Brae, a kind of loose conglomeration of huts, cabins and accommodation blocks. It has the appearance and charm of a modern-day gold town. Here live the oil men (and they are men), shipped in to heft, weld and grind, or mustering before being helicoptered out to the rigs.

I paused before crossing the forecourt of the Nordern Lights. The wind was gusting like a howling Cerberus keeping me at bay (in cahoots with the slippery ground), violently flinging the door back on its hinges each time it was opened. This was an unfamiliar Britain, where brute force and the elements still waged a daily war. And I was afraid of being an outsider among outsiders – the only person in the pub whose reason for being there was not legitimised by the contribution of physical labour.

In a brief moment of respite I dashed across, seized the door, pulled it hard and made it into the space between the outer and inner doors. Two men were huddled beneath a NO SMOKING sign, smoking. One, a giant, acknowledged my arrival with a courteous nod. The other, a short stoat-like boy-man, looked down at my hands and said, 'Look at that. Leather gloves! Who the hell are you?'

I told him about the book I was writing.

'Yes, but what's it *about*? The North Sea's a big place. It's got to have something in the title hasn't it? Something like *The North Sea: . . .*'

'*Cold Wet Cunt*?' the giant suggested.

'Or maybe *Force for Good and Ill*?'

'I haven't quite clinched it yet,' I said.

When two more men arrived for a smoke the subject was opened to the floor. *Mother of All Seas* was suggested and *Travels at the Edge of Despair*.

The tiny vestibule fumigated comprehensively, we went through the inner doors into the pub. The giant headed to a corner table at which some men were singing a song about being made to feel like a natural woman in a gruff-edged falsetto. Otherwise, excluding the barmaid this was a very masculine pub. Loud, rumbustious, brightly lit.

Danny, the shorter man, offered to buy me a drink because 'you're an author and authors are poor. Whereas me, I'm fackin' loaded.'

We stood at the bar and tried to speak. Periodically a man in his mid-twenties with short ginger hair and a beard put his arm around Danny and chanted, 'Da-a-anny! Dan-ny. Dan-ny,' before being cajoled back to the dartboard to take his throw.

Danny was apologetic. 'Oi. Leave it, Brian – this man's a fackin' author!'

Brian leaned close in to me and gave me a drunken comedy kiss.

Danny's life story tumbled out like an overdue confession. His accent was southern – London even – though he had been born in Norwich. He was a civil engineer at the Centrica gasworks five miles from Brae and responsible for all the drainage issues as the plant expanded in size. 'My job, Tom, is to fackin' take a bloody shafting from the management every time something goes tits up in this fackin' dump!' He mimed being given a shafting, one hand on the bar, the other on his pint, posterior presented submissively to his imaginary tormentor.

Danny was only twenty-six. He had had an unhappy childhood and a violent father, but pushed himself through an engineering course and found he was very good at it. He'd also been to the House of Commons – and sat on the terrace – having been elected a member of the Youth Parliament when he was a teenager. But he'd been a bit of a flash Harry, numbing early memories with prostitutes and cocaine. All the Soho tarts loved him but only on account of his cash and coke.

He hated it up here. Waiting for him in a 'shitty estate near Norwich' he had a wife and kid. He worried about the effect that being apart for weeks at a time might have on his family life, but at least he was away from the coke and the tarts, and they paid him two grand a week. His ambition was to get out of the estate, 'where half my fackin' neighbours don't even know what a day's work looks like and just hang out knocking each other up and waiting for their benefits'. When he made some proper money, he was going to get a decent house and move up the property ladder. 'I'm going to have three houses before I'm forty,' he said.

Danny surveyed the pub with a kind of fond pity. In the morning, if the weather didn't stop work, he'd be 'bossing loads of these guys around'. The ginger beard stuck his head into our conversation again, made monkey noises and pushed a shot glass full of spirits sunk into a pint glass of Tennent's in front of Danny, who raised it to his mouth and made it all disappear with a gurgle. He wiped his lips, exhaled noxiously and told me it was my turn to buy him a drink. Then he nearly doubled up, forearms clutched over his stomach. 'Fack me!' he said. 'I'm done for. See you later, mate. I'm going back to die.' And he headed out, like a spectral cripple, into the screaming night.

I had been afraid of this bar, keenly aware of imagined differences between myself and men driven by circumstance, lack of opportunity and government policy to seek a living in the northernmost tip of the United kingdom. Even after forty years of extraction, Sullom Voe remains Britain's Klondike, a place where money is made not through the regurgitation of fads and fancies or the manipulation of markets but by pitting brawn against the earth.

Here was a potpourri of dialects – Geordie, Scots, London, Dutch – but none local, for the possessors of those had real homes to go to of an evening. Perhaps half of the men present were waiting for the storm to pass; when it had they'd fly out to the rigs on a service helicopter. Their moods were largely determined by the terms of their contracts. Some were being paid a full daily rate for lounging around and some paid nothing at all.

An older man, perhaps in his late fifties, had been listening in to my conversation with Danny, whom he hadn't met before but in whom he recognised the ambitions of an earlier version of himself. Alan was from Sunderland, had served an apprenticeship in a shipyard and had anticipated leading the life his father had led – secure, working his way up to a skilled and well-paid job with no expectation that he'd ever have to move far from where he was born.

When the Tyneside yards closed, he searched out whatever opportunities he could find. First it was Sellafield and then it was the North Sea – 'Not on the rigs, mind. You've gotta be in the right clique to get a job on the rigs. If you ain't in a clique you'll never get on. And who'd want to? You'd go out of your fookin' mind with the boredom an' all. They literally befriend seagulls on the rigs, did you know that?'

He turned to a big ex-rigger from Grangemouth for corroboration, which was given. 'You give it a wee bit of y' grub every day, and it comes back when it knows the others aren't looking. Mine was called Sammy. It isn't a terribly original or imaginative name for a seagull, is it? But you do, you know, go a bit blank out on the rigs.'

Now Alan was a site inspector, a responsible and relatively comfortable job, much of it spent in an office. But the prolonged absences had destroyed his marriage. He described the heartache of having to cope with family crises by telephone, the helplessness of it. 'But there's nothing in Sunderland; I hadn't a choice.' Alan had also once believed that two decades of graft, and he'd be able to retire with a property portfolio. But his wife had kept the house after the divorce, and now lived in it with another man while he was up in Sullom saving for another. 'It's not a great deal to show for a near lifetime of work, is it?'

On the ferry heading up to Shetland I'd shared a cabin with a man called John-James Jameson. John-James was about the same age as Danny but from an old Shetland fishing family. It was natural for him to go into the oil business; that's what his generation of Shetlanders did once they were of an age to look for work. He'd used the skills he'd acquired to work around the world, spending most of his time in South Korea, where his girlfriend lived, but taking contracts in Mexico, Brazil, Philippines – anywhere there were offshore projects. 'It's been great for Shetland and for me,' he said, 'but I pity some of the blokes heading up to try and make their fortunes in Shetland. No family life. Living in those apartments or floating hotels. There's nothing for them to do but work and drink.'

Pre-North Sea oil, the argument had always run that regardless of any other obstacles to an independent Scotland, the bottom line was that Scotland simply couldn't afford to be free – her economic dependence on England gave Westminster its mandate. The discovery of oil threatened to turn that state of affairs on its head and had given a massive fillip to the nationalist movement, which had returned seven MPs to Parliament in 1973 largely on the back of a campaign headlined, 'It's Scotland's Oil.'

'The prime minister [Harold Wilson] has asked me to put two thoughts to you,' his private secretary wrote to the Department of Energy in October 1974.

> It may be that the first landing of North Sea Oil in bulk should be the occasion of some kind of official celebration, perhaps even with Royalty present. Would the secretary of state give some thought to this? [And] if the first tankerload of North Sea Oil comes direct to the Thames, the Scottish National Party is bound to use it as an occasion for protesting that this demonstrates all that they have

been complaining about: the diversion of Scotland's oil to England's pockets. Would it not be better if this first tankerload was unloaded at Grangemouth?

Wilson, aware both of the tenuousness of his own position in crisis-torn Britain and of the nationalists' growing hold on Scotland's political affections, had a dilemma. The oil had been produced in the Argyll field in Scottish waters, but the Grangemouth oil refinery at Falkirk on the Scottish coast, the facility closest to the field, was not equipped to receive crude. A second Scottish refinery at Finnart was considerably further away and would necessitate an extra two or three days' sailing and lost production time. The most cost-effective solution was to land the oil at a refinery in the Thames estuary, but this would 'in presentational terms [be] in the very least clumsy and give the SNP a field day – Scotland's oil going straight to London', according to the prime minister's private secretary Joe Haines.

Even were the oil companies and operators prepared to do so, steaming the oil around to the west-coast refinery at Finnart would, it was argued by the secretary of state for energy, be 'a transparent public relations device, and probably unproductive', given that long-term arrangements for the landing of oil from the Argyll field to Scotland were 'not practicable'. In the event, it was brought ashore at Cruden Bay in Aberdeenshire.

Civil servants pointed out that nationalist claims that Scotland would be 'better off economically' were based on dodgy figures and dubious statistics, but the importance of North Sea oil was that it had raised the issue of Scottish independence in a more acute form than at any other time since the Act of Union was passed. The Scots were not Callaghan's only headache. The oil would bring in valuable revenue, but Britain was so heavily in debt that the proceeds of the bonanza were mortgaged well in advance. The

1979 election of Margaret Thatcher in effect quelled the Scots rebellion, or suppressed it for a few decades while the nationalists mustered their forces. But in the run-up to the referendum on Scottish independence in 2014, North Sea oil, harvested from deep beneath the seabed in ever greater quantities and by more ingenious means, was critical to the Scottish Nationalist Party's argument that it would be able to afford to dissolve the Union.

In the earliest days of the oil boom the end of the bonanza was already being anticipated. The great Scottish writer Eric Linklater predicted in the late 1960s: 'Someday the oil will stop flowing and the isles will be left with the land and the sea and the old indigenous industries that have sustained them so long.' That remains true, but contrary to rumours of the industry's demise a combination of new discoveries and improved production technology suggest that the oil (and gas) will continue to flow for at least a further three or four decades. Money continues to pour into the industry. At the end of December 2013 a company called EnQuest signed a deal to invest £4 billion into an oil field called Kraken 70 miles off Shetland said to contain 140 million barrels of oil, and though local council spending is being reined in, Shetland lives will continue to be padded by oil profits.

There has however been a heavy human cost. In 1988 a North Sea production platform, Piper Alpha, exploded killing 167 men. It was the first major catastrophe in the industry and threw a painful spotlight on working practices on the rigs. Like the *Herald of Free Enterprise* ferry sinking in Zeebrugge with the loss of 193 lives, many regarded Piper Alpha as emblematic of the immorality of capitalism, of putting profits before people.

Well into the early twentieth century the lives of Shetlanders were heavily dependent on the sea. It wasn't a total reliance; from their crofts they scratched a barley-like crop called *bere*, from which they'd make bannocks, or scones, and a meagre bread. The scrawny Shetland sheep yielded fine wool and poor meat, but sufficient to salt and dry and turn into *reekit* mutton, still a Shetland staple, something like *confit de canard* and served with potatoes in broth and bannocks. Yet it was from the sea that they had come. It surrounded them; each day they negotiated their identity and survival with it, and from it there came an apparently self-replenishing abundance of fish, even close in to shore. James Nicolson noted that the 'most important of these was the saithe, especially the young fish, called up to two years old sillocks, and between two and four years old, piltocks. The flesh was dark and less inviting than that of other species, but it was the abundance of the shoals . . . that made them so important.'

One of the great merits of the piltock was that women could catch them in the coves with hand-pulled seine nets at any time of the year. In 1806 the traveller Patrick Neill visited some crofters on Shetland, recalling later, 'I inquired what they generally had for breakfast. They answered, "Piltocks."

'What for dinner? "Piltocks and cabbage."

'What for supper? "Piltocks."

'Some of them declared that they had not tasted oatmeal or bread for four months.'

Old Shetlanders did enjoy other gastronomic delights. At around the same time Edward Charlton arrived at a lodge or

buith to enjoy a true Shetland dinner. Some fresh tusk [haddock] had been brought in this morning and while the body of the fish was boiled the head was converted into 'ane crappit head', a savoury Shetland dish, prepared by stuffing that part with oatmeal and toasting it with abundance of butter before the fire. The liver too was chopped up into small pieces, and by a peculiar process dressed much to my taste, constituting another Shetland dish, the 'Livered Moggie'.

And if times were really hard, there was always a shag to be had, edible after a long soak in spring water to remove some of its gamey saltiness. Seals sometimes made it onto the menu, but were regarded with some ambivalence, on account of their mermaid-ish good looks and soulful eyes, and this often saved them from the pot.

Quite when Norn died out is uncertain. In the late 1700s the traveller George Low met a man who could recite the Lord's Prayer in Norn, and also fragments of a song that its singer couldn't understand. In the 1850s a Faroese philologist, Jacob Jacobsen, recorded some 50,000 Norse words in common currency in the Shetlands, but most were place names, and the inhabitants had lost the meaning of them. In the 1970s researcher John Graham could find only a fraction of these again. There's a consensus that the Shetland dialect includes a few Norn words, but it is in reality no less a variation of English than is Scots.

Place names apart, Norn survived longest in the employment of seafarers, not only to describe its states, but also its animal inhabitants, mythical and real. And, just as among the Hessle Road fishermen, the language of the sea provided alternatives to land words that brought bad luck used away from land, especially when out at the *haaf* (fishing grounds) – fishing from six-oared open boats (*sixareens*) sometimes up to forty miles from shore, a wildly dangerous practice even by the standards of the time. It's possible that there's a note of rebellion in this stubborn adherence to the tongue of the Vikings. One writer suggested that 'it is as if freed from the shackles of the land with all its restrictions and subservience to the Scots crown, the fishermen were at liberty to speak the language of their hearts'.

And what words. *Dekk* or *festo* was the sea bottom and *djup* the sea. *Gro*, *gula* and *gritten* were wind words in order of increasing strength. *Glub* referred to the appetite, either of man or fish – the former might lack it through seasickness, the latter might be presumed to if they failed to bite at the long line. *Mareel* was the phosphorescence on the sea, *murkavi* a blinding snowstorm and the *mirrie dancers* the Northern Lights.

It is a language both practical and poetic, a simple mirror to both the beauty and the exigencies of a hard but subtle life. *Forso* were half-boiled chewed limpets spat out on the surface of the sea to lure fish. The sands of the beach between the shore and the ebb were *sjusamillabakka*, a usefully enigmatic reply to a question as to where one might have come across a valuable supply of driftwood.

And if the Shetland bestiary is a little spare in species, it is rich in the means of describing them. For the otter alone there are half a dozen monikers: a *dratsi* is 'one that walks heavily', a *drillaskovi* 'one that drags its tail'. Or it could be a *lotate*, which walks slowly and heavily. The seal, out of the skin of which the Shetlanders once made *rivlins* – shoes – could be a *horin* – 'a hairy one', or a *kogi* – 'a peeping one'. And farmers loved the *skooie*, or skua, because he scared away the *kliksi* – eagle – which fed upon their lambs.

The favourite old Shetland phrase of Elizabeth Morewood, 'Artist, Singer and Norwegian Speaker', according to her card, is *flugga mucka*, meaning to beat one's arms around the chest to warm oneself. The old folk on the Atlantic coast of Norway use it still, she said. 'It means to shake out your wings like a cormorant.' In the late 1940s Elizabeth sang for the great ethnomusicologist Alan Lomax, pulled out of a crowd for the strength and delicacy of her voice. Ever since early adulthood she has taught and sung, while acknowledging that it is a difficult thing to define.

Shetlanders love music, and the fiddle, which can crank up a dance in a tiny croft or in the cabin of a whaler, is the instrument of choice. In 1743 a violinist called Friedemann Von Steigl jumped ship on Shetland's most northerly isle – Unst – from a merchantman and never left. Apparently he sparked the fiddle craze, which has yet to die down. Clues as to what came before the fiddle are very scant. There are reports of a two-stringed dulcimer known as a *gue* played with a bow, a reconstruction of which resides in the Shetland Museum, but like the stuffed 'dodo' in the Ashmolean it is largely based on conjecture. In the 1920s a Swedish academic scoured Shetland and beyond for traces of the *gue*, but an original has yet to surface. Neither has evidence that those traditional Gaelic instruments the bagpipe and the harp ever enjoyed any kind of currency at all. And, said Elizabeth, finding music that predates the post-Norse influx of Scots settlers, Dutch fishermen and German traders is very difficult too.

Elizabeth has been a teacher for much of her long life. Her hair is immaculate, her skin and eyes possess a kind of morning clarity and she had driven ten miles to meet me in formidable weather at formidable speed. I had been told she was indomitable.

'Which song,' I asked her, 'would you say was the oldest?'

'We-e-ell,' she said, 'it would have to be the "Unst Boat Song".'

And she sang, the melody seeming to float and curl like a silk ribbon falling in a breeze.

> Starka virna vestalie
> O-ba-dee-a, o-ba-dee-a
> Starka virna vestalie
> O-ba-dee-a monye
> Stal, stoi-ta stonga raero
> Whit saes du, da bunshka baero?
> Whit saes du, da bunshka baero?

Litra maevee drenghie

Starka virna vestalie

O-ba-dee-a, o-ba-dee-a

Starka virna vestalie

O-ba-dee-a monye

Sanya papa wara

O-ba-dee-a, o-ba-dee-a

Sanya papa wara

O-ba-dee-a monye

Starka virna vestalie

O-ba-dee-a, o-ba-dee-a

Starka virna vestalie

O-ba-dee-a monye

Many of the words, she says, are so ancient that they cannot be readily understood, but coincide with pieces of Old Norse long unspoken in Shetland.

Some days later I met Charlie Simpson at Cunningsburgh, nearly at the southern tip of Shetland. ('Are you seeing Charlie?' Elizabeth asked me. 'A dear, *peerie* man! I'd poosh him along in his pooshchair when he were a bairn!') He is retired now, a slight man with an enormous white beard, who plays music, writes books about Shetland and is an inveterate contributor to the *Shetland Times*.

'Was it true, what Elizabeth said about the pushchair?' I asked Charlie.

'Aye,' he said, *sans* smile. 'It's true enough.'

We spoke for hours in his little book-lined study – about fishing, *gues*, the Norwegian influence on Shetland aquaculture, about what would have happened to Shetland had oil never been discovered and most of all about music. And we talked about Tom Anderson, an insurance collector, fiddler, music teacher and composer who died in 1991, but hovers like a giant over Shetland for his rediscovery of its music.

Charlie's deep involvement in Shetland life was brought home by the number of telephone calls he received during our conversation, which he answered with varying degrees of broadness in his accent. 'Never retire. Never retire. Not if you want to have any time to y'self.'

Yes, said Charlie, it was possible to talk about a distinct Shetland music. But, he suggested, it wasn't so much that there was a pure strain trickling as that over time a portfolio of experiences had intermingled uniquely. Shetlanders had travelled so widely – on the whaling ships down to South Georgia and the Antarctic and up to Greenland – been press-ganged into the Royal Navy, caroused with Dutch fishermen. All of these experiences were present somewhere.

We leafed through books of Shetland songs. 'Now,' he said, 'take a look at this. The tradition was that this song was handed down through time by the *trowies*, the little people – perhaps a folk memory of the elusive Picts or perhaps stranger still. Who knows? But when a German academic came to Shetland some time ago he heard the tune and recognised it right away. "That," he said, "was the most popular dance tune in Hamburg throughout the 1860s." So there you are. You never know where you are with what's "authentic" when identity is concerned.'

I mustn't, Charlie said as I said goodbye, leave Shetland without going out on a fishing vessel. 'I'm heading out on the *Radiant Star* tomorrow.' He reassured me that that was a good boat, that I'd be fine. Charlie knew every boat and skipper on the island, having written a book about them.

To my bemusement, Victor Laurenson said he had never heard of a piltock, though it might have been that I mispronounced it. Victor's thick dialect-laced speech had led me to believe that he was old when we spoke on the telephone, but he was only forty-seven. On giving directions to his village of Hamnavoe on the island of West Burra he had to stop several times and repeat things for me as I took down his instructions. Victor skippers the *Radiant Star*, a twenty-three-metre seine-netter built for him by Parkol Marine in Whitby. When Victor's wife Pauline smashed a bottle of champagne over her bows in 2007, a 150 people were at the naming ceremony, and a Shetland band played reels.

There were Laurensons lost in the terrible Delting tragedy, when twenty-two men, crews of a fleet of *foureens* – four-oared boats – fishing at the *haaf* on a day in July 1900, drowned, the boats scattered and sunk by a sudden snowstorm. The crofts of the destitute widows and families still weigh sorrowfully upon the hills around the village of Mossbank. And Victor's father, who lives in an old whitewashed house by the quay, once chased the silver darlings down to Lowestoft and Yarmouth every summer.

The road to Hamnavoe slewed along blue-blanched valley sides, past snow-capped drywalls, croft ruins, rose to a point above Scalloway, presenting the old capital, its castle and the sea with its wishing-pond wonder and platters of islands unfolding like the denouement of a well-worn, well-told tale, and then descended past and through the town, over a bridge and up again into the hills, where it plateaued and gently alighted by the sea.

'Would you like to go fishing tomorrow?' asked Victor.

I sipped my tea and watched the long fetch of the waves, so elegantly murderous as they flung themselves upon the rocks beneath snow-mantled islands luminous against a growling sky. 'Absolutely not,' I said. But that evening I slipped aboard with a Chinese takeaway, treading carefully on the frozen quayside, afraid that I or my steaming foil container might fall and be crushed between the gunwale and the dock as I boarded the crimson-

painted, ice-trimmed *Radiant Star*, which, when I woke in my
bunk at six, had slipped out of Scalloway and was steaming south
towards the fishing grounds. Not an inch of sun, but stars still
sparkled brightly and the breeze was only the echo of a memory
of earlier gales.

This time the previous year I had been out on a boat, Andrew
French's *Valkyrie* of Mersea, to take the winter herring from the
Blackwater. Andrew (Bubby's granddad) used a gill net, like a
large badminton net suspended in the river, into which the
herring swam and became enmeshed. We set the nets, drank tea
in the tiny wheelhouse and came back to retrieve them. The
Valkyrie was a small boat, perhaps eight metres only, open save for
a cabin-like wheelhouse – a muddle of stained and chipped mugs
and old newspapers, large enough to keep two men out of the
cold, but no more. By lunchtime, the deck was filled with as
many mucusy blue and silver fish, some pristine, others gashed
and ripped at the gills, as it could be without overflowing, and
we headed back to box them up for Billingsgate, climbing onto
the quayside sequinned with fish scales like tiny, rain-wetted
petals of blossom.

The *Radiant Star* was a different beast to the *Valkyrie*, a proper
sea boat, her deckhouse saloon-like and comfortable and reassuring.
Below decks, in the galley, a cupboard was stuffed with a year's
worth of biscuits; there was a bulging fridge, and the wall was
adorned with a tasteful, no nipples, saucy calendar and a giant
television upon which I had the night before we chugged out of
port watched coverage of the funeral of Nelson Mandela.

Radiant Star wasn't as enormous as the boat I'd seen at Carstensens,
only around a tenth of the very biggest, and Victor had hinted that
to build she had cost in the region of two or three million pounds.
But she was fast, easy to work and safe, the hold big enough for
five days' fishing. Victor's dad, by contrast, only recently retired,

had started work on the old herring boats, exposed to the weather almost for the duration of the voyage.

'It must have been hell,' I said, solemnly. We were reclining in the skipper and mate's barbershop chairs staring out of the raked windscreens at the black water. The electronic chart, fish finder and other nautical toys cast a soft ambient glow, and the fear I had felt at the prospect of this trip had long departed.

'Oh no-o-o. Not at all! Imagine. Sixteen year old and stuck on Shetland all your life! How many other opportunities were there to see the world, ken? It was a great life, especially in the summer – the great sail down to the Suffolk coast, to Yarmouth and Lowestoft, meeting new pipple an' all. I think he *lo-o-o-ved* it.'

Now the darkness was being sucked away. Hamnavoe and Scalloway lay to the north. The Sumburgh Light pinpricked the dawn to the east. Far away in the west Foula sat on the horizon like the bright line of a chisel's edge. Victor told me about the *meirs*, the ancient way of navigating the inland waters around Shetland, and locating the *haafs* by giving names to visible features, lining them up and triangulating. It made sense, he pointed out, not to share the names; that way the grounds could stay secret.

A seine net grazes the sea floor, in comparison to a trawl net, which scours it, dragged by a pair of two-kilometre cables. The boat first runs out one cable, then the net, then the second cable, joins the cables together to create a long isosceles triangle and winches them in. For no reason that is clearly understood, the cables frighten the fish into the net, although they have the opportunity to swim free.

On the *Radiant Star* that morning, once the net had been drawn in, it was raised above the deck by a small derrick, and for a while the fish were suspended in green mesh while the crew got the measure of the shot's success. Victor gave a contented nod. By now an army of gulls was flanking and following, ten thousand or more wing tips calibrated to every turn of the *Radiant Star*, but so almost-static that they could have been flying through aspic. There were mollies – kittiwakes – greater black-backed gulls, a solan goose or two, each bird a keen-eyed particle in a miasmic cloud of grey and white feathers, keeping the beat, keeping time with the rise and fall of the boat.

Tope, small sharks, somehow found their way to the edge of the bulge, their puppyish heads squeezing out of the mesh. Victor pulled these and other chaff out and flung them into the sea, the birds swooping and jabbing, the fish desperate to wriggle back to the depths but with their swim bladders distended and burst, already done for. Then the net opened, and its contents with a long slippery thud, gallows-grim, fell into the chute with an incontrovertible finality while I stared down from above with the fascination of a child.

In the bright-lit hold, whitewashed, throbbing with the deafening rumble of the ship's engine, floor swilling with seawater, the fate of the fish reached its terrible conclusion. They came up a conveyor belt, those that still had the strength wriggling back into the slimy mass of each other, like kittens hiding from the cold. The herring were remarkable by their sameness, but here were quivering, whiskered, fat-bellied haddock and cod a yard long, a giant-mawed tiny-sharp-toothed monkfish, gurnard, an octopus the size of a grapefruit, a crab, saithe . . . Sometimes the little fish had fallen into the mouths of the larger.

What, I wondered, did those glistening, unblinking eyes make of the monstrousness of it all? With what kind of noise – were they able – would the mute mouths register their displeasure at being plucked from the sea into a wholly unknown element, thrust among each other, bruised, suffocated and drawn?

On one side of the conveyor belt stood the heavy-weather-suited crew, exhausted from the final stages of the shot and weary-eyed. Working quickly like fruit pickers, one gloved hand grabbed a fish and the other ripped a knife through its belly from gills to sternum, reached inside the cavity and yanked out everything that had made it vital, leaving only its carcass. By rights I should have been revolted, but it was the men who had my pity. The unremitting relentlessness of it all – grab, slice, eviscerate – and then when the fish were done and the floor sluiced of their autumn-berry blood, a cup of tea, a slice of the fudge that the wife of one of the crew had made, before preparing for the next shot.

As the day matured, the wisps of cloud thickened like phlegm. Gone were Fair Isle, Foula and Sumburgh. Gone also was my fascination with the fish. But Victor was very pleased. The weather having been so atrocious, this was the first day that the *Radiant Star* had fished in over three weeks. Better still, on account of the weather, the producers' association that manages catch allowances had distributed extra quota for cod, fishing for which is tightly controlled in the North Sea.

'You canna *not* catch de cod when you're fishing for de haddock because they swim in de same shoal. Ordinarily, we'd be having to throw all de cod away on account of de fact that we'd be above de quota.' Victor pronounced the first consonant in 'fishing' as 'vie' with a very hard v. His 'fishing' half-rhymed with 'Viking'.

I sipped my tea.

'That would ha' meant throwin' away more than half de day's catch! Discarding it! Food for de gulls, because none of it would ha' survived. De bird people should be thankin' us.'

Earlier Larry – whose wife had made the fudge – had shown me the catch book, recording what they'd landed, its value, weather conditions, fishing grounds and incidents, some at Victor's expense, like the time he had to turn back because a lad's night out the day before had rendered him incapable of anything, and the day Victor had leaped out of the wheelhouse to help with a haul only to find that he'd forgotten to put his sea boots on and was standing on the sodden deck in a gale wearing only his socks. The sums were quite remarkable, a mediocre day's catch worth nine or ten thousand pounds and a good catch closer to fifteen, although the costs of running a commercial fishing boat – not only fuel, upkeep, insurance, berthing fees, but servicing the loan to buy it – are considerable. Even so, as Victor pointed out, many of the fishermen who had sold their quotas and decommissioned their boats in the late 1980s and 90s were kicking themselves now because the Shetland waters, rich in plankton and made fecund by the swirling of currents, are full of fish, if not quite as many as there have ever been. In the late 1960s Shetland was at the epicentre of a Gadidae explosion – Gadidae being the genus to which cod and haddock belong – when, because of a peculiar and not yet fully understood confluence of tides, temperature and the movement of the Gulf Stream, numbers of prime eating fish burgeoned.

It was just as Jacob Hammer had said, after a fashion, in Skagen: the science of predicting fish numbers is sophisticated but imprecise, like shining a light into the gloom.

A boom also has its perils, turning all too easily into a glut, making prices plummet and consigning much of the catch to animal feed or, more ironically still, fishmeal to feed to farmed salmon. The regulation of fishing is fiendishly difficult and, given the conflicting agendas of environmental groups, commercial fishing lobbies, national governments, the European Union and scientists, a subject on which consensus is impossible to reach.

Victor pointed out that the Shetland fishermen had strong incentives to manage their own fisheries well. They had been fishing these waters since they arrived on the islands, and almost all the boats – at least in the whitefish fleet catching cod and haddock – were either family owned or, as in the case of the *Radiant Star*, belonged to the crew. There was a good living to be made out of it, as long as the quotas were reasonable. 'Shetland fishermen respect de resources, ken? Not like the Scots down in Fraserburgh and Peterhead. Dey're rap-a-cious bastards.'

Ironically, said Victor, winter fishing is easier. There's only enough light for four shots, and staying out to sea overnight is ludicrous. In the summer, when the sun rises above the horizon almost before it disappears, the boats will stay out for the best part of a week, shooting the nets maybe seven or eight times each day.

Returning with the net stowed and fish washed and packed down, Victor settled back into his captain's chair; the crew shed their oilskins, and I had a sense of the pleasure of returning with a full hunting bag.

There were phone calls to make and receive. First Victor's da – 'He's no' at the fishing any more, but he takes a very *active* interest in de boat' – and the other trawlers heading back to Scalloway. When he spoke in dialect, I couldn't understand Victor, but could recognise that he was downplaying success. I thought of the notion of *sjusamillabakka*. Periodically Victor glanced over and winked, indicating that what he had just told the skipper of the *Cormorant* was only half true. 'We're all de be-e-estest o' friends, but we tell each other wee half-lies – it's a part of the game of de fishing,' he said.

Soon the Scalloway light came into view. Victor's wife rang to ask what time he'd back and what he wanted for his tea. 'Not fish!' he said, and though it was now raining hard, the sea remained fair, and the *Radiant Star* scampered over the chop. On the television the news of Nelson Mandela's death began to ebb, and the flickering screen showed images of the terrible damage done across the east coast of England by the ravaging sea, upon and across which we rode in the direction of home.

'I feel for dose poor pipple down in de south,' said Victor, 'I really do.' And, feeling light and buoyant in my pilot's chair, so did I.

New Sea, New Chapters

I, last least voice of her voices
Give thanks that were mute in me long
To the soul in my soul that rejoices
For the song that is over my song
Time gives what he gains for the giving
Or takes for his tribute of me;
My dreams to the wind everliving
My song to the sea.

Algernon Charles Swinburne, 'By the North Sea'

Riding out the tail end of that storm on the *Radiant Star* in Shetland's subarctic latitudes we were safe from the tidal surge sucking along the east coast of Britain. News reports came in of the Thames Barrier literally but slowly swinging into action to save the capital, of flooded homes in Boston, Lincolnshire, stranded seal pups at Donna Nook and the evacuation of thousands of people, especially from low-lying towns such as Canvey, where six decades ago such damage had been inflicted.

I received an email from Uwe, my teacher friend on the Hallig of Hooge. It showed his Warft entirely surrounded by swirling green sea. 'It has been difficult,' he said, 'but we are all OK.'

The surge had been powerful, reproving and disruptive but not cataclysmic – a hard-hitting feint. The real body blow came later, not to the North Sea coast but to the west and south: a battery of sea-spitting, roof-ripping storms, barrelling, broadsiding . . . Soaring, tumbling towers of spray pummelled and exploded against quaysides, boulders and harbour walls, transfixing the thrill seekers who came as close – or too close – as they could to something that for once deserved to be described as awesome. Of a sudden the transformative powers of the elements were revealing themselves in ways that took a modern double-glazed nation wholly by surprise.

Climatic caprice also showed talent for mischief-making. Somerset's low-lying Levels were lost beneath flood waters, and a suite of government agencies descended to carp and finger-point, each flattering the other that it was responsible for the debacle. A seaside railway that had threaded its way along the Devon coast for a hundred years was left looking like the broken toy of a petulant child-god. Divine retribution was indeed invoked as the cause of the misery by a county councillor who blamed the British prime minister's support of same-sex marriage for the nation's woes. Insane it may have seemed to many, but the scenes of destruction, tame by the standards of even the mildest Asian tsunami or Middle East earthquake, were sufficiently Old Testament for *somebody* to make that connection.

Even for city dwellers, scarcely touched by the storms save that it tickled them to watch the drama through office windows and listen to the weather's nocturnal swirling and gurgitation, Britain was like a great barque floundering in a mountainous sea, anticipating the final lurch or the tumbling of a mast.

The weather takes, but it also gives. At Happisburgh in Norfolk soft cliffs crumbled to unveil in a stratum of sand the footprints of a small family group of pre-human beings. The prints were 850,000 – perhaps even a million – years old, their humanity strangely amplified by their antiquity. Easy and unchoreographed, they implied the presence of a foraging party – maybe gathering shellfish, seaweed or pretty stones. And in places on the coast of Wales freakish low tides pulled back to reveal the petrified stumps of oak and pine trees studded in the sand – more of the Noah's Woods that had so intrigued Clement Reid.

History never repeats itself, but patterns and ironies emerge over the course of time. Much of the farmland in the east of England reclaimed from the sea by the brawn and ingenuity of the Dutch in the seventeenth century is now worked by the industry of migrants from the new accession states of the European Union. As before, these outsiders are resented by those shamed by their perspicacity and ability to thrive despite pitiable wages and lack of foreign language skills. Support for the nationalist UKIP party is particularly high in towns like Boston, not the US city which flourished on its early diet of Irish immigrants, but the fading Fenland port which in 2011 *Daily Mail* columnist Peter Hitchens rechristened Lincolngrad on account of its being 'riven by mass immigration in its hardest and most uncompromising form'.

Who can honestly disapprove of the poor person from Lisbon, Riga or Bucharest, with a family to house and feed, tempted to uproot his or her life by the promise of wages unthinkable at home . . . [and yet who] can blame the people of this ancient place, nervous, baffled and disquieted by the sudden arrival of hundreds of people who do not speak English, who are ignorant of our customs, who move among us like interplanetary visitors, so cut off that they could not even understand a shout of 'Help!' let alone laugh at our jokes?

Even Hitchens can't quite bear to follow through on what begins as a rant, conceding by the end of his article that the high street (West Street, now nicknamed East Street) boasts half a dozen Polish, Russian and Baltic food shops – and a Latvian patisserie – and that had the migrants not set up home here 'these places would be boarded up, or charity shops'. But he qualifies the admission: 'What consolation is that to born-and-bred Bostonians who see parts of their home town transformed into a foreign zone?' The distinction between foreign and not-foreign remains as transient as it was when the Jutes arrived on the shores of Kent or the Jews of Berlin on the playground beaches of Borkum.

In the northern North Sea the national question was becoming acute as the writing of this book drew to a close. There are, say the analysts, another three or four billion barrels of oil yet to be recovered from British waters, and these could be worth £200 billion to the economy of what is still the United Kingdom. The British government says that only by sharing the custodianship of this huge resource can it be exploited fully, and that as much for this reason as any other England and Scotland should remain in the union formed in 1707. In the run-up to the referendum on independence in 2014 the Scottish government pointed to what it considered the Westminster government's shoddy record in managing North Sea oil resources and said that if Scots voted to shear themselves away from their southern neighbours Edinburgh would put in place a fund after the Norwegian model, and could put away £30 billion for the benefit of its successors. A slim victory for the 'No' campaign has pushed the debate back – but it is certain to return within a generation.

I still regard it as curious that assets so far from the land, so deep beneath the sea, unhusbanded and with origins so utterly ancient and alien, can give rise to such disputes. What right can anybody possibly have to them? And yet the stakes are high. Scots independence would have necessitated the drawing of a maritime boundary with England, with even a difference of a handful of square miles making a multi-billion-dollar difference to the coffers of the two countries. Once exhausted that particular issue will be rendered irrelevant. But what then of the wind – could that fickle, flickering resource also become subject to disputes over custody?

Ironically, while public opinion continues to tilt quixotically at wind turbines (unsightly and imposing – bad for birds) they have already consummately altered the aspect of the North Sea – always present on the horizon, in the middle distance or looming, *whump*ing, almost toppling. On Humberside wind is touted as the long-awaited successor to fishing. A joint venture between the German company Siemens and Associated British Ports is predicted to create 1,000 skilled jobs in a plant casting the seventy-five-metre-long blades for the turbines. But could wind ever provide the nucleus of a community as fishing once did? Could it create the kinds of shared references, superstitions, instincts, conventions that only a generation ago determined the identities not only of the trawler men but of their wider social sphere?

In 2009 the visionary architect Rem Koolhaas unveiled what he called a *zeekracht* – a master plan for the North Sea – which if realised would realign it wholly with the energy needs of the communities at its rim. The core of the *kracht* is a 'super-ring' of offshore wind farms. The plan demands a new kind of intimacy and engagement. Ecology and industry are integrated by 'stimulating existing marine life alongside wind turbines and other installations'; ferries provide 'eco and energy tourism' excursions; decommissioned oil and gas rigs are repurposed – reimagined – as 'cultural hubs and service islands'.

Koolhaas is Dutch and thus belongs to a nation that possesses a less adversarial, more entrepreneurial stance towards the North Sea than some others. In England we are half aghast but half enjoy the spectacle of cliff-top cottages crumbling into the briny; Dutch engineers are exploring the potentialities of water-borne homes that rise and fall with the tide, anticipating further meteorological disruption for later generations. If the future develops in this way it is likely that others will import the technology that the Dutch develop. A more conventional if ambitious British plan is afoot that would also radically alter the North Sea environment, or at least a part of it. Nicknamed Boris Island after its chief spiritual sponsor, the Conservative London Mayor Boris Johnson, the hubristically and more offically named London Britannia Airport would sit like a platter on an artificial island in the Thames estuary in imitation of Hong Kong International Airport – built on the reclaimed island of Chep Lap Kok.

The estuary has already, within the past two generations, evaded such a fate. In the early 1960s and the 1970s there emerged a series of proposals for airport and dock developments to be built close to the shore on the north side of the estuary. In 1972 a report was published with the title 'Balancing Foulness' – alluding to the location of the proposed scheme – that weighed the economic benefits against the costs and environmental impacts. A (Dutch) engineer told the authors that were the project to go ahead it would represent 'the biggest job of the twentieth century'.

Conservative Environment Minister Eldon Griffiths said at the time of the paper's launch, 'We plan to have the first runway in operation by 1980 or earlier if practicable. We want it built to the highest possible standard as a full international airport with capacity to expand up to four runways if the demand justifies . . . There is an impression, still persisting in some quarters, that the airport will never be built. If there are any doubters present today, I can assure them that we intend to build the airport.'

Griffiths, who died in 2014, will never see the airport's completion, the first desecration of the exquisite and so perfectly balanced estuary ecosystem that itsbuilding would demand.

A large number of undersea habitats have already been destroyed, among them the reefs of coral and sea-fans that graced the bed of the North Sea's southern basin until the middle of the nineteenth century, when it was scoured by steam trawlers dredging for the ever-delicious oyster. Now climate change campaigners warn that global warming is raising the temperature of the North Sea, disrupting the natural cycles of the phytoplankton at the base of its food chain. They predict that a number of North Sea fish – cod and haddock among them – will be pushed further north in search of cooler ambient water temperatures. Rather than leaving a vacuum in their wake, the changes will draw in more exotic creatures, joining the dramatis personae of invaders – like North American slipper limpets – that have hitched rides in the bilge tanks of ships like rail-riding hobos.

Marine biologists believe that there could be at least eighty such aliens in North Sea waters, many long-settled and raising again the perennial question of who or what constitutes a stranger. Some were brought hundreds of years ago on the hulls of Mediterranean caravels or longboats from the Baltic. And nor is it one-way traffic: the dastardly green shore crab *Carcinas maenas* has been charged with the crime of 'gigantism and strong predatory effects' off the coasts of California and Tasmania, to which its larvae were inadvertently introduced in ballast water.

Inexorable as global warming may be, it appears to take the occasional step backwards, illustrating the truism that just as a trend becomes apparently fixed, an event occurs that confounds it. In the Easter of 2013 I travelled to the Neuk of Fife to visit the puffins that breed on the islands of the Firth of Forth, but I saw only their little corpses tangled in the kelp. Every so often another would roll in on a wave, the sea nudging it gingerly onto the beach as a soft-mouthed hunting dog might bring game. The colour had leached from their ridiculous beaks, and their bodies lost their puff.

The cause of the carnage was a cold spring following a cold winter, which in turn had followed from an edgy, saturnine autumn. Sustained chill and unforgiving easterlies sap the puffins' strength and leave them without the wherewithal to dive below the surface for the sand eels on which they depend, and thus they starve or collapse while fishing. On a quarter-mile stretch of beach between the villages of Elie and Largo I found nineteen dead puffins, three guillemots, a cormorant and a razorbill. This, said the ornithologists, could have been the largest puffin wreck, as such a disaster is called, for over sixty years. Thousands, perhaps tens of thousands, had washed ashore on beaches from Banffshire to Yorkshire.

Despite such glitches the mercury nudges upwards. Some foresee the return of bluefin tuna, which – though nobody knows why – were so plentiful off the coast of north-east England in the 1920s that during a halcyon interwar period Hollywood moguls and the international glitterati rerouted their big-game fishing adventures from Key Largo and Havana to Bridlington and Scarborough. Yet the North Sea is too substantial, too terrible, to be glamorous. Yes, in places it can sparkle with sufficient intensity to attract the interest of the beau monde, but these are patches of fluorescence on a great elemental force that shrugs and shirks the qualities we vainly strive to etch into its surface.

I felt proprietorial about the North Sea on adopting it as a writing adventure, as I suppose any biographer might about their subject. But I have yet, despite my profligate use of mood words en route, to find anything in it that can be anthropomorphised or indeed vested with an identity other than the sum total of its cold blue-grey mass.

Words can only fail the North Sea. It divests itself of abstraction; falls apart as a singularity. This beast that tickles my calfhairs cannot be the self-same thing that stretches hundreds of miles (enfolding octopussies, whales, the *Radiant Star* and Lewis the cook) and fathoms deep – or at least not within the span of a single human consciousness.

In the moment of striving to fold the North Sea into those two short syllables, the effort reveals something of the shoddiness of language at large. But here is the rub: that self-same thing, the shadow gap between words and the world they reach out towards, that grey, grave, terrible discrepancy – a dreadful chasm – looks something like the North Sea itself.

Here, perhaps, I'm taking large clumsy steps towards the end of my North Sea journey, up to my thighs in churning moss-green spume-flecked unfriendly uncertainties, but (curious that we ask the question so seldom) is this why the sea possesses a siren's charm for those who know, by dint of age or infirmity, that their mortal days are quickly counting down? The elderly on the pier or the esplanade, in their sea-view care homes, are they searching the horizon, listening in the softly soughing, sawing of the tides for a hint, an intimation, of what oblivion might have in store?

I have spent many hours on the North Sea's shores, and what I know is that it is everything we say it is and none of those things, that it exists inside us and yet transcends us – possesses no boundaries other than those we inflict upon it, neither moral values, nor narrative structures. They are all with us and not the sea. That is what I know of it.

Further Wading

The following is not an exhaustive bibliography but lists by chapter sources implicitly or explicitly referred to in the text – or otherwise of assistance to the reader looking to wade a little further into the waters of the North Sea...

Chapter 1: A North Sea Crossing

Childers, Erskine, *The Riddle of the Sands*, Smith, Elder & Co., 1903

Conrad, Joseph, *The Mirror of the Sea*, Doubleday, New York, 1924

Roding, Juliette and Van Voss, Lex Heerman, eds, *The North Sea and Culture 1500–1800*, Verloren, Hilversum, 1998

Hay, David, *No Star at the Pole: A History of Navigation from the Stone Age to the 20th Century*, C. Knight, London, 1972

Kirby, David and Hinkkanen, Merja-Liisa, *The Baltic and the North Seas*, Routledge, London & New York, 2000

Taylor, E. G. R., *Haven-finding Art: A History of Navigation from Odysseus to Captain Cook*, Hollis & Carter, London, 1956

Trinder, Ivan F., *The Harwich Packets 1635–1834*, Ivan Trinder, Colchester, 1998

Van de Noort, Robert, *North Sea Archaeologies*, Oxford University Press, Oxford, 2011

Chapter 2: In Defence of the Estuary

Author Unknown, *The Wreck of the "Princess Alice", on the Thames, September 3, 1878, with a list of the principal calamities which have happened on water during the last 100 years, etc.*, A. Heywood and Son, Manchester, 1879

Author Unknown, *The Official Guide to Canvey Island*, British Publishing Co., Gloucester, 1965

Carter, H. M., *The Fort of Othona and the Chapel of St. Peter-on-the-Wall, Bradwell-on-Sea, Essex*, Provost and Chapter of Chelmsford, Chelmsford, 1972

Cekota, Anthony, *Entrepreneur Extraordinary: The Life of Tomas Bata*, University Press of the International University of Social Studies, Rome, 1968

Defoe, Daniel, *A Tour through the Eastern Counties*, London, 1772

L'Estrange, Robert, *The Life of Michael Adrian de Ruyter, Admiral of Holland*, Newman, London, 1667

Leather, John, *The Northseamen: The story of the fishermen, yachtsmen and shipbuilders of the Colne and Blackwater Rivers,* Dalton, Lavenham, 1971

Pollard, Michael, *The North Sea Surge: The Story of the East Coast Floods of 1953,* T. Dalton, Lavenham, 1978

Weaver, Leonard T., *The Harwich Packets: The Story of the Service Between Harwich and Holland Since 1661,* Lindel Organisation, Seaford, 1975

Chapter 3: The Question of the Scheldt

Belloc, Hilaire, *The River of London,* T. N. Foulis, Edinburgh and London, 1912

Bindoff, S. T., *The Scheldt Question to 1839,* G. Allen & Unwin, 1942

Great Britain: Parliament, A collection of Papers relating to the expedition to the Scheldt, A. Strahan, London, 1811

Howard, M. R., 'Walcheren 1809: a medical catastrophe', *British Medical Journal,* 1999; 319(7225):1642–1645.

Rawling, Gerald, *Cinderella Operation: The Battle for Walcheren 1944,* Cassell, London, 1980

Rodger, N. A. M., *The Command of the Ocean: A Naval History of Britain, 1649–1815,* Allen Lane, London, 1980

Chapter 4: With Ensor and Octopussies in Ostend

Department of Transport, *Herald of Free Enterprise Formal Investigation:* https://assets.digital.cabinet-office.gov.uk/media/54c1704ce5274a15b6000025/FormalInvestigation_HeraldofFreeEnterprise-MSA1894.pdf

McGreal, Stephen, *Zeebrugge and Ostend Raids 1918,* Pen & Sword Military, Barnsley, 2007

Southern Railway, *Ostend and the Coast of Belgium,* London, 1924

Swinbourne, Anna (ed.), *James Ensor,* Museum of Modern Art (Moma), New York, 2009

Van den Bussche, Willy, *Ensor and the Avant-gardes by the Sea,* PMMK, Brussels, 2006

Chapter 5: Shapes and Shingle on the Naked Shore

Benfell, Roy, *Spurn Lifeboat Station: the First Hundred Years,* R. Benfell, Hull, 1994

De Boer, G., *A History of the Spurn Lighthouses,* East Yorkshire Historical Society, York, 1968

Jarratt, George A. (revised Welton, Mike), *Memories of Spurn in the 1880s,* SKEALS, Easington, 2010

Leach, Nicholas, *Lifeboats of the Humber,* Amberley, Stroud, 2010

Mathison, Phil, *The Saint of Spurn Point: Wilgils, father of St Willibrord,* Dead Good Publications, Newport, 2010

Neal, Geoff, *The Birds of Spurn – a comprehensive checklist*, Spurn Bird Observatory, Kilnsea, 1996

Ostler, Gordon, *Lost Villages of the Humber Estuary*, Hull College of Further Education, Hull, 1990

Van de Noort, Robert and Stephen Ellis (eds), *Wetland heritage of Holderness: An Archaeological Survey*, Humber Wetlands Project, University of Hull, 1995

Chapter 6: Last Resorts

Borut, Jacob, *Antisemitism in Tourist Facilities in Weimar Germany:* http://www.yadvashem.org/download/about_holocaust/studies/borut_full.pdf

Corbin, Alain (trans. Phelps, Jocelyn), *The Lure of the Sea: The Lure of the Seaside in the Western World 1750–1840*, Polity, Cambridge, 1994

Dickens, Charles, *Sketches by "Boz", Illustrative of Every-day Life and Every-day People*, John Macrone, London, 1837–1839

English Tourist Board, *The future marketing and development of English Seaside Tourism*, 1974

Granville, Augustus Bozzi, *The Spas of England, and Principal Sea-bathing Places*, H. Colburn, London, 1841

Hannavy, John, *The English seaside in Victorian and Edwardian Times*, Shire, Princes Risborough, 2003

Walton, John K., *The English Seaside Resort: A Social History*, Leicester University Press, Leicester, 1983

Chapter 7: Mare Frisium, Fris Non Canta

Black, William George, *Heligoland and the Islands of the North Sea*, W. Blackwood & Sons, Edinburgh and London, 1888

Ring, Jim, *Erskine Childers*, John Murray, London, 1996

Schultze-Naumburg, *Sylt: The Dream Island*, Sun & Health, Harrow, 1966

Storm, Theodor (trans. Boyden, George), *The Rider on the White Horse*, Pen Press, Brighton 2011

Chapter 8: Myths of Origin – a Land Beneath the Sea

Flemming, N. C. (ed.), *Submarine Prehistoric Archaeology in the North Sea*, Council for British Archaeology, York, 2004

Gaffney, V., Fitch S. and Smith, D., *Europe's Lost World: The Rediscovery of Doggerland*, Council for British Archaeology, York, 2009

Hygen, Anne-Sophie and Lasse Bengtsson, *Rock Carvings in the Borderlands*, Warne Förlag, Gothenburg, 2000

Reid, Clement, *Submerged Forests*, Cambridge Manuals, Cambridge, 1913

Spanuth, J., *The Atlantis of the North*, Van Nostrand Reinhold, 1980

Sprague de Camp, L., *The Atlantis Theme in History, Science and Literature*, Dover, New York, 1970

Chapter 9: A Postcard from Atlantis

Black, William George, *Heligoland and the Islands of the North Sea*, W. Blackwood & Sons, Edinburgh and London, 1888

Buckle, G. E. (ed.), *The Letters of Queen Victoria, 1886–1890*, Vol. 1, John Murray, London, 1930

Drower, G. M. F., *Heligoland, The True Story of German Bight and the Island that Britain Betrayed*, Sutton, Stroud, 2002

Gatke, Heinrich, *Heligoland as an Ornithological Observatory: The Result of 50 Years' Experience*, David Douglas, Edinburgh, 1895

Chapter 10: A North Sea Outrage

Credland, Arthur G., *Harvest from a Common Sea: The North Sea Fishery, 1870–1940*, Association of North Sea Societies, 1997

Gilchrist, Andrew, *Cod Wars and How to Lose Them*, Q Press, Edinburgh, 1978

Gill, Alec, *Lost Trawlers of Hull: 900 Losses Researched and Listed Between 1835 and 1987*, Hutton Press, Beverley, 1989

—, *Superstitions: Folk Magic in Hull's Fishing Community*, Hutton Press, Beverley, 1993

—, *Village Within a City: the Hessle Road Fishing Community of Hull*, Hull University Press, Hull, 1986

Jónsson, Hannes, *Friends in Conflict: the Anglo-Icelandic Cod Wars and the Law of the Sea*, Hurst, London, 1982

Politovsky, E. S., (trans. Godfrey, Major F. R.), *From Libau to Tsushima: A Narrative of the Voyage of Admiral Rojdestvensky's Fleet to Eastern Seas, Including a Detailed Account of the Dogger Bank Incident,* John Murray, London, 1906

Report on the British Fishing Industry: Distant Water Trawlers, British Trawlers' Federation, Hull, 1956

Starkey, D., Ramster, J. and Reid, C., *England's Sea Fisheries: The Commercial Sea Fisheries of England and Wales since 1300*, Chatham, London, 2000

The Fishing Industry: Its Economic Significance in the Yorkshire and Humberside Ports, Yorkshire and Humberside Economic Planning Board, Leeds, 1977

Tunstall, Jeremy, *The Fishermen*, MacGibbon & Kee, London, 1962

Chapter 11: In the *Halligen* or an Axolotl in the Almost-Islands

Jenemann, Christiane, *Halliglüüd – Erzähltes Leben*, 2011

Storm, Theodor (trans. Boyden, George), *The Rider on the White Horse (Schimmelreiter)*, Pen Press, Brighton, 2011

Storm, Theodor (trans. Jackson, Denis and Anja Nauck), *Journey to a Hallig*, Angel Classics, London, 2000

Chapter 12: Where Two Seas Meet

Edwardes, Charles, *In Jutland with a Cycle*, Chapman & Hall, London, 1897

Ebbesen, Lisette Vind and Mette Bøgh Jensen (eds), *The Skagen Painters: Introduction to the Skagen Painters and Skagens Museum*, Skagens Museum, 2009

Svanholm, Lise (trans. Jones, Walton Glyn), *Northern Light: The Skagen Painters*, Gyldendahl, Copenhagen, 2003

The Hedtoft sinking: http://www.hanshedtoft.dk/

Chapter 13: The Fishing Game

Author Unknown, *A representation of the state of the English oyster fisheries, and of the hardships and discouragements the oyster-dredgers of this kingdom labour under*, London, 1737

Author Unknown, *History of a Great Industry: Twenty-one years of trawling*, reprinted from the *People's Journal*, John Leng & Co., Dundee, 1905

Barker E. J., and J. P. MacCrum, *Grimsby Trawlers*, Oxford University Press, London, 1961

Burroughs, John (Sir), *An Historical Account of the Royal Fishery of Great Britain*, E. Curll, London, 1720

Company of the Royal Fishery of England, *A Collection of Advertisements, Advices, and Directions, relating to the Royal Fishery within the British Seas, &c*, London, 1695

Credland, Arthur G., *Harvest from a Common Sea: The North Sea Fishery 1870–1940*, Association of North Sea Societies, 1997

Gilchrist, Andrew, *Cod Wars and How to Lose Them*, Q Press, Edinburgh, 1978

Kirk, Hans (trans. Linder, Marc), *Fiskerne*, Fǎnpìhuà Press, Iowa City, 2000

Perry, W. H. (ed.), *The Fisherman's Handbook,* Fishing News, Farnham, 1980

Report on the British Fishing Industry: Distant Water Trawlers, British Trawlers' Federation, Hull, 1956

Sicking, Louis and Darlene Abreu-Ferreira, *Beyond the Catch: Fisheries of the North Atlantic, the North Sea and the Baltic 900–1850*, Brill, Leiden, 2009

Starkey, D., J. Ramster and C. Reid, *England's Sea Fisheries: The Commercial Sea Fisheries of England and Wales since 1300*, Chatham, London, 2000

Walmsley, Leo, *Three Fevers*, Jonathan Cape, London, 1932

Wood, Walter, *Men of the North Sea, Tales of the Dogger Bank,* Eveleigh Nash, London, 1904

Chapter 14: *Radiant Star* of Shetland

Barnes, Michael P., *The Norn language of Orkney and Shetland*, Shetland Times, Lerwick, 1998

Byron, R., *Burra Fishermen: Social and Economic Change in a Shetland Community*, Social Research Council, London (undated).

Charlton, Edward, *Travels in Shetland 1832–52*, Shetland Times, Lerwick, 2007

Knooihuizen, R., *Fishing for Words: The Taboo Language of Shetland Fishermen and the Dating of Norn Language Death*, Transactions of the Philological Society. Vol 106; No. 1, 2008, 100–113, Blackwell Publishing Ltd, 2008

Linklater, Eric, *Orkney and Shetland: An Historical, Geographical, Social and Scenic Survey*, Robert Hale, London, 1965

McGrandle, Leith, *The Story of North Sea Oil*, Wayland, Hove, 1975

Neill, Patrick, *A Tour Through Some of the Islands of Orkney and Shetland, etc.*, A. Constable, Edinburgh, 1806

Nicolson, James R., *Shetland and Oil*, Luscombe, London, 1972

Owen, Olwyn (ed.), *Things in the Viking World*, Shetland Amenity Trust, Lerwick, 2012

Simpson, Charlie, *Water in Burgidale: Shetland Fisheries in a Pre-Electronic Age*, Shetland Times, Lerwick, 2010

Chapter 15: New Sea, New Chapters

BBC News, 'UKIP Councillor blames floods and storms on gay marriage'. http://www.bbc.co.uk/news/uk-england-oxfordshire-25793358

Hitchens, Peter, 'Boston Lincolngrad: Peter Hitchens investigates the troubling transformation of a sleepy English town after mass immigration from Eastern Europe', *Daily Mail*, 18 September 2011. http://www.dailymail.co.uk/news/article-2037877/Boston-Lincolngrad-The-strange-transformation-sleepy-English-town.html#ixzz3prLIxoqj

Koolhaas, Rem, *Zeekracht*. http://oma.eu/projects/zeekracht

Regional Studies Association, *Balancing Foulness* – Comprehensive Development Planning for the Thames Estuary, 1972

Acknowledgements

I'd dearly like to thank all those who have actively facilitated, made suggestions or criticisms, or otherwise indulged me in the writing of *The Naked Shore*: starting close to home, my partner Marie Francis for her indulgence – and Mark Cusick for his. Hugh Barnes, Alex Schneideman, Derek Johns, Henry Olsen and Edward Woodman all deserve thanks for their support and company on various legs.

I'm also enormously grateful to Tim Bates of Pollinger, for his spot-on comments and suggestions (pulling no punches, but always enthusing), Michael Fishwick at Bloomsbury for bearing with me – and Anna Simpson for helping carry the book through to completion.

So many people have shown interest and hospitality on my travels, but to Herman Vuijsje and Wilhemyn, Arend Maris, Jacob Hammer, Victor Laurenson, Andrew French, Uwe Jessel, Mathias Piepgras, Ben Davies and Jill Franklin, Anne Paulsen, Hark Martinen and Richard Haward – I owe particular gratitude.

Index

A Note on the Type

The text of this book is set in Bembo, which was first used in 1495 by the Venetian printer Aldus Manutius for Cardinal Bembo's *De Aetna*. The original types were cut for Manutius by Francesco Griffo. Bembo was one of the types used by Claude Garamond (1480–1561) as a model for his Romain de l'Université, and so it was a forerunner of what became the standard European type for the following two centuries. Its modern form follows the original types and was designed for Monotype in 1929.